# THE POLITICS OF MYTH

*SUNY series, Issues in the Study of Religion*
*Bryan Rennie, Editor*

# THE POLITICS OF MYTH

*A Study of C. G. Jung, Mircea Eliade, and Joseph Campbell*

Robert Ellwood

STATE UNIVERSITY OF NEW YORK PRESS

Published by
State University of New York Press, Albany

For information, address
State University of New York Press,
State University Plaza, Albany, N.Y. 12246

Production by Dale Cotton
Marketing by Anne M. Valentine

*Acknowledgment*
Portions of this book previously appeared in Robert Ellwood, "Why Are Mythologists
Political Reactionaries?" published in Jacob Neusner, ed., *Religion and the Social Order: What
Kinds of Lessons Does History Teach?* © 1994 by the University of South Florida and published
by Scholars Press for the University of South Florida, the University of Rochester, and Saint
Louis University, and reprinted here by kind permission of Scholars Press, Atlanta.

**Library of Congress Cataloging-in-Publication Data**

Ellwood, Robert S., 1933–
    The politics of myth : a study of C. G. Jung, Mircea Eliade, and
Joseph Campbell / Robert Ellwood.
      p.  cm. — (SUNY series, issues in the study of religion)
    Includes index.
    ISBN 0-7914-4305-1 (hc. : alk. paper). — ISBN 0-7914-4306-X (pbk.
: alk. paper)
      1. Eliade, Mircea, 1907–  —Views on politics. 2. Campbell,
Joseph, 1904–  —Views on politics. 3. Jung, C. G. (Carl Gustav),
1875–1961—Views on politics. 4. Mythologists—Attitudes—
History—20th century. I. Title. II. Series.
BL303.5.E44  1999
291.1'3'0922—dc21                    98-54277
                                     CIP

10 9 8 7 6 5 4 3 2 1

# Contents

# PREFACE

Amid the horrors of world war and the exponential expansion of technologies and economies, the mid-twentieth century saw also a late modern upsurge of popular and academic interest in mythology. Three persons were primarily associated with this development: the analytic psychologist C. G. Jung, the historian of religion Mircea Eliade, and the widely read public mythologist Joseph Campbell. The interest was not merely aesthetic: these interpreters of ancient myth said much to lead their public to believe that a rediscovery of meaning in myth could contribute to solving the personal and social problems of those tumultuous times. At the same time, all three mythologists have at times been associated with the politics of the extreme right, even, according to some charges, with sympathy for fascism and anti-Semitism. The present book refers to these serious accusations, while chiefly endeavoring to extract the political and social philosophy presented explicitly and implicitly in the entire lifework and published corpus of the three persons.

The introductory chapter, "Myth, Gnosis, and Modernity," treats of the nature of "modern" belief in progress and the unity of knowledge. It portrays the mythological movement as, like fascism and communism, representing an extreme case of modernism even as it was highly critical of many aspects of it: of materialism, "mass man," and the uprooting of traditional societies. For the modern mythologists could only critique the modern from out of the context of modern sciences, academic institutions, and means of communication. The ambivalence of their "reaction" and their "gnosticism"—seeking a "hidden" wisdom in the remote past—is sought for, as is the relation of modern mythology to romanticism and German "volkish" thought.

C. G. Jung presents a paradigmatic case of this paradox, for though he was a modern medical doctor he came increasingly to believe that his patients—and the modern world generally—needed to get in touch with the "archetypal" powers that lay beneath its rational surface, powers both individual and collective. It is here that Jung came dangerously close to enthusiasm for the German National Socialist revolution. In the end, though, the political stance of this difficult and sometimes contradictory thinker was closer to Burkean conservatism than to fascism.

The Romanian Mircea Eliade, a brilliant young intellectual in his homeland in the 1930s, and for a time an admirer of its fascist Iron Guard, suffered exile and a radical disjuncture in his life after 1945. Despite the early context, in the end it was the experience of exile that shaped what there was of political thought in Eliade: it gave him the freedom to be nostalgic for the unities of the distant past, while allowing him to see the sacred in the secular of the modern world in diverse places, and to appreciate guardedly the kind of institutions he found in his adopted homeland, the United States.

Joseph Campbell, the only of the three born in America, came to extol the heroic radical individualism he perceived in the American past and its traditions. A student in Germany during the Weimar period, he absorbed the influence of such thinkers and writers of that era as Spengler, Frobenius, and Mann, as well as the psychoanalysts Freud and Jung, with their pessimistic view of the future of civilization as the modern world knew it. Like the other two, while supporting the political right he chiefly saw the saving of the world not in "collective" institutions, but in the transformation of individuals with the help of the power of myth.

The book's conclusion points to the way in which the whole concept of myth which underlay the work of these three mythologists is a modern construct. We can, it will be said, certainly listen to their wisdom, but we need not hold that it contains a unique "gnosis" that will save us from the obligation to chart our own human future.

It is important to make clear what the book is and is not about. *The Politics of Myth* is not *primarily* an assessment of charges that Jung, Eliade, and Campbell were sympathizers with, and involved in, Nazism, fascism, or anti-Semitism. To deal with all the charges that have been made would require book-length studies in themselves, and that is not the task to which I have set myself. Rather, my real purpose is to discuss somewhat more abstractly the political philosophy that seems to emerge from the published writings of the three on mythology; I view the afore-mentioned inflammatory charges essentially as matters that must be faced and dealt with in the course of proceeding on to the real agenda. Thus I do not claim that my treatment of those issues is exhaustive or final; what I hope to do, at best, is to put the 1930s and 1940s in the context of each man's total life and work, and see where that leads. In the course of this project it will be necessary to confront the difficult and often highly charged issue of asking precisely in what way are such accusations, and evidence, important—as they certainly are—to assessing the overall work, even the overall political philosophy, of any intellectual figure, including Jung, Eliade, and Campbell.

A task like this involves careful definitions of terms. Anti-Semitism, for example, cannot be imputed to one who simply differs theologically with Judaism in the same way that a Catholic might differ with a Baptist, or a Christian or Jew with a Buddhist. The pejorative label anti-Semitic is rightly used when it is clear that the feeling of difference extends to Jews as persons as well as to their supposed beliefs: when Jews appear to be held in some generic sense to be unchangeably different psychologically and even biologically from others, so that they could never "fit in" to the rest of a society, and their influence and even mere presence is therefore destructive to the unity of society. This anti-Semitic way of thinking involves stereotyping in terms of a generic quality that all Jews, regardless of individual differences, are supposed to have. Therefore the anti-Semite presumes that his antipathy toward Jews requires words—and actions—that are directed toward Jews as a whole.

We must acknowledge that it is possible to use terms like *fascist*, *anti-Semitic*, or *rightist* (especially in the European sense) as though they enabled a blanket condemnation of a person and all his work, sometimes even when the condemnation is really for other ideological reasons. Without denying the moral seriousness of the issues raised by such terms, one must still be prepared to examine honestly the quantitative and qualitative importance of that which evokes the charges relative to a writer's total corpus. The critic must then come to clarity on just how those accusatory words may be connected to other aspects of the person's intellectual work. Certainly there are unities in all of a major thinker's endeavors—deep structures, paradigms, polarities, values that run through them. A tendency to think in generic terms of peoples, races, religions, or parties, which as we shall see is undoubtedly the profoundest flaw in mythological thinking, including that of such modern mythologists as our three, can connect with nascent anti-Semitism, or the connection may be the other way. A negativity toward Judaism, for example, seen as a religion of a personal monotheistic deity acting in the history of a particular people, may well resonate elsewhere in the writer's pages with a general negativity toward divine personality, toward the notion of history as the defining framework of human experience, toward historical ways of thinking in general, and toward any sense of religious mission by any particularized group. But it is important that such intellectual continuities not be just assumed, but—as difficult as that may be in this case after Auschwitz—assessed freely and fairly on their own terms, not only by a kind of intellectual guilt by association unless the association is clearly evident. Some structures, some generic categories, are probably necessary to any intellectual work and can be found in writing, including writing about Judaism, far removed from anti-Semitism. These are hard things of which to write and speak; I can only hope that the remainder of this book will make my meaning in respect to them clear.

For there is no doubt that the three mythologists here under consideration have intellectual roots in the same spiritual climate as that in which early fascism and sometimes anti-Semitism flourished: Nietzsche, Sorel, Ortega y Gasset, Spengler, Frobenius, Heidegger, the lesser Romanian nationalists and German "volkish" writers and, before his courageous rejection of Nazism and exile, Thomas Mann. Most of these just named were not full-blown partisans of their respective national fascist parties; some, such as Nietzsche, would have condemned political fascism as utterly contrary to the heroic individualism for which they stood. So also, by their own later testimony, did the three mythologists. Yet there is in that climate and the three mythologists an unmistakable common intellectual tone: antimodernism and antirationalism tinged with romanticism and existentialism. This subset of modern thought is deeply suspicious of the larger modern world, as that world was created fundamentally by the Enlightenment (despite, as we shall see, their embracing of some themes, like nationalism and the purifying revolution idea, carried over from the Age of Reason's turbulent finale). Above all, the romantic antimoderns decried modernity's exaltation of reason, "materialistic" science, "decadent" democracy dependent on the rootless "mass man" its leveling fosters.

In contrast, they lauded traditional "rooted" peasant culture, including its articulation in myths that came not from writers but from "the people," and they no less praised the charismatic heroes ancient and modern who allegedly personified that culture's supreme values. Above all, one felt in these writers a distinctive mood of world-weariness, a sense that all has gone gray—and, just beneath the surface, surging, impatient eagerness for change: for some tremendous spasm, emotional far more than intellectual, based far more on existential choice than on reason, that would recharge the world with color and the blood with vitality. Perhaps a new elite, or a new leader capable of making "great decisions" in the heroic mold of old, would be at the helm.

This flavor was in the air to a remarkable extent in the United States during the ten years or so after 1945. Any overtly fascist overtones were, needless to say, well disguised in those years after the great victory over that lost cause. But in a sense it was not so much that the larger antimodern intellectual context in which fascism flourished was lost, as that, willingly shedding its bastard fascist form and redressed in new apparel, it came back to haunt a world weary from the struggle against fascism. For the root dissatisfactions of the modern mind were far from laid. Reformatted, wistful versions of Spengler and Nietzsche and Heidegger and the mythological mood suited the spiritual and intellectual fatigue many felt after the great war and the ideological battles of the 1930s. Traditional religions were on the rise. Purposeless amidst abundance, people felt "decadent" and alienated from something crucial, which had probably been better known in the remote past. This spirit also consorted well with the emerging anticommunism of the 1950s, since Marxism presented itself as quintessential modern and "scientific" politics at the opposite pole from such reactionary nostalgia; and much in the reactionary mood also fitted well with the antirational discourse of then-fashionable existentialism, despite the fact that many existentialists, especially the French, claimed to be politically left. Above all, nostalgia for lost values provided a platform for those of both the elite right and the elite left critical of emergent 1950s "mass culture": the new world of television, the automobile, and suburban tract houses. The 1950s "Beats" liked Spengler, and the same sort of ideas at least were savored by rightist critics in the mold of William Buckley, Russell Kirk, and B. I. Bell. It was also around 1950 that the vogue for Carl Jung, Mircea Eliade, and Joseph Campbell began to accelerate in the United States.

In dealing with these matters, as well as what might be called the cumulative political philosophy of these three figures, much will have to be taken into account. I will plead guilty to the charge that the three main chapters of this book, one on each of the three figures, cover several domains: the mythologist's personal and intellectual biography, a consideration of his late modern times, a summary of his view of myth and its explicit and implicit political ramifications, and here and there my own critical response. But to my mind this is simply unavoidable. These are complex persons and issues. None of these strands can be separated out from a study such as this is intended to be because they are all profoundly interlinked. Whatever they may have thought, the mythology of the three was not from the perspective of eternity, but as much a product of its times as any intellectual endeavor, and was interwoven with the subject's own life and political context. To bring this out is very much the point of this book.

Even the terms that force themselves into a discussion like this may be controversial. For convenience, I have repeatedly referred to Jung, Eliade, and Campbell as mythologists. Some will no doubt protest that the three were not really mythologists (or folklorists) in a strict academic sense. They did little field work, it will be said, or serious textual and philological work on myth; rather, depending largely on the labors of others, they employed myth—sometimes selectively and cavalierly—in the service of other agenda: promoting a school of analytic psychology, establishing a history of religion academic discipline, addressing the spiritual problems of the day. It will be pointed out that there are other "working" mythologists, including some now active in the scholarly world, who undoubtedly do not share the politics of Jung, Eliade, or Campbell. I take the point, but will have to ask that for the purposes of this book we accept the term *mythologist* on the grounds of their intense interest in myth and their avid concern for promoting awareness of it.

For a time I thought of labeling the three reactionaries. Even "conservative" did not seem strong enough. Like its antonym *liberal*, the word *conservative* is often slippery in meaning, and has had somewhat different connotations in Europe and America. Furthermore, the surface meaning of just keeping things as they are hardly does justice to the radical overtones, as over against their contemporary world, of some of the visions involved.

Reactionary is also not quite right, if it implies merely a Colonel Blimp sort of yearning for days that are no more, or a Bourbonlike passion to recover lost aristocratic privileges. Yet all three men did in fact want to draw wisdom from wells sunk deep in pasts they deemed preferable in crucial human respects to the present. I do not say they wanted simply to return to those pasts, for they were well aware that was not possible, or even desirable. They were also profoundly modern, even if they embraced traditionalism and antimodernism as ideological stances within the modern spectrum. As scholars and intellectually engaged persons, they were also aware that the differentiated consciousness of the modern world had its value. It could even be argued by their partisans that the stance of the modern mythologist, with one foot in each world, archaic and modern, was the ideal. At the same time they knew there was much in modernity to react against, even though in some ways they were more modern than they realized; they knew that one could do worse than look backwards with contemplative if not nostalgic eyes upon cities and centuries well tempered by stories and rites that (ideally) made human society like a great dance, itself integrated smoothly into the dance of the universe.

For them this kind of reaction was an urgently felt ideological and even spiritual cause, which would bring them no economic or social gain, and indeed much obloquy in some quarters, but which they felt entailed a message the world desperately had to hear. The past they evoked was no subject of mere nostalgia, much less of material benefit, but a time when values and spirituality, now almost forgotten, reigned.

Still living and workable pasts were in fact twofold for each of the mythologists. On the one hand, like a lingering earthly paradise an undated primordial golden age when myths were strong and human life was meaningful lay shimmering on a distant horizon; on the other hand the mythologists also discerned a more immediate secondary silver age within the last few hundred years, more fallen but also perhaps more accessible, for which they pined: Jung for a medieval harmony of symbol and life before it was fractured by the triple evils of the Reformation, the Enlightenment, and the Industrial Revolution; Eliade for the silver years of Romania's nineteenth-century cultural renaissance; Campbell for an idealized early America of moral virtue and sturdy individualism.

To put it another way, all cast passionate (though not always uncritical) eyes upon the primitive, believing that, largely through the power of myth and ritual, primal humanity was better integrated spiritually and cosmically than moderns, and they also held that enough recent examples obtain to suggest that primal integration can be recovered at least in part, though perhaps only on a individual basis. In their own terms, they were not so much reactionary, then, as integrationist: holding that the mythological past needed to be integrated fully into the subjective lives of modern persons. To ascertain what that meant for the subjectivty out of which political actions flow will be the major theme of this book.

# 1

# MYTH, GNOSIS, AND MODERNITY

## THE MIDCENTURY MYTHIC TRINITY

Myth, mythology, and the idea of myth have had a remarkable place in the intellectual and spiritual awareness of the twentieth century. Amidst the troubled days and nights of those years have been heard sweet and seductive words from out of the past, not seldom transmitted and interpreted by men widely regarded as living sages. Tales of creation, of heroes and timeless love fascinated many actors on the stage of a world bound by time and history, by war and cold war. "Myth" took its place in contemporary consciousness alongside expanding economies and genocidal horrors.

To be sure, events of the contemporary drama itself reached nearly mythic proportions in the century's battles of light against darkness, and the introduction of weapons drawing their power from the same awesome energies that light the sun and stars. Myths provided models for the world around, yet at the same time offered avenues of eternal return to simpler primordial ages when the values that rule the world were forged.

Three "sages" above all were foundational figures of the twentieth-century mythological revival: C. G. Jung, Mircea Eliade, and Joseph Campbell. Their work stimulated belief that the recovery of meanings enigmatically encoded in ancient mythologies could do much to heal deep midcentury wounds in both individual and collective psyches. Moreover, the words they transmitted from out of the past resonated with an antimodern counterpoint to the century's giddy devotion to "progress," with its terrible shadowside of war, devastation, and destructive ideology.

Their teachings in the twentieth century had a role rather like that of gnosticism in antiquity. Both eras confronted dazzling change and baffling contradictions that seemed unmanageable in their world's own terms. Whether in Augustan Rome or modern Europe, democracy all too easily gave way to totalitarianism, technology was as readily used for battle as human comfort, and immense wealth lay alongside abysmal poverty. Faced with a time of rapid changes some accounted progress, yet also surveying suffering too profound to be self-healing, gnostics past and present sought answers not in the course of outward human events, but in knowledge of the world's beginning, of what lies above and beyond the world, and of the secret places of the human soul. To all this the mythologists spoke, and they acquired large and loyal followings.

The elder of the modern popular mythologists was the Swiss analytic psychologist Carl G. Jung (1875–1961). In his later years, his gentle, white-haired features suggested a modern master of forgotten wisdom as he prodded a troubled world to look inward through widely read books like *Modern Man in Search of a Soul* (1933) or *The Undiscovered Self* (1958). They inevitably pointed to sicknesses of the contemporary soul that could well be diagnosed and alleviated through recourse to the lore of myth. For have we not all within us, struggling to declare and rightly align themselves, something of the "archetypes" he identified in both myth and modern dream? Far too often, hardly knowing what we are doing, therefore doing it badly and without balance, we and the tormented human world around us act out the parts of the Warrior, the Wizard, the Mother, and the many sinister guises of the Shadow.

By the late 1950s, Jungian interpretations of myth were ascendant forces in the intellectual and spiritual worlds, even as the regnant

Freudianism was beginning to fade. The distinguished literary critic Northrop Frye, who read Jung assiduously in the late forties, did much to make "myth analysis" of Shakespeare and other literature an academic vogue.[1] Theologians like Victor White (*God and the Unconscious*, 1952) and David Cox (*Jung and St. Paul*, 1959) took Jungian ideas seriously in relating Christianity to contemporary consciousness.

Nor was regard for Jung limited to academic circles. *Time* magazine, in 1952, did a story on the sage of Zurich that presented him as "not only the most famous of living psychiatrists," but also as "one of the few practitioners of the craft who admit that man has a soul." Jung was "an unabashed user of the world 'spiritual,' " who held that the "religious instinct is as strong as the sexual," though the news magazine did acknowledge that Jung was odd, in a perhaps lovable though perhaps also slightly disturbing way: "His home is filled with strange Asiatic sculptures. He wears a curious ring, ornamented with an ancient effigy of a snake, the bearer of light in the pre-Christian Gnostic cult."[2]

This piece, and the general tendency to adulate Jung as one of the world's wise men in the fifties and after, was much in contrast with a notorious article only three years before in the *Saturday Review of Literature*. Robert Hillyer's "Treason's Strange Fruit" was mainly a protest against the awarding of the Bollingen Prize by the Library of Congress to Ezra Pound for his 1948 *Pisan Cantos*. Hillyer's impassioned essay raised the matter of Pound's well-known anti-Semitism and apologetics for Mussolini, but also pondered the curious fact that this prestigious American prize was named after Carl Jung's home in Switzerland, Bollingen.

The reason was that the award was funded by the Bollingen Foundation of New York, which also happened to be the sponsor of the Pantheon Press, Jung's major American publisher. Joseph Campbell was editor of the Bollingen Series of Pantheon books on mythology and comparative religion. All these Bollingen works were offered ultimately by grace of the wealthy Paul Mellon, son of Andrew Mellon, Twenties-era Secretary of the Treasury. Paul Mellon's first wife had been a patient of Jung's, and Paul was dedicated to the Swiss doctor's name and fame.

But Hillyer, unimpressed, remarked caustically that it was appropriate to give Pound a prize with a Jungian name, given his perception that they were two of a kind; what was shocking was that the award was granted by an American committee. Hillyer went on to claim that Jung was hardly less pro-Axis than Pound, citing a number of sayings by the former, not all in context, to support the notion that "for a time Dr Jung's admiration for Hitler was warm," and that this enthusiasm also included "racism in general, the superman, anti-Semitism, and a weird metaphysics embracing occultism, alchemy, and the worship of Wotan." The article provoked a barrage of letters to the editor, largely but not entirely in defense of Jung.[3]

Quite interesting also was Hillyer's mention of a new "literary cult to whom T. S. Eliot and Ezra Pound are gods." Jung presumably was virtually a third member of what would then have become a divine trinity. This was the "cult" of the "New Criticism" which, in profound reaction against the brutal ideological wars of thirties and forties literary discourse, sought to see only what was in a poetic or fictional text itself, in its own texture of mood, image, and internal allusion. It deliberately detached the printed page from social and doctrinal context. The imagist Pound and the nostalgic Eliot (who had been a member of the controversial Bollingen Prize committee, and whose political and social views have also not gone unquestioned), both considered consummate craftsmen on the level of words and sentences, fitted into the New Criticism canon well despite their baggage of ideas unsavory to holdover Depression-era liberals. Jung, or works influenced by him like Joseph Campbell's 1949 book, *The Hero with a Thousand Faces*, were then able to make modern poets speak the "timeless truth" of archetype and myth. In the immediate postwar period Jung and the New Criticism were only parts of a larger mood of selective nostalgia for times and values, including forms of spirituality, out of ages past before the disastrous upheavals of the twentieth century: one also recalls Aldous Huxley's perennial philosophy, the pilgrimage of Thomas Merton to his Trappist monastery, and Zen. Moreover, after 1945 the Nazis and fascists had been replaced by another enemy, communism. All lovers of traditional things, though they might have equivocated before the half-archaic, half modern world of fascism, could freely hate this foe with singleness of heart.

The fifties were only an anticipation of the heady countercultural atmosphere of the sixties. Then Jung and the mythological mood definitely won out, over both Freud and the pragmatic style of modernism that saw progress measured by elongated freeways and better bombers, in the decade's flourishing countercultural circles. But that triumph required a curious movement of myth, archaism, and

Jungianism from political right to left in its perceived place in the intellectual spectrum, leaving behind people like Eliot and Campbell. In those days when, in the image of a popular song, magic was afoot, revolutionaries even more than reactionaries were likely to dream of earlier times when myths were strong. According to a 1967 *Time* essay on the "New Left" of those days, the radicals wanted to repeal "big-ness"—the mark of modernity—and yearned for small, self-contained idyllic villages of such nineteenth-century visionaries as Charles Fourier and Robert Owen—"New Harmony computerized." This would be "the totally beautiful society," and the article categorized the move-ment as really "not political but religious."[4] Extremes of consciousness met, and found common ground in opposing what passed for moder-nity. Talk of archetypes and return to the archaic world seemed to fit when people dressed like figments of myth or dream, and wanted to establish communes where they could live close to the earth.

It was during the sixties that I had the privilege of studying the history of religion with the second of the three mythologists under consideration in this book, Mircea Eliade (1907–1986). The Romanian-born scholar came to my attention in 1962, when I was a Marine chaplain stationed on Okinawa. Okinawa and Japan had been my first experience of a non-Western culture, and I had naturally been at pains to come to an understanding of the relation between Western religion and the Shinto and Buddhism I saw around me. I could not help but believe that some indefinable spiritual presence lingered in the lovely sylvan shrines of Shinto, or that there was more than mere atmospher-ics in the great peace that filled temples of the Buddha. One day I came across a review of one of Eliade's books. Something about the account led me to believe it might help. I ordered the slim volume, read it, and suddenly the significance of a wholly new way of looking at religion rose into consciousness: not theological, but in terms of its phenomenological structures, its organization of sacred space and time, its use of myth as models of how things were done in the ultimate sacred time of origins. It was one of those books that make one think, "This was really true all the time, but I didn't realize it until now." Soon I had left the chaplaincy and enrolled as a graduate student under Mircea Eliade at the University of Chicago Divinity School.

Eliade was a kindly and conscientious teacher, at his best in a small seminar of highly motivated docents. I recall engrossing discus-sion of such fascinating topics as shamanism and initiation rites. His

luminous books taught that myths were from out of *illud tempus—that*
time, the other timeless time when the gods were strong and made the
world, and when the primordial "gestures" of heroes set the patterns
for what is still sacred in our fallen "profane" world. Few rumors had
as yet arisen concerning the aging professor's relation to the profascist
and anti-Semitic Iron Guard in his native Romania thirty years before,
and I recall remarkably little discussion of concrete political implications of his concept of history of religions, despite the intensely political nature of the sixties decade. It was as though Eliade's world was
a place of welcome escape from the turmoil all around.

The third mythologist, Joseph Campbell (1904–1987), was American born and bred. He was of Irish Catholic background, and a natural
rebel who early began to make his own way in religion and life. But
he ended up an academic, teaching at Sarah Lawrence College in
suburban New York. On the mythological front, he early made his
mark with *The Hero with a Thousand Faces* (1949), a tendentious if brilliant and sometimes magical study of the hero myth in all its varieties
and commonalities; it was followed by a four-volume series on myths,
*The Masks of God.* Fundamentally Jungian in temperament and approach, Campbell was for a time also under Freudian influence, chiefly
by way of Géza Róheim, the psychoanalytic anthropologist. A widely
traveled lecturer as well as a popular writer, Campbell acquired a
large following, above all from the posthumously aired series of television interviews with Bill Moyers. The response to that series of six
interviews was remarkable. It seemed as though the world was waiting for someone to tell stories that undercut the modern narratives of
urbanized meaninglessness and despair, and yet at the same time
reinforced the worth modern times put on heroic individual achievement and realization of selfhood. But questions were also asked about
how much of the mythic meaning was Campbell and how much was
in the myths themselves, and what a world of Campbellite heroes
would really be like. For Campbell, the mythic hero was a timeless
model of an original ideal humanity that could be set against
modernity's fall into ambiguity.

For Jung, Eliade, and Campbell, mythology was nothing less than
a grand, ultimate source for the "timeless truth" undertow against the
modern tide. Even older and more universal than the great religions,
than Trappist monasteries or Huxley's "perennial philosophy," myth
seemed a true voice of the primordial and eternal world, the ultimate

nonmodern pole of human experience. Then, at least in the eyes of the exemplary mythologists and their docents, the human psyche was fresher and purer, and timeless truth could be hidden in its stories. Yet the mythologists, essentially both academics and curés of the soul, were in an ambivalent posture between the primordial world and modernity. They were not dropout Beats or monks, but professors and physicians, inside the modernist camp, credentialed by its most characteristic institution, the modern university. For them, in the end, myth had to become mythology to be useful; it had to be studied and analyzed, and from it extracted what was universal and as applicable today as ever. This was tricky, for in fact myth in its original packaging is *only* particular and one dimensional. It is always a myth *of* a particular tribe or people, originating from some particular time in history, full of allusions to matters that would be best known to people of that time and place. Moreover, except in later literary versions ancient or modern, myths do not usually spell out the moral at the end. The reason why it is told, what it is about, must simply be *known*, perhaps without words.

Jung, Eliade, and Campbell, however, spent countless words in the telling both of the stories and the meanings. Like the nineteenth-century romantics, whose world of the spirit was their true home, they believed first and final truth to be located in the Distant and the Past, or in the depths of the self. The return to the supposed world of mythology was a return really to the premodern world *as envisioned by the modern world*. Mythology in the nineteenth and twentieth centuries was grounded on the modern world's fantasy of the premodern. For the mythologists, as for their romanticist progenitors, the mythological revival meant spirituality that was close to nature and the soil, that was symbol based, that expressed itself in accounts of heroes and other archetypes rather than individual figures. It was the world of Plato's cave, and the shadows on the wall were cast by the pure light of primordial dawn. The mythologists' myths were myths selected and related to fit modern need.

This is not unusual; religion reconstructs itself in every generation and must. The question is, what were the needs of the modern world understood to be? It is significant that in their own mythological reconstruction of religion, these three, especially Carl Jung, paid particular attention to ancient Gnosticism; and that a recent literary critic has provocatively argued that modern America, which by far contained the three mythologists' largest and most enthusiastic audiences, is fundamentally gnostic in spiritual style. We will now turn to the matter of gnosticism in the modern world, in this writer's view a touchstone for interpretation of the modern mythological vogue and much else as well.

## MODERN GNOSTICISM

The answer to the "needs of the modern world" question was, in mythological eyes, that what the world needed was a wisdom outside itself, for its problems could not be resolved on their own terms. What human wisdom from outside the human present could better be received and applied by modern humans than that contained in myth? It came from elsewhere, yet it did not require the difficult faith of dogmatic, exclusivist religion. It seemed rather, as packaged and interpreted by modern mythologists, to be universal and self-validating. This is the kind of wisdom known as gnosticism: a saving wisdom telling a universally important secret, but one which has to be received by one who has undergone right initiation (or perhaps has sufficiently suffered, and has right intent and sincerity), and which has been revealed by the right savior.

Ancient gnosticism was generally part of the Christian movement though related to Neoplatonism, Zoroastrianism, Mithraism, and other activities stirring in the spiritual melting pot of the Hellenistic world. A traveler to marketplaces of ideas like Alexandria or Athens would have heard of the various gnostic schools of teachers like Valentinus, Basilides, or the Ophites, and would also have found related Jewish movements inculcating the sort of mysticism that would eventuate in the Kabbala. Manichaeanism, commencing in the third century C.E., put gnostic-type beliefs on a world-religion basis.

What were the core beliefs of the ancient Gnostics? Typically, that this world was created by a "demiurge," a lesser god somewhere on the chain of intermediaries between the ultimate Light and material earth, who bungled the job. The true God is pure uncreated light, utterly transcendent and without parts or passions,. The inner nature of at least some humans is the same as that of the true God but, owing to the Bungler, the uncreated light is entrapped in our physical envelope. We humans are suffering because we were not made for this world but are caught in it anyway. Salvation releasing us back to the light from whence we came is attained through knowledge, or gnosis, of our true origin, nature, and destiny. This knowledge must first be shown to us by a savior or enlightened being, whose revelation then enables us to discover its truth within ourselves; as we shall see, Richard Noll has argued that Carl Jung believed himself to be such a gnostic savior for the modern world.

This gnostic "monomyth," to borrow Joseph Campbell's term, was then populated with numerous colorful if not bizarre names and details. Gnosticism speaks the language of myth even as it helps one understand the modern fascination with myth. But the fundamental point is always the same: salvation is essentially inward or intrapsychic, and entails the possession of secret, saving knowledge. Its basic assumptions then are:

1. We are inwardly of a different nature from the surrounding evil world, in which we are entrapped through no fault of our own.

2. Salvation must come from a source outside the present evil environment, which cannot overcome its contradictions on its own terms.

3. Salvation is in the form of secret knowledge or gnosis.

The "secret" aspect meant that gnosticism was often taken to be, in the words of a modern authority, "a knowledge of divine secrets which is reserved for an elite."[5] Some gnostic schools taught that only certain humans had the divine light within; most held that only some were now ready to receive the fullness of wisdom. At the same time, an authority like Hans Jonas, in his classic *The Gnostic Religion*, stresses the universality at least of the gnostic quest, comparing the gnostics' desperate search for meaning in an alien world to that of existentialism in modern times.[6] The widely read scholar of gnosticism Elaine Pagels has emphasized gnosticism's compatibility with contemporary psychological and therapeutic thought. She quotes, for example, this strikingly modern-sounding passage from the gnostic teacher Monoimus:

> Abandon the search for God and the creation and other matters of a similar sort. Look for him by taking yourself as the starting point. Learn who it is within you who makes everything his own and says, "My God, my mind, my thought, my soul, my body." Learn the sources of sorrow, joy, love, hate. . . . If you carefully investigate these matters you will find them *in yourself.*[7]

Such lines make the likelihood that modern gnosticism could come to us in the form of a combination of mythology and popular psychology appear not at all far-fetched. Why is it that ancient gnosticism sounds both distant and contemporary? The thought-worlds generally are different, despite the above, but the historical settings display similarities. In both, people experienced rapid change and some degree of progress. The Romans, for all their faults, had brought relative peace and prosperity to the Mediterranean world, and built their famous roads and spectacular cities. The "progress" of the nineteenth and twentieth centuries goes without saying. Enough progress had been experienced to suggest that someday, just past the cutting edge of the most advanced physics, we might learn the innermost secret of the universe and its manipulation—the ultimate gnosis.

Yet these were also times of anxiety and despair—Rome's routine cruelty and enslavement, modernity's wars and holocausts—suggesting that the secret was not in plain sight, but must be found through cunning, and needed a larger stage than the present. The new gnostics, like those of old, thus came to conclude that the great secret was not to be found *within* the same world that brought mixed progress and disaster in their hopelessly self-contradictory entanglement. It could not be located in the same science, engineering, social science, or medical-based psychology that made the roads and staffed the schools. It would need to come from sources far deeper and older than the one-dimensionality of the present, even if such a message might be capable of reaching no more than an elite. This was the role that the modern mythologists, well aware of gnosticism and quite sympathetic to it, saw for ancient myths recovered by them.

Actually, for several centuries Europe and America have harbored a veritable gnostic underground of intellectuals ready to sabotage any too facile celebration of progress and materialism. Writers like William Blake, Herman Melville, and Friedrich Nietzsche are among the spokespersons of a gnostic strand in Western thought that is temperamentally antimodern. This current sought to undermine exoteric belief in the world's ever-increasing technical knowledge with the help of secret but eternal wisdom.

Mainstream thinking, from Voltaire and de Condorcet to Herbert Spencer, believed that an age of rationality had dawned with the eighteenth century, bringing an end to superstition and injustice. Rational religion based on science would replace priestcraft, democracy would overthrow aristocratic tyrants, and in time vastly improved machines and medicines would bring a far better life to all. But the underground had its doubts.

Blake decried the emerging modern world's "number, weight, and measure." He was frankly gnostic in his exaltation of the eternal human Christ over against the tiresome old God called Urizen or Nobodaddy, he of the staunch loins and frozen scowl in Blake's drawings, who represented Enlightenment "reason" no less than patriarchal tyranny. Melville was also a gnostic who took for granted that this world was wrongly made by an incompetent spirit, and most of its quests like Captain Ahab's ultimately vain searches for white whales. Finally, nothing could be more at odds with modernity's essentialist view of progress and universal knowledge than Nietzsche's notion of eternal recurrence, in which all that we make is unmade and remade, over and over in a world without end, and all that is truly of worth is the eternal affirmation of the hero in the midst of change and decay.

Nor is the modern gnostic spirit necessarily precious or cultic. The literary critic Harold Bloom asserted:

> And the American religion, for its two centuries of existence, seems to me irretrievably Gnostic. It is a knowing, by and of an uncreated self, or self-within-the-self, and the knowledge leads to freedom, a dangerous and doom-eager freedom: from nature, time, history, community, other selves.[8]

The idea that American religion is fundamentally gnostic in structure, as unexpected as it may sound, is based on consideration of the importance of the conversion experience, the subjectivizing of religion that goes with religious freedom and separation of church and state, the prevalence of new revelations and inspirations, and the general importance of inner feeling and inner reward in the republic's religious life. The United States is indeed a wholly different religious environment, far more different than many Americans realize, from the religious situation almost anywhere else past or present since the Hellenistic age of the first gnosticism. Elsewhere one usually found only a single religious institution, a state church, or at the most two or three violently clashing bodies, dominating the situation. Here arises opportunity for rampant diversity, and with it the need to anchor faith not in a historic church, but above all within the depths of oneself. Though the inner self may also be shifting and elusive to the grasp, it is at least more firm a foundation than a myriad of sects. Together with this was the American theme, also addressed by Eliade, of return to the beginning, to the time of origins. Nineteenth-century churches wanted to return to the New Testament, abolishing if possible the legacy of the many centuries between then and now. Literature was full of the theme of reversing history and starting over in a new Eden. The mythologists, then, claimed to be bearers of stories direct from that time when the human world began. They said that, even if Eden cannot be rebuilt of modern brick, at least one can recover it in the inward places well known to American gnosticism. It is little wonder, then, that the gnosis of the mythologists, addressed to the self from out of time far behind either the modern puzzle or sectarian proliferation, was in the end especially well received in America.

But the sword of gnosis is double edged. We need to take into account another perspective on the term, that of Eric Voegelin's 1952 work, *The New Science of Politics*.[9] Voegelin, a political philosopher seeking to discover the root causes of the ills of the twentieth century, pointed his finger at troublemakers he labeled "gnostics." They were those who strove to rise above nature and find salvation through hidden knowledge of the political and psychological laws by which history secretly works. Modern examples of the gnostic were Comte, Nietzsche, Sorel, and of course the Nazis and the Communists, with their ideological credence that through understanding the "secret" laws of history and nature—those of, say, the metaphysical meaning of race or "dialectical materialism"—human nature could be radically changed and perfected. According to Voegelin, Gnosticism led to World War II and Russian armies in the middle of Europe, all because gnostic thinkers and leaders refused to see moral barbarism when it was there, preferring instead their dreams of how the world should be. Political gnosticism substitutes dreams for reason because it disregards the facts of the world that actually exists. The gnostic elite, no doubt fired by ideological myths, fantasizes that by human effort based on suprarational knowledge of the ultimate goal, their kind can create a society that will come into being but have no end, an earthly paradise equal to God's.[10] On the other side are those who recognize sin and the limitations of human nature, and for that reason are on the side of freedom, limited government, and a society unburdened by an imposed totalistic ideology. They believe, we are assured, in some kinds of "progress" but not in human perfectibility.

Voegelin went so far as to define all modernity as gnosticism, a term which encompassed such diverse phenomena as progressivism, Marxism, psychoanalysis, fascism, and National Socialism.[11] Later he clarified the position to the extent of revealing that modern persons who hold to "the Gnostic attitude" share six characteristics: dissatisfaction with the world; belief that the ills of the world stem from the way it is organized; surety that amelioration is possible; belief that improvement must evolve historically; belief that humans can change the world; conviction that knowledge—gnosis—is the key to change.[12] In his most memorable statement, Voegelin, who had himself lived under the Third Reich before going into exile and knew Europe's ideological wars at close range, put it well enough when he alluded to "the massacres of the later humanitarians whose hearts are filled with compassion to the point that they are willing to slaughter one-half of mankind in order to make the other half happy."[13]

Were the mythologists gnostic in Voegelin's negative sense of the word? Some of the same attitudes, even some of the same people (Nietzsche), appear in both his catalog of modernist gnostics and in our account of antimodern gnosticism. In both cases one finds the theme of secret knowledge of how the universe really works that is accessible only to an elite, and the idea that by the power of this knowledge one can reverse, or at least stand outside of, the stream of history. The basic problem with Voegelin, of course, is that he applies the term *gnostic* to speculative nostrums that were essentially political, whereas ancient Gnosticism, together with gnosticism as revived in the modern era by antimodern poets and mythologists, was apolitical if not antipolitical, scorning any this-worldly salvation.

In a real sense, Voegelin is not at odds with the mythologists, for what he calls gnosticism is what they might have called, in Jungian language, "ideological inflation." Both regarded the ills of modernity as fundamentally spiritual diseases. As Robert Segal has pointed out, Voegelin recognized that what defined modernity is confidence in its ability to master the world. The modern "gnostics" of Voegelin's demonology, from Sorel to Lenin and Hitler, shared that confidence even as they rejected ordinary nonspiritual, nonideological modernity's means of saving itself—science, technology, industry, and democracy. Like the poetic and mythological gnostics, they knew that modernity could not be saved on its own terms. They contended that the social cost of those means was too high; they had seen the ravages of bourgeois capitalism and the anomie behind modern urbanization and "democracy."[14] As technological antimodernists and totalitarian futurists, they wanted to combine the best of what modern science and secular thought had to offer with some form of a secret, gnostic, "spiritual" wisdom and power, whether of Marx or Mussolini.

For Voegelin held, that at base, modernity's confidence did not rest in science and technology so much as in a gnostic belief that supreme power lay in knowledge of the true nature of the world. That knowledge, ultramoderns assumed, could now be within the grasp of at least a modern elite. Physical science gave modernity part of that ruling knowledge, of course. But the human engineering aspect of managing history called for another science and other means of knowing. To the true gnostic, ancient or modern, the ultimate knowledge which is power is not about elemental forces but is intrapsychic; it is knowledge of the true nature of humans and so of right politics and social organization. But these studies were also becoming "sciences" in modern times.

Assuming that the idea that humans can irreversibly change the world for the better is essentially modern, the social ideology of the political antimoderns is paradoxically very modern at the same time, for the fascist and the communist takes to the ultimate degree the notion that by secret knowledge—*political* and *historical* gnosis—they could transcend history and make a new and irreversible paradisal world. They had a true believer's confidence in their ability to know the world secret, whether enshrined in Marxism or myth. As Stephan A. McKnight has put it, for Voegelin the key gnostic belief is that the gnostic has direct knowledge of ultimate human nature, and so knows how to overcome alienation. Therefore thought such as that of Comte or Marx is no more than political gnosticism, and modernity is not truly secular but a new form of religion, with its appropriate myths and rituals.[15]

A comparable situation can be seen in Japan, where the Marxist infatuation of many intellectuals came rather abruptly to an end with the triumph of militaristic nationalism in the 1930s. A congruent romantic literary cult emerged emphasizing classical Japan, the aesthetics of death, and the denial of modernity; it was clearly aligned to the neo-Shinto that envisioned a primordial Japanese paradise of simple living and heroic virtues, practiced close to the kami or gods, and now accessible primarily through myth and ritual.[16]

It is clear that these romantic dreams were not so much archaic as a way of both protesting modernism and preparing a nation spiritually for success in the thoroughly modern contemporary world of political and military power. The secret of such success, Japanese at the time felt as well as Europeans and others, lay in the gnosis of a past accessible through myth and an antimodern mood capable of generating power for modern triumphs. The mythologists obviously were in the same camp so far as the value of myth was concerned; the question is, how concerned were they with its political, in contrast to its personal, application?

The political world of the Roman Empire in which the ancient gnostics lived was rarely named in their writings; it was clearly and utterly part of the realm of fallen power and matter from which they sought escape. To them gnosticism was the opposite of a this-worldly ideology. It was a way *out* of the world of society, politics, and power into higher realms of being. Or, in the translation of modern mythological gnostics, it was a way to uncover realms within the psyche that can never be touched by the powers of the outer, political world.

The gnosticism of the mythologists, of Jung, Eliade, and Campbell, then, turns Voegelin on his head; what Voegelin means by gnosticism is what mythological gnosticism, closer to the ancient meaning of the term, seeks to save people from. It saves them from entrapment in the false hopes of worldly political fantasies. It instead unfolds compensatory fantasies, or intrapsychic realities, which show the self that its true recovery of wholeness lies within. If the mythologists' neognosticism had lasting political ramifications, they lay in the way that any ostensibly nonpolitical psychotherapy by default supports the existing order. Or, at best, it sustained spiritually the efforts of those prepared to make changes on the grubby level of everyday, nonideological politics by helping them get their lives clarified, and so do their useful work better.

The three mythologists under study, C. G. Jung, Mircea Eliade, and Joseph Campbell, were no doubt modern gnostics all the way through, and they were not unacquainted with both political and intrapsychic gnosticism. But my sense is that in the end, and only after some unfortunate dallying, they came down to an intrapsychic, not a political, gnosticism. They were certainly tempted at times by some version of the political gnostic myth in Voegelin's sense, usually in its fascist form. But they came through bitter experience to agree implicitly with the ancient gnostics that gnostic wisdom was intended for the soul rather than the state, and they did not present any full-blown mythical models that could be enacted on the political stage. Their political philosophy was finally that the state and society can do no more than safeguard the practice of intrapsychic gnosticism, and they wished of them only that they and their sort of people remain free to read and teach mythology, practice mythology-based therapies, and act out their personal myths in their private lives.

But to understand why they dallied and may have come close to presenting political models based on myth and gnosis, it is necessary to look at their social context and intellectual heritage.

## ANTIMODERNISM

Why mythological gnosticism? And why did political gnosticism become inner gnosticism? We must look again at the social and intellectual world of the mythologists. Despite war and worldwide depression, in the first half of the twentieth century the prevailing wisdom was that the future would be better, perhaps almost unimaginably better, than anything humanity had so far known. Somehow, after the wars and depressions, after the problems had been solved, a shining new world like that adumbrated by the 1939 World's Fair in New York would appear: a world of democracy, of ever-expanding scientific knowledge, of humming factories and universal prosperity, perhaps even space flights to other worlds. This was the vision, in caricature, of what has been called "modernism."

There was, of course, another side. This was the modernism of mind-numbing assembly-line jobs cursing the lives of people uprooted from familiar fields and villages. Now faceless in their bleak smoke-stack environments, these "masses" were less paragons of democracy than "atomized" individuals without extended family or significant place, prey to any demagogue who came along. Conservative observers bemoaned the loss of local cohesion found in common myths and sacralities, the loss of social hierarchy, the loss of moral and traditional values amid the modern wastelands.

What then did *modern* mean? Here it will suffice to present some qualities of modernism particularly useful for understanding the mythologists; these can be summed up in the two "metanarratives" Jean-François Lyotard has offered as the essence of modernism: the metanarrative of the emancipation of humanity by progress and the metanarrative of the unity of knowledge.[17] The first means, briefly, that cadres of educated elites since the effective beginning of modernism in the Enlightenment have believed that history controlled by persons like themselves was capable of freeing humanity from all its shackles through more and better knowledge and its application. The second metanarrative tells us that this knowledge which emancipates is found through the generalized, abstract, rational ways of thinking characteristic of science and social science. Under this rubric the particular is subordinated to the abstract category; the old is generally inferior to the new; the local submits to the universal.

The mythologists were far from alone is sounding alarms at excesses of modernism, though they may be regarded, in a particular but authentic sense, as the most radical of antimoderns. Others also sought to call those wandering on the spiritually stony ground of modernism back to some true faith, or to take vengeance upon its hateful philistines through a cause like fascism. But difficulties lay along the path of those, from T. S. Eliot to Billy Graham, who sought to correct modernity by appeal to one of the "great religions" like Christianity. For those faiths had fraternized with the enemy—indeed *were* the enemy as much as not. Actually the "great" religions, above all Judaism and Christianity, with their ancient founders and long histories, are world prototypes of what modernism really means. Before state or university went modern on anything like the same scale, they had their reasoned universal truths, their elites and bureaucratic institutions, their beliefs that history was, despite often dismal appearances, an arena of emancipation through progress: in this case through revelations of God or universal truth at specific historical moments, leading up to a supreme consummation.

The Hebrew scriptures present God as revealing law and truth successively to Noah, Abraham, Moses, and the prophets; to this Christianity adds the manifestation of God in Jesus Christ; both traditions look to an ultimate historical and metahistorical fulfillment in God's creation of a new heaven and earth. Beyond doubt Western modernism is to no small degree the secularization of Judaism and Christianity. At the same time, fascism was patently no less half modern and half antimodern, using radios, railroads, and bombers, together with dreamily utopian visions of paradisal racial futures, on behalf of Atilla the Hun agendas.

Moreover, on the local level, modernism was often experienced as only the newest mask worn by exploitation. Peasants who had common lands taken from them to make factory sites, and whose children then had to work for pennies in front of pitiless machines in that factory, did not see the modern dream at its best. Although themselves of different background, the mythologists were temperamentally attuned to the rhythms and values of the rural, peasant life in which living folklore seemed to have best survived. They were therefore at odds with all that was destroying that heritage.

The other side was not seldom comprised of the sort of modernist capable of imposing progress regardless of cost and whether desired or not. Although democracy was among the most deeply held ideals of modernism, the modern regimen also called for effective power by knowledge-holding elites. These were people particularly adept at the second of Lyotard's criteria of modernity, the unity of knowledge, pointing toward ability to organize all particular knowledge under universal and abstract categories like those of law, science, or social science, and to utilize that knowledge through industrial or social engineering. The kind of education that did this well prepared modernity's professionals, industrialists, enlightened civil servants, teachers, and often religious leaders.

There were also those whom modern progress left behind in the byways of rural life and local folklore, and they had their advocates. The mythologists were persons of modern education, really more interested in literary mythology than local folklore. But their sympathies were understandably often with those outside the progressive mainstream, from Native Americans to Romanian peasants.

The rural-roots-versus-modern-industry divide paralleled a more strictly in-house mythological chasm. Some students of myth, heirs of the Enlightenment, saw the mythical world as quaint and interesting, but long since superseded as a serious intellectual force. Others, including our three mythologists, protested that myth contained a powerful critique of modernity, one to which the world must listen. The divide was clearly between the Enlightenment spirit and romanticism.

*Romanticism* is as slippery a term as any to define precisely. As a school of thought and literary or artistic expression, it is based on the conviction that what excites the feelings and inspires the imagination is as valid, and even as true, as factual or rational knowledge. Its political expressions have ranged from romantic revolutionary ardor to reactionary dreams of an idealized medieval past. What both have in common is the characteristic romantic sentiment that political truth, like artistic truth, is known less by rational considerations than by its capacity to fire the passions and configure awesome visions of the heavenly city in the imagination. Political truth, along with artistic and spiritual truth, is therefore very apt to be found, at least in its ideal type, in the distant and the past, or the future, for that which is other serves well to charge the visionary imagination of the romantic temperament. Romanticism is not quite modern gnosticism. While it has a feeling for the reception of truth from the distant and the past, unlike the gnostic the romantic does not necessarily have a definite social or intrapsychic message from far away or long ago; sufficient is the sense of wonder evoked by that which is far away and long ago. Pure romantics would be more in tune with the musings of Henry David Thoreau:

> While the commentators are disputing about the meaning of this word and that, I hear only the resounding of the ancient sea, and put into it all the meaning I am possessed of, the deepest murmurs I can recall, for I do not in the least care where I get my ideas, or what suggests them.[18]

## The Romantic Roots of Modern Mythology

This is the source from which modern mythology sprang. The three mythologists arrived well after the first and most powerful wave of the romantic movement, but they were heirs of its spirit and, indeed, benefited from being able to receive from it living but mature doctrine, already hardening into partisan positions over against the confident progressive, scientific world of late Victorianism.

The modern revival of interest in myth began in the study of classical Greek and Roman texts, which was foundational to the early modern university. That in itself reminds us that myth in the European mind has never been free from ideological agenda. The medieval and early modern divide was between biblical "truth," and the human and divine worlds of myth "back then" in the classical writers or "out there" in India or elsewhere. Distinguishing myth from accepted belief enabled one to fabricate from myth an "Other" offering context, contrast, and profound corrective to the foreground spiritual patterns. Patristic and medieval religionists set the inferior temper of the pagan gods over against the claims of Christ.

The renaissance brought a major shift in the politics of myth, one that really laid the foundations of something like Joseph Campbell's view of myth. Unlike the serious Christians of the middle ages, the renaissance humanists who busily revived mythological learning often hardly bothered to conceal their enthusiasm for the robust sensuality and passion of the Greek gods and heroes, and their disdain for the asceticism of the saints except as an occasional subject of pious art. The tension between the sensual and the ascetic impulse was next expressed in the Puritan's inner asceticism versus outer prosperity, and the romantic poet's proverbial inner spiritual abundance versus outer deprivation. The energies generated by tensions like these were among the wellsprings of modernity.

The romantic mythological revival of the nineteenth century, insofar as it held up the romantic/mythological way of thinking as an antithesis to modernity, often continued the Christian/classic conflict by viewing much of the Christian past as antagonist, just as it saw the modern present in the same adversarial role. Both cross and smokestack seemed repressive and hard compared to the simple, joyous and free life promised by pagan myth. Mythology's pilgrimage might nonetheless pause to admire the middle ages, whose art and knightly spirit they often appreciated when presented in the spirit of Sir Walter Scott romanticism. But then the quest drove still deeper into the mists of lost Edens. During the Enlightenment religion as a major unifying cultural reality had steadily disappeared to become either philosophy or superstition. Romanticism, and the romantic view of myth, endeavored to salvage the inner and cultural meaning of religion under other names, as art, as nationalism, as mythology. This whole enterprise very much lived on the three mythologists here under study; Joseph Campbell, for example, was full of praise for both primal and medieval myths. He liked above all the quest for the Holy Grail, while scarcely hiding his dislike of much of Judaism and Christianity. But where he, and others, looked for the best of any religion was not in its preaching or rites, but in its art and stories.

The romantic founders of modern mythology took the quest behind the Renaissance by seeking out not only "classical" Greek and Roman myth, but increasingly myth from Germanic, Asian, and "primitive" sources. They accepted the romantic view of myth of German thinkers like Johann Gottfried von Herder, Friedrich W. J. Schelling, and the "folk psychology" of Wilhelm Wundt. That position, often embraced far too uncritically, insisted that myths stand apart in an entirely different category from other styles of folklore, such as legends, fables, or allegories. Those were stories; myths were collective creations of an entire people, and expressed in story form the basic worldview, and view of human nature, of that people.

It is important to realize that the categorization of myth as different from folklore and fairy tale is *modern*. It comes out of a modern need to see, in the archaic world, societies unified by common foundational stories believed by all. Unlike mere fables, these stories present a comprehensive cosmogony and model of the social order. Moderns yearned to believe that their ancestors perceived unity between the human and natural orders, a symbiosis pregnant with symbols and alive with significance—all unlike the painful modern schisms they sensed between the city and nature, or the human and the "dead" cosmos. In this belief in the uniqueness of myth they were influenced by Kant, for whom faith lay in the realm of emotion, not of reason. Faith and knowledge were therefore separate, as they were for Luther, at least as his beliefs were understood in nineteenth-century interpretations of the great reformer.

Thus faith could have its own nonrational but emotively powerful means of expression: myth. As interpreted by Jan de Vries, the romantic mythologists considered that "the spiritual power of myth over the human soul is precisely what makes it impossible to see in myth something invented or thought up by poets or philosophers."[19] Myth, now a powerful instrument of romantic consciousness, became a magic potion by which one could again drink of the rejuvenating power of humanity's primal vision. A second-rank representative of this perception, Joseph von Görres (1776–1848) offered this rhapsodic if confused recovery of the first humans admiring the wonders of their cosmos; he placed this scene in India, on the banks of the Ganges and Indus:

> They looked from the earth upward. There in heaven was the real realm of fire. There was the sun burning continually. There the stars, the planets and the fixed stars both, pierced through the darkness like flames. There the fires which only shine sparsely on earth were burning for ever unconquerable. Then the cult of fire became a cult of stars and the religion became pantheism. . . . And because all the nations were together in this great primordial state, these world views . . . form the inheritance which they bore with them on their long, later journeys.[20]

According to romantic mythology, myths were not the products of individual poets or philosophers but of "the people." They presented a deep wisdom, based on experiences of nature and the cosmos, and of human feeling often conflated with nature, that in humanity's earliest stage of development could only be communicated in stories. Myth instilled a sense of wonder and an almost indefinable kind of insight, like mystical experience. In the end its exaltations transcended the individual, and even the dualism of the human and the natural.[21]

The "folk psychology" of Adolf Bastian and Wilhelm Wundt postulated that collective folk wisdom adhered in all distinctive, "rooted" peoples. The idea of "rootedness," suggesting the superior worth and wisdom of peasant agricultural peoples who lived generation after generation on the same soil, was important and was to have a baleful influence. Different folk, according to Bastian and Wundt, have diverse national or cultural ways of thinking, expressed in national myths.[22] A community is more than a collection of individuals. It has a life of its own, and its products are distinctive both from individual creativity and from those of other nations. This was believed to be supremely the case among primitive peoples, who at the time were assumed to have only a collective mentality. Pronounced individuals were rarely if ever found among them, although hero figures in myth could singly embody a "people's" characteristics.

One illustration of this sort of romanticism that was politically reactionary, and important to our study, is the German movement known as "volkish thought," familiar to many through its reflection in the operas of Richard Wagner and in the propaganda of the Third Reich. Originally a romantic reaction against the international world of reason, science, and progress adumbrated by the Enlightenment and reinforced by the industrial revolution, volkishness called for Germanic distinctiveness and a simple, close-to-the-soil way of life.

Here are a few examples. In the 1860s Wilhelm Heinrich Riehl, in *Land und Leute* [Land and People], argued that the German Volk constituted an organic society that could not be separated from the native landscape on which they dwelt. Moreover, this society was to be hierarchical, patterned after medieval feudalism; the commercial, bourgeois tasks, of which Riehl was more suspicious, were to be managed by craft guilds fashioned on medieval lines. To be sure, the former exploitative relation of lord and peasant, or master and apprentice, could be improved upon; Riehl admired the idealistic British industrialist Robert Owen for his experimental enterprise at New Lanark, in which that capitalist cared for the welfare of his family of workers in the manner of a kindly patriarch. Workers, in turn, were not to be the dehumanized automatons of the modern factory, but creative individuals rooted in the Volk like the artisan of old.

The shapeless proletariat of the upstart modern industrial city, Riehl argued, was unstable, removed from the soil, antivolkish and almost beyond redemption. That class could only be repressed if not destroyed. The rootless urban mass included not only the wandering job-seeking worker pulled away from soil, kin, and native village, but also such products of modernity as the journalist and the ideologist who argued against the ancient ways of the Volk. Jews were particularly to be found in this group, which had to be extirpated before healthy volkish life could be recovered.[23]

The establishment of the German empire in 1871 gave a boost to volkish thought, both because it was a triumph of long-held dreams of German patriots, and also as a consequence of reaction against the disappointingly unromantic, bureaucratic, commercial nature of Bismarck's imperial state. There were those who yearned for something more, something medieval, oriented chiefly to rural peasant life, and at the same time deeply spiritual. As volkish motifs developed, these spiritual yearnings found voice in efforts to isolate a distinctive German religion apart from the universalistic aspects of Christianity and its Judaic roots. Volkish writers like Julius Langbehn (1851–1907), before his ultimate conversion to Roman Catholicism, embraced Swedenborgian and other doctrines of the theosophical type. Emanuel Swedenborg appealed to Langbehn particularly because of his belief that societies and the world as a whole constituted real organisms, while the individual reflected the living universe within.

Meister Eckhart, the great medieval German mystic in the neoplatonic tradition who spoke of a gnostic kind of idea of "God above God," was viewed by radical Germanic religionists as a representative of a deeper perspective than that of the Judeo-Christian scriptures. Indeed, in their eyes, all authentic Germanic mystics, imbibing the pure volkish spirit and living close to nature and the common people, like the gnostics of old dwelling on a plane far above that of the literalist and legalist, were attuned to a direct and intuitive realization of the oneness of being.[24]

Spirit, *Geist*, was an important idea. It was embodied not only in the world of ancient myth but also in a current figure like Friedrich Nietzsche. Nietzsche was interpreted by German volkish writers like Karl Joel as a supreme embodiment of *Geist* or spirit. No less significantly, his doctrine of eternal recurrence undercut as profoundly as any could modern notions of progress as eternally or eschatologically significant.[25] The deeply anti-Christian character of Nietzschean thought was also seminal. For Nietzsche as for his sometime friend, the brilliant recreator of myth on the operatic stage Richard Wagner, myth was the distinctive archaic medium of communication, the true voice of Geist and Volk. So well was the job done that the mere mention of Germanic myth all too easily now suggests the entire world of nineteenth-century, antimodern, volkish values.[26]

Such sentiments, at their height in the century roughly from 1850 to 1950, were by no means limited to the Germanic world. Everywhere, amid the dramatic scientific, technological, and political changes of that era, sensitive souls, Januslike, looked forward and backward, forward to the vistas of progress without end promised by modernity, then, seized with anxiety, back to the spiritual comforts of mysticism, medievalism, nationalism, and myth. One need think only of Slavophilism in Russia, Shinto nationalism in Japan, the Hindu renaissance in India, the "Celtic twilight" mystique of Yeats and others in Ireland, and the combined Arthurian cult of chivalry, empire, and the English gentleman in Britain.[27] In England the late Victorian and Edwardian periods to which we are chiefly referring were also the high point for the cultural influence of theosophy and Christian mysticism in the spirit of Evelyn Underhill. In the United States, it was the heyday of the schoolbook apotheoses of such heroes as Columbus and Washington, and of a glorification of the westward-marching frontier that gave little more consideration to the aborigines behind that frontier than any Germanic quest for *lebensraum*. In most of these and many other examples, one finds a rediscovery of founding myths and national heroes, an idealization of rural "rootedness" and peasant or pioneer life, an exaltation of feudal hierarchies and values, and a sense that the nation is not just a political entity but a spiritual reality as well. Some of these patriotic mysticisms are now in better odor than others. Some were certainly brought into the service of national independence movements and democratic reform in the progressive era ("make the nation truly worthy of its heroes") as well as of reactionary agendas. German volkish thought, though it contained much nonsense and will always be stained in retrospect by its association with the evils of the Third Reich, at the beginning was often no better or worse than the others.

By the last decade of the nineteenth century, however, volkishness was acquiring an ominous harshness, especially in its attitude toward Jews. Popular novels like Wilhelm von Polenz's *Der Büttnerbauer* (1895), in which a peasant loses his land through debt to a Jew and sees it turned into the site of a factory, pictured Jews as exploiters, as bringers of the evils of capitalism, industrialism, and modernity. Above all, whatever their virtues or vices, they were increasingly portrayed as irretrievably Other, alien to the organic unity of the Volk. Hitler once said that this work had influenced him. The nationalistic historian Heinrich von Treitschke claimed that Germany was a young state searching for self-awareness, and therefore Jews should not complain if that awareness was sometimes expressed in making distinctions between Germans and Jews.[28] It was von Treitschke who also first uttered the oft-repeated line, "Die Juden sind unser unglück" [The Jews are our misfortune].

Anti-Semitism was by no means limited to Germany. Until the rise of the Nazi regime it took its most brutal forms in Russia and eastern Europe. At the same time, it was hardly unknown in the English-speaking world. "Restrictions" in housing, education, and club memberships affected "Semites" everywhere, and one could hear endless anti-Jewish "jokes." Anti-Semitism was a dark side of the glorious mythic dimensions of race and nation. Against their bright images Jews were alien, dark shadows on the margins of social reality. One could praise them, do business with them, resent them, hate them: whatever the attitude, they were regarded them as different, other, and so a problem or potential problem.

In the German-speaking world anti-Semitism gathered with ominous force. Not all "real Germans" advocated the physical elimination of Jews. But the idea that they were different, foreign, "other," not real Germans, in a land that truly belonged only to real Germans, was widely accepted. How one should respond to the reality of their presence—whether to like them or hate them, welcome them or make them unwelcome, tolerate them or exterminate them, were secondary matters, though of course crucial to Jews, and on them one might find differences of opinion.

Eugen Diederichs, a notable volkish writer, editor, and publisher from the turn of the century until his death in 1927, espoused one possible opinion. Carl Jung had on his shelves several books on Gnosticism published by Diederichs. A colorful personality who lived in the small university town of Jena, this individual reportedly held court at the legendary Greek feasts of his "Sera circle" wearing zebra-skin pants and a turban as he proclaimed a "new romanticism" to counter the simplistic naturalism and rationalism of the times. His new romanticism emphasized the oneness of the world, and within it the unity of land and Volk; but Diederichs also rejected anti-Semitism as he understood it. While he portrayed Jews in accordance with current stereotypes as given over to arid legalism and intellectualism, he also saw them as a distinctive people with their own spirit and organic cohesion, a culture to be set alongside others. As we shall see, the vacillations of Jung, and in their way also of Eliade and Campbell, on the Jewish issue seem at root to reveal an internal cognitive struggle between some degree of liberal democratic sensitivity and a visceral feeling that the Jew is "other." Enthusiasts of the "rooted," traditionalist, organic society, so closely aligned to the world evoked by mythology, sensed that Jews were in its terms alien and different, more a part of the forces destroying traditionalism than an antidote to the evils of modernity. But like Diederichs they were pulled both ways on the matter, unable to give up either volkishness or liberalism, or to follow either firmly and consistently to its ultimate logical outcome.

Diederichs's new romanticism could see in other peoples besides Jews counterparts to what volkishness meant to Germans. Slavs, Celts, and even non-Europeans like Indians, Chinese, and the Islamic peoples could also be "rooted" in their own land, culture, and myths. Here lay an opening to another significant dimension of the new mythology: its attitude toward non-European and non-Christian peoples. This terrain has been disputed in the wake of Edward Said's much-discussed *Orientalism*, with its argument that European scholars essentially constructed the East they purported to study in the colonial period.[29] Did Europeans approach Asian cultures with genuine openness, or did they seek there only what they wanted to find—exotic civilizations with values quite different from those at home, reservoirs of ancient wisdom like that embodied in myth, perhaps, but whose people were barely capable of abstract, rational thought? Did they merely project onto them the primitive world or the Orient that Europe required for its own completion? Did they want to see along the Ganges or in the Congo societies "arrested" yet for that very reason less fragmented than their own, offering visions of constricted wholeness which, while obviously not to be taken in their entirety by more advanced persons, presented resources for the healing of the West?[30]

Any "organic" society calls insistently for an Other to clarify its self-definition. But the Other can be, perhaps must be, both alien and reinforcing. It can function as a negative confirmation of one's own "organic" identity and values, as the Jew so served the Volk. Occasionally—but significantly—the Other can offer a superior model of civilization that confirms one's aspirations, and pointedly reinforces criticism of one's own society, as did the idealized Orient for some romantics from Thoreau to Diederichs. Luis O. Gomez has noted that Carl Jung, in his studies of India, was "also seeking in the other, in India, a self-confirmation . . . almost as if one needed to recognize in an other parts of oneself that could not be seen as self, and would otherwise remain totally other, inaccessible, and unacceptable."[31] India represented something hidden in the European psyche, that needed the experience of India to be discovered and held up as a mirror to Europe.

The idea of the primitive and the archaic obsessed romantic mythologists. On the one hand the lost world was a glory hole holding all the most profound and most authentic sentiments of the human race, or of particular races, with which what is best today must resonate. On the other hand the primal world was too undifferentiated to be brought over whole. But there could be selective reaction.

One could of course proclaim a radical political eschatology like the utopian or Marxist envisioning a consummation that, like all great eschatologies, was mythology-fueled return to the paradise of ultimate beginnings. But political radicalism had a destructive side with which the romantic was not entirely comfortable. Furthermore, twentieth-century futuristic utopias required confidence in the scientific, industrial, democratic, and cultural "progressive" tendencies of the modern world they would presumably fulfill, and that was a confidence the real romantic lacked. Political reaction is and was a more immediate possible consequence of modern romantic thinking. If the modern world was fallen, the shortest road to paradise might lead backward. Either way, myth contained something modernity needed.

## THE MEDICINE OF THE MODERN WORLD

By the late nineteenth century, then, romantic mythologists had made myth potentially available to thinkers requiring such a resource as medicine for the ills of the modern soul. Myth was an elixir very different from those fashioned in the laboratories of modern individualism. To recapitulate, there were three main differences: the mythic world pointed to a collective, not individualistic, society, and so its creativity was likewise collective rather than individual; in the world of myth nature was not alien inert matter merely subject to technological use, but possessed subjectivity continuous with the human and the divine; and this alternative universe, recovered from the springtime of humanity, like romanticism itself exalted nonrational, intuitive, "poetic" ways of knowing. Myth connects the self to society and world, unlike rationality, which depersonalizes and objectifies that which is other than self.

But what of the "lost" modern proletarian, so deprecated by W. H. Riehl? What of the lowly modern urbanite, whom José Ortega y Gasset and C. G. Jung were to call "mass man," whose rootlessness and depersonalization amid the masses of the modern industrial city seemed like a dark parody of tribal collectivity? Volkish writers and their allies exalted the "rooted" rural classes while deploring the empty, wandering lives of urban masses in the gloomy new cities built by the industrial revolution.

Here comes a paradoxical but very important twist in the dialectic of myth. Mythologists worshiped at the shrine of tribal collective consciousness in the beginning, holding that myth was not composed by a single person but was the voice of the "people." But in the modern world, at least until racial consciousness was again gathered into the "single will" of the people on which the Nazis harped, collectivity simply became "mass man." Glory lay with the individualism of one who, patterning himself on ancient hero myths, won solitary triumphs on behalf of all. Modern humanity was no longer the primordial well of collective inspiration, but had seriously fallen from it into "mass man." Out of that pit salvation can only be individual, yet it must reflect values larger than the individual if the mythic dimension of the modern hero's calling is to have any meaning. The paradox of collective and heroic in myth was never fully resolved.

Even in primordial tribal societies the hero's role was ambivalent, for the hero must emerge out of an organic society that has a rich collective consciousness. The hero who transcends that collectivity must also be a part of it, so that it is the tribe's values that are made visible and timeless in the grand and authentic gestures of the hero, the Odysseus or Siegfried. Today the collective has degenerated, through a false uprooted individualism wrought by commerce and industry, into the depressed counterfeit collectivity of the modern city. It can only be rescued, modern mythmakers might argue, by new heroes who retrieve the power latent in ancient symbols, not excluding the fasces, the swastika, the hammer and sickle.

The possible political concomitants of this kind of mythology are almost too obvious: one wants a homogeneous, largely rural, and "rooted" society with a hierarchical superstructure; this society should possess a religious or mystical tendency able to express its unity ritually and experientially. Today such a society could only be recovered through a new enactment of the hero myth by one able to awaken the primordial but slumbering values of this people and call them into being again. This is one direction mythology could go, and has gone, in the modern world: nationalism, especially when based on a single leader embodying the people's *Geist* and idealized to heroic stature.

The two major apertures available to generic myth in the modern world were in individual psychological procedures and in nationalism. Other possibilities were preempted. Liberal or radical reform was taken over by secular myths such as Marxism or by the myths of specific relevant religions, as in the Christian social gospel. Social roles had their indigenous mythic models already staked out in the earlier mythic revival: Victorian reconstructions of chivalry provided models for the English gentleman, Daniel Boone epitomized and idealized the American frontiersman. The catastrophic twentieth century called for something more: myths to radically transform nations; myths to transform, not merely legitimate, individual roles.

On the face of it, tools were available for both individual and national courses. The very individualism on which twentieth-century mass man quixotically prided himself, together with the notion of progress, made people want to progress inwardly, to inwardly simulate growth and evolution, by moving from one psychic state to a better one. In the hands of Jung and Campbell, mythic scenarios were ready-made models for individuals in the process of inner transformation.

Nations also could move on to what they trusted were higher stages of their own development through attaining the inner cohesion

and unity of purpose afforded by a mythic model, with reference back
to the "organic" society supposedly realized in mythic times. This is
what Eliade meant by "Romanianism" in the 1930s, and what Jung at
the same time called "Wotanism" in regard to Germany.

These two processes, the individual psychological and the nationalistic, were ostensibly at odds with the fundamental character of
modern society—its scientific, "statistical" homogenization, its pro-
fessedly democratic institutions. Moreover, the modern mind cannot
really countenance the possibility of any sort of large-scale change
except through the political process. The mythology movement therefore had to be in some way (maybe only a mythic one) political.

But it could not be liberal or progressive in the ordinary sense,
since that implied only more of the same, scientizing and bureaucra-
tizing human life rather than mythologizing it. It could not be conservative in the usual sense either, since that also implied more of the
same science and bureaucracy, save now more in the hands of business corporations than of government. A radical change, such as the
mythologists required, could only be reactionary, returning in significant
ways—maybe only individually, maybe nationalistically—to an idealized traditional world.

But here is where the approach of the mythologists needs to be set
carefully against that strand of thought which led to Mussolini, Hitler,
and Stalin. In fact, the gnostic mythology of Jung, Eliade, and Campbell,
contemplative in fundamental intent, contrasts significantly with the
apocalyptic definition and use of myth in the political wing of modern
mythology. In the end, Jung, Eliade, and Campbell turn out to be more
oriented toward individual than national transformation, though no
less significantly political for that reason.

## APOCALYPTIC AND GNOSTIC MYTH

The cleavage between Enlightenment and romantic views of mythology is but a special case of a larger divide in modern thought
between the Enlightenment and romanticism. That is between the
Enlightenment perception of the individual as autonomous; and a
second school, which arose together with romanticism, that affirmed
the determinative role of history and society on individual lives. The
first was the gift of Locke and his followers, the second of Hegel,
Marx, and their heirs. The latter emphasized the extent to which one's

very *consciousness*—the favored term—is shaped by one's place in the unfolding of history, or by one's socioeconomic status.

No more than a glance at the horrendous slums and industrial conditions of the nineteenth century was needed for those persuaded by the communitarian or organic view of society to posit certain situations as considerably more disadvantaged or oppressed than others. Justifiable in its original setting, this finding was ultimately to lead both to salutary democratic reforms from the abolition of child labor to the legitimization of unions, and to the twin evils of twentieth-century Marxist and fascist totalitarianisms.

The intellectual roots of communism and fascism were profoundly intertwined. The foundation of both was rejection of the liberal, Enlightenment belief in the autonomous individual. The individual was instead essentially identified as a part of a larger community or group. This identity was believed to shape one's consciousness and destiny inescapably for better or worse. Finally came the practical assumption that many if not most persons are inextricable parts of oppressed communities. If communities are to overcome oppression, it must be first of all through conscious realization of the group identity and the nature of the oppression. Thus workers in their common economic plight as laborers with nothing to sell but their labor must first of all assert that identity. Their solidarity with their socioeconomic class, from the Marxist perspective, takes precedence over those of culture or volk or religion or individual personality or anything else.

It is only at this point that Marxist communism and fascism part company significantly. The Marxist identification was with socioeconomic class, emphasizing the oppressed proletariat; the fascist identification was instead with the oppressed nation or race. We have seen how the volkish approach to mythology was interwoven with the latter consciousness.

But although the community identification theme arose in its modern form along with romanticism, it would not be true to say that Hegelianism and Marxism were no more than romanticism. These philosophies and romanticism were both reactions against enlightenment autonomy, but they were not the same thing. Romanticism possessed not only warm feelings about community, especially primordial "organic" communities, but it also bestowed its benediction on a rich individualism that exalted in personal dreams, raptures, and agonies, and which offered much scope for the fulfillment of the hero's calling in accordance with one's own vision. Idiosyncratic individual heroic dreams could only be regarded with deep suspicion in the iron-clad societies of totalitarian salvation.

The divergence of the merely romantic or volkish mythologist from the fascist/communist use of myth may be illumined by turning to the work of Georges Sorel (1847–1922). That ambivalent French social thinker, beginning as a Marxist, became very interested in the social uses of myth and of revolutionary violence. He influenced Mussolini and, at least paradigmatically, articulated the mystique of the twentieth-century cult of revolution as redemptive and purifying.

Sorel added to Marx's sometimes dry analysis the dynamic antirationalism of radical romanticism, holding that heroic myths and violence were wellsprings of social transformation, and so profoundly moral. In this circumstance they, and the doctrines behind them, were not to be judged for their veracity so much as for their use as weapons for struggle. For Sorel myths were "systems of images" that enable people who participate in social combat to conceive of their endeavors as battles that would end in triumph and redemption. Like sound-bites and propaganda posters, myths, or mythic images, were less to be considered intellectually or historically than in their relation to feeling and action. Sorel was opposed to discursive thought, and to descriptive or rationalistic kinds of thinking; he was concerned with what drove revolutionary action and change. For Sorel, the fundamental revolution was the oppressed against the oppressor, the Marxist struggle of the proletariat against the capitalist. He made this conflict antirational, mythical, apocalyptic, and so religious in the functional sense of the word.

It is important to realize that, while volkish and other nineteenth-century recoveries of myth may have had a place in the background of the twentieth century, it was the Sorelian concept of myth that was the dynamic of twentieth-century revolutionary Marxism and fascism, insofar as they are mythology in action. This is true whether the debt was explicit, as it was to a significant extent in the case of Mussolini, or whether it amounted to a more or less independent discovery of the same principle, as it may well have been for communism and Nazism. For Sorel and the Sorelians, the social function of myth was key to the understanding of the term: its value lay in its religious, indeed apocalyptic, character; in its orientation to world transformation.

Because its apocalyptic picture of change was total, it was antirational, for it brooked no standard of truth or judgment outside itself. It had to be an incitement to absolute action free of any doubt or qualification. It is sufficient to think of the Nazi and communist myths of racial or class oppression followed by dramatic revolutionary redemption. On the level of concrete mythic symbols, one may recall the swastika flags dipped in the blood of Nazi martyrs paraded at the Nürnberg rallies, or the undecaying body of Lenin preserved and virtually worshiped at Red Square in Moscow. For the role of stimulating total commitment, so comparable to the dynamics of religious conversion, myths and their associated symbols were extraordinarily effective, for they cannot be undercut—since the ground of belief in a mythic reality is transcendent and not subject to mere human critique.[32]

However, Sorel's idea of myth differed from that of the three mythologists. Theirs might be called a gnostic view (in the non-Voegelin sense), and Sorel's apocalyptic. The gnostic concept is Platonic and contemplative; it emphasizes the way myth functions in individuals and society as a means to profound understanding. Far from immediately inciting revolutionary action, it often undercuts actions through its appeal to a wider and more accepting wisdom. Indeed, the work of the three mythologists could be, and has been, accused of offering the oppressed heavy doses of Marx's opiate of the people by carrying their thoughts away to dreamy inward-looking or escapist mythological worlds. For better or worse Jung, Eliade, and Campbell were essentially Platonic or gnostic in their *use* of myth. They may have unearthed some of the same root myths, or types of myths, that Sorelian marxists and fascists sought to use in the service of radical social transformation. But the mythologists' apocalypses were inward or intellectual, and so stood in a different relation to the political realm from the Sorelian. The latter is action driven, valuing myths for their prophetic-religious value in imaging and inciting absolute change. The mythologists' goal instead was deep wisdom, above all about the self and its symbolic life; if there were political consequences of this knowledge, in the end the three came to realize they would be indirect, and sometimes counsels of restraint rather than of action.

A second but related difference was the question of original goodness versus original sin. A lineage of thinkers from Mencius to Marx has taught that human nature is good, peaceable, and sociable in its true and original form. The evil of the world is due to evil structures of society rather than inherent individual evil; most people, apart from a few saints, will be no better than the society in which they find themselves. But make society better and people will become better in their nature, recovering more and more of their original goodness. Understandably, this view has been sympathetic to the "right of revolution" in political thought; when evil social structures are changed, if need be violently, human nature can permanently be changed to good.

The other side, with a lineage from Augustine and Calvin through Freud, Voegelin, and Reinhold Niebuhr, argues that evil, or the mindless selfishness of the id, is inherent in the individual as well as society. This line of thought is compatible with the gnostic view that the world itself was made by a blundering god, the creation and the fall one and the same event. It leads to the more pessimistic view that even if the social order is changed for the better, people will find ways to be as unpleasant as ever. After the revolution, the cadres of the triumphant group or party, themselves no better than they ought to be, will soon enough become "more equal" than others and take over the office of the former exploiters, like the pigs moving into the house in Orwell's *Animal Farm*.

The mythological position on this matter was in some ways ambivalent, but in effect tended toward the Augustinian side. This was first of all because, in Eliadean language, it put a clear line between cosmos and history. Cosmic religion and spirituality, embodied in the oldest myths, was pure in that it was pristine, fresh from the hands of the gods. But history, leading down to modernity, was a kind of fall, which has meant that, as Augustinians and Niebuhrians would say, all attempts to change society for the better within history meet with only ambiguous and partial success. While it is necessary to try to make the world better, efforts to do so entail the danger of people believing they can act again as if in the mythical purity of cosmic times. It would be better to try to improve conditions through small and pragmatic steps. Those who advocate revolutionary change as though enacting mythologies of apocalypse are not aware, the gnostic mythologists would insist, of how powerful are the primordial forces they are unleashing. Painful experiences of their own had been the mythologists' first teachers of this lesson. The energies of the first creation are not at home in modern civilization; they are like the proverbial bull in a china shop;

they are likely to run out of control and work as much harm as good. Thus Jung remarked, "If Communism, for instance, refers to Engels, Marx, Lenin, and so on as the 'fathers' of the movement, it does not know that it is reviving an archetypal order of society that existed even in primitive times, thereby explaining, incidentally, the 'religious' and 'numinous' (i.e. fanatical) character of Communism."[33]

Like all believers in original sin, the mythologists would say in effect that salvation must be first and foremost individual, a personal act of divine grace, not merely engineered through social reform. On these grounds too they would favor the gnostic over the apocalyptic use of myth, for mythological "contemplation" is the first step to individuation or personal salvation. Gnostic salvation for the ancients was individual liberation from the stream of historical time in a suffering world back to the our true home, the timeless halls of light. The best hope for society is that enough persons would be sufficiently interested in the inner quest to forego outward greediness, and that nostalgia for Eden might lead one to make this world more of a paradise for the sake of its recollection.

So it was that while all three of the mythologists dabbled at least ideologically in political mythology, even on occasion romanticizing its apocalyptic expression, finally for them myth came to be internalized as a means of cohesion with one's true self rather than with soil and social movements. One could even make bold to say that, in the end and only after some missteps, the three mythologists managed to save what was best in volkish mythology and its romantic roots from fatal contamination with unsavory politics, and redirected those dangerous energies to make of them an inward therapeutic, even as early Christianity allegedly translated disappointed apocalyptic expectations into otherworldly salvation. Let us now turn to the mythologists themselves for confirmation, or disconfirmation, of such an idea.

# CARL GUSTAV JUNG AND
# WOTAN'S RETURN

## BOY AND MAN

The psychology of C. G. Jung rests on psychic biography. Biography in this case means the narrative of the subject's inner life, above all as it is expressed in dreams and fantasies. For from the Jungian perspective, the real life of an individual, as of the world, is inward. So it was, at least, that Jung himself saw his own work, which is profoundly autobiographical in its genesis. From the Jungian perspective, real life is not, on the profoundest level, one's worldly life of homes, marriages, or jobs, but is the flow of a mighty underground river to which life's surface phenomena are but reflections or diversions. Politics as such are the least of concerns to the god of this river, yet the river is the ultimate source of all that happens in politics, as in everything else. Seen or unseen, the underground river of the unconscious makes occur what occurs.

If there is anything that Jung's eighty-seven years teach us, it is that projecting the passions of the gross political realm onto the psyche, or conversely allowing the psyche to adventure into the realm of outward politics armed only with its archetypes, is bound to be disastrous. Better to let the psyche blossom in its own way in its own internal soil and under its own sun, and keep politics plain and low to the ground, as they were in Jung's native Switzerland. Times there were when Jung let the borders between politics and psyche fray more than he should have. But in the end he seems to have learned that only the most rigorous separation between soul and state is safe for real people. If the kind of energy and archetypal symbolism that go into making up the psyche were allowed into political affairs, and one tried to make the outer world work like the affairs of dreams and myths, the results would be as disastrous as if fish tried to live on land, or birds in the depths of the sea. Some birds can of course dive, and fish leap briefly into the air, but such excursions are appropriate only for a short nourishing moment, not as a way of life.

Statecraft ought therefore to be kept at a minimalist, pragmatic level in order to let souls be souls in their own free way. Nonetheless, the maintenance of religious and mythological tradition is important in societies, for these are the treasure houses of resources in story and symbol that souls need to complete themselves. Moreover, as souls go about their own business of finding psychic completeness they may discover themselves, as it were inadvertently, making history.

Thus it is not easy to keep psyches out of politics in Jungian thought, for according to this school psyches ultimately create the world, and the history, in which politics happen. Compared to the psyche, the outer realm is a pale reality, only a screen on which to project the trailings of the soul's inner weather, its turbulence and light. One must learn to see and let be. Here Jung differed from his sometimes mentor, Sigmund Freud. In the terms of Jung's own system, Freud was an extravert, who saw the outer world as the hard, solid "reality principle" against which one batted one's head in vain. "Maturity" meant to accept it and deeply discount all religious and other systems that would cast specious illusion over the adamantine actuality. But for Jung, myth and religion were flesh and bones of what was real because they were integral to the psyche, and the psyche was in the last analysis the only reality we can know. Looking outward, we see—or make—a soft and shifting "reality" put there by the psyche.

By the logic of his worldview, Freud was basically a pessimist about history and human civilization; they were not so much positive goods as desperate stratagems to contain with acceptable limits the powerful irrational energies of the libido, the essentially sexual inner self, yearning to break free and express itself in all ways at once.[1] Over that volcano civilization and the history made by its measures are necessary but repressive caps, and the repressed is seething beneath the polite veneer. Indeed, the legerdemain of politicians could draw as much from what was beneath the lid as cover over the boiling pot. The position of Freud's anthropological disciple, Géza Róheim, has been described in this manner:

> For Róheim, politics was a kind of black magic. the political leader, far from being descended from the gods (as in traditional hierarchical theory) had risen from the depths of hell. The politician was the modern descendant of the sorcerer, and political science, therefore, was most accurately treated as a branch of demonology.[2]

The Hungarian Róheim, a central European contemporary of Jung, had like the latter no lack of observable evidence to support the most demonological theories of politics imaginable. Yet, though Jung came, after hesitation, to develop his own version of political deviltry at work in respect to the most egregious case of all, National Socialist Germany, his ultimate position was a bit different from the Freudian.

Freud was modern in his own self-conscious assumptions about science, religion, and society, even though he tortured modernity into directions unfamiliar to heirs of the Enlightenment. The channels had been cleared by romanticism, but to hear a medical doctor talking about dreams and the unconscious in 1900 and later fell as strangely on nineteenth-century ears as the new century's new unmelodic music. Yet the radical modern agenda was still there for Freud: progress, materialism, health through secularization and science. Despite the Austrian Jew's well-earned skepticism about European civilization, one could still envision a scientific and perhaps socialist earthly paradise once humanity, in a mighty psychoanalytic spasm, sloughed off its repressions.

Jung was antimodern in a way Freud was not, for he substantially sought to understand and correct the modern from standpoints outside of itself, like a gnostic aware that the true history of an individual or a world began immense aeons above and before its present experience in time. Such a stance could of course have opened the door for endorsement of explicitly antimodern political movements, and we will look at controversies concerning the extent to which he did this. But Jung saw himelf chiefly as a doctor of the individual soul, and of civilization on a very deep level, who increasingly came to understand that in this world nothing is quite what it seems. For all experience has been projected through the distorting lenses of psyches whose real realm is not the outer world. This brings us to Jung's autobiography, *Memories, Dreams, Reflections*.[3]

The psychic autobiographical base of Jungianism is eminently evident in this late book, wherein he probed in himself, as the grandest case of all, what he had prospected in the subterranean mineshafts of so many other psyches. This strange and wonderful volume is assembled from autobiographical and other writings interwoven with leisurely reminiscing conversations recorded and substantially edited by Aniela Jaffé, his secretary. The end product is less photographic autobiography than painterly self-portrait, with the symbolic enhancement one might expect in such a work from the hand of a master of self-creation. Peter Homans called it "a special genre of its own"—"automythology."[4] After so many years the details of dreams and fantasies may be smudged; what remains is the image of a life interpreting itself as fired to an extraordinary degree from out of the depths of its being. It is the vibrantly alive unconscious that drives the engines of this individual and is the real "hero" of this narrative; it is overwhelmingly powerful dreams which, like underground explosions, mark each stage in this career.

Few readers will soon forget Jung's terrifying nightmare allegedly at the age of only three or four years, when he came into an underground chamber and in the dim light saw there enthroned a gigantic phallus, a single luminous eye at its tip. Nor will they soon let sink into oblivion the pubescent fantasy in which God dropped a huge turd on the beautiful sparkling roof of the Basel cathedral, shattering the sacred structure. All this was against the backdrop of years in which Jung was in a complex relation with his parents, especially his father, a pastor who struggled with religious uncertainty.

Carl Jung thought it was partly because of these inappropriate doubts that the clerical Jung was often edgy. Not a few stormy scenes disrupted family life, though the son also remembered hours of love and of trying to understand one another. Yet as is often the case in such homes, especially when one is as obviously a congenital introvert as Carl Jung, the boy maintained a rich and secret inner life. Indeed, as he set off for college, Jung saw himself as twofold. "No. 1" was "a rather disagreeable and moderately gifted young man with vaulting ambitions, an undisciplined temperament, and dubious manners . . . in his innermost essence a hermit and obscurantist." "No. 2," on the other hand, "regarded No. 1 as a difficult and thankless moral task, a lesson that had to be got through somehow," but in his own nature this strange being "had no definable character at all," but was "born, dead, everything in one; a total vision of life," and that specter pursued the visible Jung like a shadow.

There was also something medieval about No. 2, in the sense that he seemed to belong to the occult world evoked by Goethe's *Faust*. At the time, characteristically guided by a dream, the young man believed he should follow the light of consciousness and leave the shadow to itself. He was haunted nonetheless to the end of his years by what he took to be No. 2's ultimate nature, the Void, which embraces all beginnings and endings, and which could hold its own against final darkness.[5]

In college Jung took up the study of medicine. But he also took time to scan the German intellectual world of his time. He read not only Faust, but also Nietzsche's *Thus Spake Zarathustra*; though that philosopher probably influenced him more than any other writer outside of professional psychology, he later said he saw in Nietzsche an unbalanced genius who had made a dangerous mistake when he "fearlessly and unsuspectingly let his No. 2 loose upon a world that knew and understood nothing about such things."[6] The student Jung also absorbed with profit Schopenhauer, Kant, and Swedenborg. For a time he was intensely engaged in the study of spiritualism and psychical research, not only through reading, but also by attending seances, including those of a mediumistic cousin of his, Helene Prieswerk. Those observations became the basis of his dissertation for the medical degree, "On the Psychology and Pathology of So-Called Occult Phenomena."[7]

For as his specialization Jung had selected psychiatry, partly because he believed it would allow him to combine his humanistic and philosophical interests with medicine. In December of 1900 he commenced his career by taking up a post as assistant at the Burghölzli Mental Hospital in Zurich. That same year Freud's epoch-making *The Interpretation of Dreams* was published, introducing his intensely controversial theories of psychoanalysis to the profession and the general public. Jung read the book, recognized Freud's importance, and took up his cause. Jung later claimed that even then he did not accept the opinion of the father of psychoanalysis that sexual trauma was the origin of all repression, and had a higher view of religion and spiritual things than the older man. Nonetheless he became a partisan of Freud at a time when the Viennese doctor enjoyed little respectability in the psychiatric world, and such discipleship could offer few career benefits. Jung met Feud in 1906; for a time the two men were close, Freud not hesitating to anoint the younger as his chief docent and heir apparent.

In 1913 they broke with each other, one immediate cause being Jung's 1912 work *Wandlungen und Symbole des Libido* (*Transformations and Symbols of the Libido;* translated as *The Psychology of the Unconscious*).[8] In that work Carl Jung went beyond his senior's "unendurably narrow" conceptual framework, as Jung called it in the forward. Casting his gaze well beyond Freudian narrowness, the Swiss disciple fraternized with premodern and antirational themes as well as with the Age of Reason. Images from the volkish and Nietzschean mythological vogues, in all their reaction against the Enlightenment spirit, began to suggest in Jung's *Wandlungen* that modernity itself was the problem, and that European humanity needed to return to very ancient wells for renewal. Yet at the same time Jung was a man of his time and place, and he was not alone. As we have seen, in the decades before World War I a form of late romantic nationalism—volkish, Wagnerian, Nietzschean, sometimes anti-Semitic—was shouldering its way in alongside modernity, battening on modern discontents. It could not easily be argued with, for it conceded little to the canons of rationality. Like Jung, and Freud too in his way, this cause knew that the real king, the psyche, rules by other rules.

Jung was comfortable with much of mythological late romanticism, for he was well aware of modernity's inner demons. He knew how much had been pared off the fullness of a human psyche to make it fit the needs of Enlightenment rationalism and industrial production. He saw all around symptoms of the modern alienation, rootlessness, and spiritual emptiness that the volkish theoreticians talked about. Jung was concerned that modern men and women find ways back to the resources of other times and places where what was missing might be recovered.

The whole massive work of *Wandlungen* was based on the "Miller Fantasies," the charming journal of dreams, imaginings, and poetry left by a young American woman then traveling around the Mediterranean, who wrote as "Miss Miller." We are reminded how much of Jung's interest in universals started as a therapist involved in the psychic processes of individuals. *Wandlungen* presented psychic process as movement toward "individuation," or rebirth as a new person in whom all unconscious constituents, which appear to deep consciousness as "archetypes" analogous to those of myth and dream, have been balanced off.

His basic task in the study, as he saw it, was to ransack the resources of archaic myth and religion for models by which to conceptualize and understand the many permutations the Freudian libido took in its quest for freedom and full expression. Jung correlated "Miss Miller's" personal images with those of universal myth and dream, and in that light found their meaning. As he excavated mighty archetypes from out of the subject's ephemeral dreams and poetic thoughts, Jung was aware he was dealing with strong medicine, but he left it all on the level of the psyche's inner life. The closest *Wandlungen* came to political material was in illustrative references to archaic sacred king myths, including the wounded king of the grail legend. But these sovereigns were inevitably turned into individual models for moderns in search of a kingly soul.[9]

This seminal book was clearly the foundational work of a mind too teeming with originality to be forever acolyte to another. It put the analytic project on a much more broadly humanistic and less medical footing than the Freudian. The exclusively sexual definition of the libido was presented by Jung as one-sided.[10] Still uglier issues than this book had arisen between Freud and Jung as well. By 1915 Freud was claiming that Jung's defection was connected to a crisis involving both religion and anti-Semitism. He said in a letter of July 8 of that year to an American supporter, James Jackson Putnam, that he had liked Jung until the latter was taken over "by a religious-ethical 'crisis' " which the younger man apparently felt had endowed him with "higher morality, rebirth," and which had led Jung to present "lies, brutality and anti-Semitic condescension toward me.' "[11]

The rupture was acutely painful and consequential for both. The less well-known Jung withdrew into semiretreat, exploring inward storms and vistas during times that roughly converged with the terrible years of World War I. Sometimes his dreadful dreams seemed to parallel or prophesy the outer horrors of that bloodletting. The spiritually afflicted

Swiss doctor pressed the quest for the ultimate nature of the sovereign psyche very far indeed, on occasion veering toward the margins of madness. But he came out of this dark passage with his own life on a firm footing, and with a book, *Psychological Types* (1921), that gave him a recognized independent place in his profession. Containing terms that have moved into popular culture, such as *extravert* and *introvert*, *Psychological Types* is widely regarded as Jung's most original contribution to general psychology by those who do not accept the full Jungian system.

Jung's emerging basic position was that the goal, individuation, meant becoming who the person really is inwardly, not the *persona* fabricated by convention and expectation. The pilgrimage to the real self is long and winding, but may be enlivened by encounters with denizens of the well-populated intermediate ranges. The archetypes— the Wise Old Man, the Great Mother, the Hero, the Maiden, the Shadow, the Marvelous Child who is the hoped-for individuated self—are all really facets of the self, fragments one can become or repress, or better configure harmoniously into a mandala, or balanced pattern, out of the center of which the new self arises victorious.

That nativity is aided by the guiding presence of the archetypes in the lore and religions of all peoples as well as in the dreams of the individuating individual. This was, according to one of the most controversial of Jungian propositions, because they are parts of a "collective unconscious" as well as an individual font of forms. Jung thought that levels of the unconscious—family, clan, nation, race, primate, and animal in general—lay like geological strata between the individual and the "central fire" that energized them all.

By collective unconscious Jung thus meant mental contents shared with others, either the entire human race or a subdivision of it, such as a culture or nationality. Being unconscious, this collectivity obviously did not mean a people's articulated beliefs, ideas, or vocabularies, but rather pointed to the preconscious mental energies that activated them. Being preconscious, those powerful forces could express themselves only in camouflage, usually through emotions bearing symbolic archetypal forms: a culture's particular versions of the Father, the Mother, the Hero, the Shadow. In a traditional society, these images were best found in its religious or folkloric myths and symbols. As Robert A. Segal has pointed out, Jung uses myths and the universality of their themes to establish the existence of the collective unconscious.[12]

Nothing is more important than the collective unconscious idea for a Jungian understanding of politics and history. The collective unconscious, expressed through individuals great and small, is the ultimate and supreme source of historical and political consequences, as various nations and periods exalt particular archetypes and so play their parts on the stage of time. This is of descriptive significance; it may also raise possibilities of historical therapy. Jung wrote:

> When we look at human history, we see only what happens on the surface, and even this is distorted in the faded mirror of tradition. But what has really been happening eludes the inquiring eye of the historian, for the true historical event lies deeply buried, experienced by all and observed by none. It is the most private and most subjective of psychic experiences. Wars, dynasties, social upheavals, conquests, and religions are but the superficial symptoms of a secret psychic attitude unknown even to the individual himself, and transmitted by no historian; perhaps the founders of religions give us the most information in this regard. The great events of world history are, at bottom, profoundly unimportant. In the last analysis, the essential thing is the life of the individual. This alone makes history, here alone do the great transformations first take place, and the whole future, the whole history of the world, ultimately springs as a gigantic summation from these hidden sources in individuals. In our most private and most subjective lives we are not only the passive witnesses of our age, and its sufferers, but also its makers. We make our own epoch.[13]

In these lines, as clearly as anywhere, is the foundation of Jung's theory of history and politics. If history is *au fond* a play of projections of consciousness from out of the multitudinous psyches of humanity, it would be surprising if history were not really psychohistory and archetypal history. Jungian history, like the Trojan War, is a tale of gods as well as heroes.

If we make our own historical epoch by projecting history out of our collective psyches, can we make it what we want, or are we only at the mercy of the hidden gods?

This all-important question was, I think, long on the margins of Jung's mind, and was one with which he half-consciously wrestled. But, having seen too many disastrous attempts to awaken and harness those gods—or demons—deliberately, and to make history into triumphs of the will, caution generally prevailed. In the end, he thought, it would probably be better to keep the gods tame and balanced off against each other, so that ordinary everyday life could proceed, and persons ravaged by modernity could find what they needed of the gods within.

But for that story, we must start at the beginning of human consciousness.

## PRIMITIVE CHILDHOOD AND MODERN MATURITY

From out of the psyche, by way of the archetypes, then, one "projects" the contents of the psyche onto the world, seeing its objects in terms significant to the sovereign psyche. In Jung's view, primitive man lived in a state of almost total projection; he sent out his inner emotions onto external objects and persons, seeing them there more than in himself—his anger becoming a carved jaguar-god, his fear an accursed witch, and so forth—and consequently he lived in a condition of minimal analytic self-consciousness or self-knowledge. How vividly is that state described in "The Role of the Unconscious":

> The country he [primitive man] inhabits is at the same time the to-pography of his unconscious. In that stately tree dwells the thunder-god; this spring is haunted by the Old Woman; in that wood the legendary king is buried; near that rock no one may light a fire because it is the abode of a demon; in yonder pile of stones dwell the ancestral spirits, and when any woman passes it she must quickly utter an apotropaic formula lest she become pregnant, for one of the sprits could easily enter her body. All kinds of objects and signs mark these places, and pious awe surrounds the marked spot. Thus does primitive man dwell in his land and at the same time in the land of his unconscious. Everywhere his unconscious jumps out at him, alive and real.[14]

That is indeed another world. Just as "primitive man" could hardly have understood the modern "Western" way of being in the world, so do we find it hard to recover what it meant to our remote ancestors.

> How different is our relation to the land we dwell in! Feelings totally strange to us accompany the primitive at every step. Who knows what the cry of a bird means to him, or the sight of that old tree! A whole world of feeling is closed to us and is replaced by a pale aestheticism.[15]

But the former immediacy of projected unconscious contents was at the expense of critical distance, rational analysis, and the individuality which inevitably accompanied these developments of thought. "The further we go back in history," he wrote, following Lucien Lévy-Bruhl's now-discredited idea of primitive "participation mystique," "the more we see personality disappearing beneath the wrappings of collectivity, and if we go right back to primitive psychology, we find absolutely no trace of the concept of an individual."[16]

But if individual consciousness in the modern sense was not shared by our primitive ancestors, dreams were. For Jung as for Freud and Nietzsche, dreams appear as the royal road to recovery of the archaic way of thinking. In *Wandlungen* he wrote, "infantile-thinking and dream-thinking are simply a recapitulation of earlier evolutionary stages." He quoted Nietzsche's *Human, All Too Human* to the effect that, "In sleep and in dreams we pass through the whole thought of earlier humanity..." and Freud from "Creative Writings and Day-Dreaming": ". . . it is extremely probable that myths, for instance, are distorted vestiges of the wishful phantasies of whole nations, the age-long dreams of youthful humanity." Otto Rank is cited as regarding myth the collective dreams of a whole people.[17] Such statements with their late-romantic sweep and their feel of indefinable profundity, may or may not ring true, but they epitomize the perspective psychoanalysis sought to bring to history and, by extension, to current affairs.

The emergence of modern consciousness came about when, as history moved ahead, changing circumstances brought the gradual withdrawal of projections and a consequent increase in individual awareness, together with enhanced knowledge of both self and world in the West. Physical science caused the withdrawal of "the most distant" projections, reducing moon, sun, and stars to rocks and gasses. Echoing Max Weber's concept of disenchantment, Jung referred to this as the first stage in the despiritualization of the world.[18] The libido that had flowed out to all those natural or social objects now had to the stifled—or transferred to other, perhaps more dubious, attachments.

It is worth noting that Jung considered Eastern civilizations, such as India, to represent a different sort of movement, in which a complex and subtle culture was constructed on the basis of much greater continuity with the primordial way of thinking. India was far more on the unconscious level than the West: ". . . the Indian . . . does not think, at least not what we call 'think.' *He rather perceives the thought.* He resembles the primitive in this respect. I do not say he *is* primitive, but that the process of his thinking reminds me of the primitive way of thought-production. The primitive's reasoning is mainly an unconscious function, and he perceives its results. We should expect such a peculiarity in any civilization which has enjoyed an almost unbroken continuity from primitive times"—in great contrast to the West, which must suffer both the bane and blessing of the abrupt "invasion" of a "higher" level of psychology for which it was not yet truly ready. That intellectual forced march could only be made at the cost of "dissociation between the conscious part of the mind and the unconscious."[19]

Again, that consciousness leap was by no means wholly beneficial. Much could be said for the view that the earlier natural, easy flow of the libido out and back was the way it ought to be, and that when it is constricted the cost will in the end outweigh the gain. In another writing on India, Jung mused, "It is quite possible that India is the real world, and that the white man lives in a madhouse of abstractions." India is "perhaps the real life, life as it was meant to be, the life of the earth. Life in India has not yet withdrawn into the capsule of the head."[20] And that head-capsule could be full of snakes, for the world of primitive feelings—which Jung did not idealize either—lives on, hissing just beneath the surface, in the modern unconscious. Because it is repressed, it has all the more pathological power: "This lost bit of nature seeks revenge and returns in faked, distorted form," in the "crazes and crudities" of the modern age, above all in the reversion to tribalism on a monstrous scale in the mad devastation of modern war. For this there is no anodyne except on the level from which the horror comes. In the last analysis modern madness derives from snakepits deep within the psychologies of individuals, and can only be healed through individual therapy. "Our rationalistic attitude," he wrote in 1918, "leads us to believe that we can work wonders with international organizations, legislation, and other well-meant devices. But in reality only a change in the attitude of the individual can bring about a renewal in the spirit of the nations. Everything begins with the individual."[21]

At this point we must underscore the extreme discontinuity in consciousness that Jung perceived to obtain over geographical space and human time. The "primitive" mind was unimaginably different from the modern European—accessible perhaps only to the trained and expansive imagination of a scholar of the soul like himself—and the mind of India today hardly less so. In large part, of course, that way of thinking was characteristic of the times, full of evolutionary *kulterkreis* (cultural stages) and nationalistic *völkspsychologie* theories, which not seldom finished off their Hegelian equations with the proponents' own century and city at the apex. One product of this European mentality was what has more recently been called colonialist if not imperialist scholarship, or "Orientalism," readings of non-European peoples in terms that justified the political and spiritual hegemony of the imperial powers. The two-tiered world was in place, even if a sensitive savant like Jung could occasionally indulge in nostalgia for primal simplicity or purity of consciousness, above all when the primordial paradise was also identified with one's own antecedents. In no small part Orientalism was doubtless only a example of the mind's natural tendency to think in dichotomies, but in the nineteenth and early twentieth centuries it was unchecked in both the political and scholarly worlds by compensating voices, for the European's last redoubt was the unquestioning faith he put in the arcana of his own linguistic and ethnographic sciences.[22]

With typical flourish, Jung carried such notions very far toward ultimate separatism, holding that the profoundest structures of thought could be radically different in humans of one time and place from those of another. Then, with no less bravado, he turned the theories on their heads by suggesting that the West also, for all its light, exhibited pathologies as profound as any disquieting the most superstitious "native." He was far from alone in such judgments, especially after the devastation of World War I, which should have suggested to even the dimmest dolt that something was wrong in Europe. But Jung was fairly distinctive in linking the critique to the new "medical" discipline of psychoanalysis on the one hand, and to the vogue for mythology and folk psychology on the other, bringing the two together. The combination could be explosive, and brought Jung onto dangerous ground. The process by which he came to his distinctive style of critique is of considerable interest.

In a well-integrated culture, he said, like that of primal humanity, or indeed (in Europe) of humanity up through the Middle Ages, the archetypes—including the Shadow, representing destructive forces—are adequately balanced off in myth scenarios and symbolic symmetries, creating mandalas. Those symbols then provided for the orderly release of the irrational energies that welled up from the unconscious fountains of the deep, and so kept society on an even keel. For Jung was quite convinced that rationality is a precious but precarious epiphenomenon on the surface of human life, that our real drives are irrational and far more powerful than reason.

There is a severe imbalance, Jung thought, between the overdeveloped conscious intellect and its instinctive, unconscious roots in modern Western man. Myths can be compensation for that which is lacking in a psyche or a civilization, and so provide clues to the nature of the lost. The hidden gnostic truth, when found again, can awaken deep levels of understanding of the roots of both literature and current events. Faust, Jung asserted, stands as unconscious but protean Shadow over against Goethe's conscious attitudes as a child of the Enlightenment moving toward Romanticism.[23] UFOs are a "modern myth" of circular objects representing the wholeness moderns so grievously lack.[24] Jung considered the 1950 papal promulgation of the dogma of the Assumption of the Blessed Virgin Mary into Heaven to be "the most important religious event since the Reformation," because of its completion of the masculine Christian Trinity with a feminine component, making it a perfect and balanced quaternity.[25]

More ominously, Jung later reported that as early as 1918 he had begun to notice a "peculiar disturbance" in the unconscious of his German patients, which had suggested to him that the "blond beast" was stirring.[26] Indeed, in the same fateful Armistice year he had written that, as the Christian view of the world declined, the Germanic monster could "be heard prowling about in its underground prison, ready at any moment to burst out with devastating consequences."[27]

Jung had little faith in modern notions of development and progress, for he did not think that such superficial changes in the conditions of human life could really change the equation between the rational and irrational, so heavily skewed toward the latter. In fact, like the volkish thinkers, he saw the situation as actually getting worse, for what modern developments from the Reformation on had done was break up harmonious symbolic outlets for psychic energy, therefore separating people from their unconscious and instinctual natures. The Reformation shattered the symbolic unities of medieval Catholicism; the Enlightenment, by creating the illusion that life could be rational and its worse illusion that the psyche is a tabula rasa, further alienated moderns from life's powerful and rich but irrational sources; the Industrial Revolution augmented the damage as it alienated humanity's conscious and psychic natures from each other through its one-dimensional and robotlike occupations, and by herding people into the sterile life of urban centers where they were torn from nature, and from traditional communities in which healthy instincts and symbolic harmonies can be nourished.

The result was what Jung, following Ortega y Gasset, called "mass man," humans isolated socially from others, while also separated from their unconsciousness and their instincts. José Ortega y Gasset's celebrated *The Revolt of the Masses*, one of the last important frank and unapologetic apologies for an aristocratic mentality, fed into the antidemocratic critique of modernity such lines as these:

> There is one fact which, whether for good or ill, is of utmost importance in the public life of Europe at the present. This fact is the accession of the masses to complete social power. As the masses, by definition, neither should or can direct their own personal existence, and still rule society in general, this fact means that actually Europe is suffering from the greatest crisis that can afflict peoples, nations, and civilization.... It is called the rebellion of the masses.[28]

Elsewhere in the same book, Ortega wrote of a new type of man—"I call him mass-man"—whose main characteristic is that, feeling himself "common," he proclaims the right to be common, and refuses to accept anyone as superior to himself.[29] Yet "mass men" cannot really do anything by themselves, so they organize the state—"the greatest danger, the state"[30]—and with it specialization, combining to form the bureaucratic webworks of modern society, but without a moral code.

In the same vein, in "The Undiscovered Self," Jung spoke of "modern man" in terms of "mass-mindedness," "mass role," "the blind movement of the masses," "the infantile dream state of mass man," and the like.[31] Mass man is always less real than the individual, only a statistical average, easily becoming the victim of modern authoritarianism. Jung not seldom counseled a return to something of the past though within the context of contemporary society—but not mass man society. So it was that Jung reminded us in 1945, in language highly reminiscent of the volkish "rootedness" versus urbanized wandering though now with an antiNazi thrust, that one condition of a "state of degradation" is "the accumulation of urban, industrialized masses—of people torn from the soil, engaged in one-sided employment, and lacking every healthy instinct, even that of self-preservation. Loss of instinct of self-preservation can be measured in terms of dependence on the State, which is a bad symptom." This condition means that these sorry masses seek dependency rather than personal responsibility. They become parts of "a herd of sheep, constantly relying on a shepherd to drive them into good pastures." And the shepherd can easily turn into a wolf, as when in Germany a "megalomaniac psychopath" took over that role, "to the collective sigh of relief of the sheep."[32]

To some extent these fulminations simply represent views characteristic of the political right, with which Jung certainly identified himself, though he claimed in a nonpartisan sense. As a man of the right he instinctively favored social class and stability, and a rather abstract ideal of individualism, over the interests of labor and the benefits of the welfare state. He was vociferously anticommunist, highly sceptical of socialism, a believer in governance by a powerful elite (insofar as that was compatible with Swiss democracy, though beyond the borders of Switzerland his rightism could at times embrace admiration for the likes of Franco in Spain and Mussolini in Italy), and held to such typical rightist positions as advocacy of firm treatment of criminals, including capital punishment. Yet in Jung there is always a little more than stereotyped thinking reflecting one band or another on the usual political or intellectual spectrum. As elitist and condescending as his views of the common man and woman may be, he deserves to be heard out. The notion that modernity has meant atomizing and then reassembling once well-rooted souls into sheeplike herds ready to follow any "shepherd" who will promise then more and still more on material and psychic levels, though a gross caricature of democractic liberalism, helps to interpret all too well some twentieth-century events.

These rootless sheep are eminently susceptible to "psychic epidemics," the virulent expression of this extreme inner imbalance. As we have seen, according to Jung the catastrophes of human history are not physical or biological events, but psychic happenings.[33] The epidemics are most likely to take political form, because Enlightenment rationalism inculcated that the sources of good and evil are to be found in the objective social environment rather than in the psyche, and so require political rather than religious solution; and because mass man's urban social isolation urges him to deal with his inner demons through some kind of compensating collective expression.

For what mass man's alienation had done was to leave a vast cloud of unreleased and irrational psychic energy floating in the air, so to speak, not tied down to benign symbols or understood through living myths, but just there, capable of working tremendous destruction and waiting to be employed at the whim of any demagogic personality—most likely political—who knew how to harness it. For as Jung perceived, mundane life alone is not likely, in practice, to be able to resist the psychic and social drives seducing one into conformity with the herd and the state, to "mass-mindedness." True, "spiritual and moral autonomy" can only be anchored in "an extramundane principle capable of relativising the overpowering influence of external factors." This amounts to religion—except that religion can be seduced too. "The dictator State has one great advantage over bourgeois reason: along with the individual it swallows up his religious forces. The State takes the place of God."[34]

The seducing figure would be what Jung called a "mana personality," like Napoleon, whose excess of psychic energy magnetically draws others into its pattern, and then is able to organize and direct the flow of their own energies in one direction.[35] This process will produce a collective psychic "inflation" as rough new channels are cut, modern alienation is short-circuited, and a group again identifies with the archetypes of its collective unconscious—or rather, because of the sudden and violent nature of this preemptory operation, the psyche is likely to so identify with only one or two of its archetypes in an unbalanced way; the group is also likely to project the "shadow" archetype on its perceived enemies and demonize them. Salvation then must be gnostic—from elsewhere, psyche-level—not a one-dimensional political solution operating on the same level as the problem. Richard Noll, in *The Jung Cult* and *The Aryan Christ*, has contended that Jung saw himself as a modern "Christ" or gnostic savior. While far from convincing as serious biographical interpretations of Jung, these books do call attention to the profound interaction between his often self-dramatizing inner life and his understanding of the dramas of the world.[36]

## REACTIONARY MODERNISM

The emergence of truncated "mass men" was now ready for one of several possible responses. One would be sheer reactionism, like that of Ortega y Gasset or volkish thought in its pure form. Another would be the modernism, or gnostic pseudomodernism, of totalitarian Marxism. But Jung, obviously intrigued by the volkish critique of the evils of atomistic modern life and fascinated by the persistence of the collective in the unconscious, yet not prepared to give up his modern role as a member of the medical profession, was now moving toward a third way. That is the intellectual world, with which Jung clearly had more than a nodding acquaintance, which Jeffrey Herf has aptly named "reactionary modernism." It was, basically, "the embrace of modern technology by German thinkers who rejected Enlightenment reason." These philosophers, some of whom were precursors of National Socialism, did not think of themselves as reactionary but "viewed themselves as cultural revolutionaries seeking to consign materialism to the past. In their view, materialism and technology were by no means identical."[37]

That of course has much in common with Jung's perspective—if within technology we include the "scientific" training and methods of the medical psychiatrist and analyst. Again, we are forcefully reminded that a motif of all fascism was its ideological rejection of materialism and its claim to be spiritual. Along with their professed rejection of atomistic individualism, the common mark of mass man and of much-scorned bourgeois democracy, fascists favored a "spiritual" view of nationhood based on common myths, archetypes, and *Geist*. The thought of Friedrich Nietzsche was compatible with this line of thought, as that half-mad genius of a philosopher galvanized many of the reactionary, romantic dreams of revolutionary apocalypse and spiritual transformation that emerged as outer Europe careened toward world war. Those dreams lighted up in the subterranean consciousness of European society, fascinating an elite with madness and genius and supposed antimaterialistic spirituality, while the bourgeoisie maintained their comfortable life and the working class contemplated revolution. Nietzsche raved of a Christian "slave morality" and called for the appearance of a masculine elite, the beautiful "blond beast" beyond good and evil. Jung drank deeply of such visions even while considering that something was tainted in them, and he heard the psychic restlessness they invoked.

It is important to note what Jung had in common with the precursors of fascism and National Socialism, and what he did not. He shared with Ortega y Gasset and Nietzsche much of their critique of modern mass man and his problems—though to be sure Jung's tone was more moderate than their shrill and extreme tirades. Jung had always a capacity, uncommon in persons of the antimodern party, for balance and self-correction. He was aware that he was dealing with subtle levels of soul, not street politics. Undoubtedly in Jung, as in Ortega, there was too much of the self-dubbed aristocrat; both came from an old-fashioned Europe in which scholars and intellectuals were spiritual aristocrats or pretended to be. Both the Swiss and the Spaniard had the nobleman's unfortunate readiness to oversimplify and stereotype the subjective life of the "common" masses. Jung preferred that his psychiatric clients be from the educated genteel classes. Yet the analytic psychologist could in the end—after some initial fascination—express anger and despair at those mana personalities, like the one across the border in Germany, who took advantage of mass man's psychic deprivation to promote their own megalomania. Jung may have shared the intellectual's tendency to overemphasize the helplessness of the masses, but he approached them, at least on the professional level, with the heart of a healer, not of a tyrant.

Perhaps for this reason he did not also share the frenetic and overaesthetic mood of what Andrew Hewitt has called, in the title of his book on the subject, *Fascist Modernism*—the style of fascist worldview that proved so attractive and exciting to a generation of writers and artists of the "avant garde." Such poets and painters as Ezra Pound, Tommasso Marinetti, and the "Futurist" school loved the "postdecadent" irrationalism and imperialism they saw encapsulated in powerful machines, spectacles, the dramatic gesture, the aesthetics of struggle.[38] Their view of art was better expressed in dynamic movement than the nineteenth-century sort of stationary scene; they thereby adored technology, movement, the new art of the cinema, all well exploited by the propaganda of the new order. This side of fascism was admittedly more Italian than German, but certainly not unknown in the staged dramas being unveiled north of the Alps. But Jung was more interested in deeper matters.

The terrible trauma of Germany's defeat in World War I pushed those who thought about their nation in volkish terms in the direction of reactionary modernism: the mists of myth with technological teeth in them, but little regard for democracy. Books came out like Oswald Spengler's famous *Der Untergang des Abendlandes* (*The Decline of the West*), with its calls for the defeat of democracy, liberalism, and money in favor of a "life energy" that is "blind and cosmic" but racially bound to the soil, and carried by an elite of "higher men" who make "great decisions." The writer Ernst Jünger shared with others of his type the *fronterlebnis*, front-line experience, in the Great War, and found—as did Adolf Hitler—that war could be the forge of heroes and a profoundly liberating and transformative adventure. In such books as *Der Kampf as inneres Erlebnis* (*Battle as Inner Experience*; 1922) and *Feuer und Blut* (*Fire and Blood*; 1926) Jünger celebrated the heroic dimensions of war together with the technology of modern combat, with its "storms of iron" and vulturelike bombers. He did much to prepare German consciousness for Nazidom, though he himself never joined the Party; he found the Nazis a bit plebeian, lacking his level of aristocratic refinement in contemplating the aesthetics of blood and death on the field of honor. (After the war he was to establish the journal *Antaios* with Mircea Eliade and Ortega y Gasset and, himself avoiding all the century's storms of iron, died in 1998 at the age of 102.) Carl Jung, as a neutral Swiss, had no combat experience in either war and, apart from his role as a medical officer in the Swiss Reserves, no special interest in combat beyond the archetypal hero myth. But he shared in the world of spiritual crisis in which an Ernst Jünger could find a voice.

Perhaps the reactionary modernist whose role most paralleled Jung's was the world-class philosopher Martin Heidegger, whose brief career as a public exponent of Nazism in 1933 and 1934, while he was rector of the University of Freiburg, has been much discussed. In his notorious inaugural address as rector in April 1933, and in subsequent pro-Nazi speeches, Heidegger stressed, in language comparable to Jungian inwardness, the radical subjectivism and collectivism of the Party, as over against the rationalism and individualism of other politics. Hitler, he said, had awakened the will of the German Völk "and brought this will together into a single decision."[39] As a recent biographer has put it, "Heidegger's Nazism was decisionist,"and in this sense he was not anti-Semitic, "certainly not in the sense of the ideological lunacy of Nazism."[40] Although Jung never embraced the newly triumphant ideology and its political practitioners as openly as did Heidegger, it was in the same years that the Swiss psychiatrist made what compromising utterances he was to make; like the German (although Heidegger remained a member of the party to the bitter end), by 1939 he was well into disillusionment. Both Heidegger and Jung found themselves unable to accept crucial aspects of the new Reich: Heidegger, what he saw as Nazi compromise with technology;[41] Jung the way in which the "single decision" appeared to be a new a terrible manifestation of mass man rather than a purifying archetype of the nation.

## THE GERMAN PROBLEM

Like not a few romantics, including Nietzsche, Jung was of two minds about Germany. At its greatest it was a land of incomparably exalted culture and vision. At the same time, it boasted the deadliest of bourgeois civilizations, and beneath all ran dark and terrible undercurrents. In his 1918 essay "The Role of the Unconscious," Jung declared that the source of the "German problem" lay in the way Christianity had "split the Germanic barbarian into an upper and a lower half, and enabled him, by repressing the dark side, to domesticate the brighter half and fit it for civilization." But, needless to say, the lower half, the caged but restless "blond beast," was still there, awaiting its hour of return and revenge.

Plowing ahead with his summary treatment of Germany's unconscious in that year of her greatest defeat to date, Jung turned his attention to the country's highly visible Jewish population. For them, he said, the German split-unconscious problem did not exist. Rather than precariously living half civilized and half barbarian, they had taken over the culture of the ancient world, and on top of it had placed the cultures of the nations among which they dwelt. This meant that the Jew "was domesticated to a higher degree than we are, but he is badly at a loss for that quality in man which roots him to the earth and draws new strength from below"—a "chthonic quality" which was, on the other hand, "found in dangerous concentration in the Germanic peoples." The Jews had too little of this, the Germans too much.[42]

"Rootedness," that staple of volkish thought, emphasized the differences in the thought processes of different peoples, claiming that a special quality of mind obtained in those who, like the Germans of the countryside, had a particularly close bonding to the land on which they dwelt. Jung professed only to be saying that different peoples had different methods to attain psychological wholeness. The concept of racial psychospiritual differences did not necessarily imply that one race was innately superior to another, and Jung spend a lot of time in the middle thirties, and after, explaining that that was not what he meant. But the apologetics were required because "rootedness" and racial differences in the unconscious were ideas the moved disturbingly close to treacherous terrain. Surely it was unfortunate that Jung took racial and national psychologies and collective strata of the unconscious so seriously, particularly at the expense of as much attention to individual differences within them. (These were progressively harder to see, the farther from one's own kind one got.) But on the other hand such notions were parts of the intellectual world in which he lived, all too lightly taken for granted as part of what "everyone knows."

But if ideas like these were dangerous yet not serious, what was the cause of the virulent evil, above all the deadly anti-Semitism, culminating in the unspeakable holocaust of Jews, which swept Germany in the twelve years of the Third Reich? Numerous theories have been advanced, from demonic possession or dark occult enchantment to notions that it was nothing more than an acute case of ordinary politics, or no more than an expression of an anti-Semitism that had been a firm fixture of the "ordinary" German mind, and German life, for centuries.

This is not the place to sort out all the factors in this dreadful conundrum. But here are a couple of reflections that may be of some relevance to the mythological issues, and the politics of mythologists, at hand. First, the point must be made that evil is, by its intrinsic nature, irrational. If it were not so, if an occasion of evil, even one as vast and horrifying as the holocaust, could be found to have a complete and wholly satisfying rational explanation, then it would be less than what evil appears to be as it confronts us—that which should not be, yet is: the mystery of iniquity, the abomination of desolation standing where it ought not. While of course it is appropriate to look for the causes of evil with a view to understanding and healing, one will never follow all threads to the end and uncover all causes. Answered questions lead to new questions, first-level causes to deeper causes, until one comes up to ultimate mysteries built into human nature and the universe itself. It is important to understand this, for too-easy a finality will not quiet all the demons.

Second, on the plane of first-level causes, it is necessary to accept another perhaps unsatisfying but profoundly human observation: that what happens does not usually happen out of irresistible destiny, implanted malignant viruses, or supernatural curses, but out of ordinary human choices, more or less freely made but, like all such, colored by predisposition and limited by imperfect wisdom. If anything is clear about the political machinations that led to the Nazi seizure of power in January 1933, it is that it did not have to happen, and was not meant to happen, in the sense of being predetermined by some transcendent cause. Of course Nazidom was made possible by flaws in both national and individual character. The later Jung emphasized the German "inferiority complex" calling for redress by psychic inflation, and the need for compensation—a major Jungian term—for the humiliation of the Versailles treaty. But as witless and unscrupulous as the principal players—von Hindenburg, von Papen, von Schleicher, Brüning—may have been, the Hitler state was not what they had intended. In its fully developed form, perhaps it was not even what the millions who cheered that winter night had intended. Yet it happened. Beyond pure happenstance, short of the full-blown demon theory, maybe Jung was as right as anyone, as he folded those ominous developments into his psychic theory of history, that outer events are expressions of the movement, and successive emergence, of archetypes in the collective unconscious. At least that view places any explanation in the realm of the nonrational, while relating it to what was at least possible in the psychic context of Germany in those years.

So it was that Jung's particular theory of German culture, expressed back in 1923, contended that a "mutilation" of the Germanic soul had resulted from the grafting of "a wholly incongruous Christianity, born of monotheism on a much higher level," together with a veneer of Mediterranean civilization, onto the primitive German religion. But the superficial southern polish concealed a plethora of barbarian attitudes, a problem that was to plague Germanic culture down through the centuries: "There is a whole lot of primitivity in us to be made good." Further progress toward civilization could involve going back to those neglected primitive roots and "giving the suppressed primitive man in ourselves a chance to develop."[43] Here are the tangled roots of a deep tension in Jungian thought, one which will be seen to have profound political implications—the collective unconscious versus therapeutic individualism. Any notion that letting the primitive out might be healthy was in conflict with another: the idea that "all human control comes to an end when the individual is caught in a mass movement," as Jung put it in an essay soon to be considered, "Wotan."

In the Europe of his time Jung had considerable occasion to observe the processes of mass man and of mana personality, and to see
his views apparently confirmed, the most egregious case being across
the border from his native Switzerland in National Socialist Germany.
In 1945, in the red light of Germany's Götterdämmerung, Jung described the age's own mana personality vividly and bitingly enough:

> Hitler's theatrical, obviously hysterical gestures struck all foreigners
> (with a few amazing exceptions) as purely ridiculous. When I saw him
> with my own eyes, he suggested a psychic scarecrow (with a broomstick
> for an outstretched arm) rather than a human being. . . . A sorry lack of
> education, conceit that bordered on madness, a very mediocre intelli-
> gence combined with the hysteric's cunning and the power fantasies of
> an adolescent, were written all over this demagogue's face. His gesticu-
> lations were all put on, devised by a hysterical mind intent only on making
> an impression. He behaved in public like a man living his own biography,
> in this case as the somber, daemonic "man of iron" of popular fiction.[44]

Jung's words at the time of the hysteric's rise to power were less
dismissive though deeply uneasy. In a 1933 interview on Radio Berlin,
Jung had commented:

> As Hitler said recently, the leader (Führer) must be able to be alone and
> must have the courage to go his own way. But if he doesn't know himself,
> how is he to lead others? That is why the true leader is always one who
> has the courage to be himself, and can look not only others in the eye but
> above all himself. . . . Every movement culminates organically in a leader,
> who embodies in his whole being the meaning and purpose of the popu-
> lar movement.[45]

By the time of his remarkable 1936 essay "Wotan," Jung could
describe more fully the volcanolike upsurge of raw long-repressed,
irrational psychic energy that had produced the Hitler state.[46] This
famous and controversial piece of writing displays an obvious poetic
feel for the Wotan archetype in all its Nietzschean power. Wotan is the
restless wanderer (like Ahasuerus, the Wandering Jew), the god of
storm, and capable of possessing persons. In the new Germany, one
man, "who is obviously 'possessed,' has infected a whole nation to
such an extent that everything is set in motion and has started rolling
on its course toward perdition."[47] Jung here appears to me to treat that
nation's pretentious Germanic spirituality movement with amused

contempt, though he had once given joint seminars with J. W. Hauer of Tübigen, founder of one of its instruments, the neopagan German Faith Movement, which had attemped a literal revival of Wotanism. Now he saw such fundamentalists of the new regime as themselves also victims . . . of whatever may come next. (Andrew Samuels, however, states that "It is hard to assess what Jung really thought about the German Faith movement, as he spoke of its adherents as 'decent and well-meaning people,' but also 'possessed' by the 'god of the Germans' "—Wotan; Samuels sees these lines as "in no way a repudiation or condemnation of Hauer."[48])

Despite his own inflation with some of the intellectual roots of National Socialism, it seems clear that Jung knew well enough—at least as well as anyone of comparable placement—what was really going on. But he was not sure what response to make to this monstrous yet seductive enchantment worthy of Wotan. It must be recalled that most German Protestant pastors—of the culture of Jung's ultimate roots—welcomed the accession of Hitler; they generally despised the Weimar regime for royalist reasons, because of the godless new culture arising under its aegis, and because of their denominations' relative loss of status over against Roman Catholicism in the new secular state.[49] For somewhat similar reasons of heart and status, a great number in Germany's traditionally conservative legions of scholars and professors likewise hoped for good things from Hitler. They too had found themselves in an unfamiliar land after 1918, a strange country, which had impoverished them and taken from them the unquestioning prestige they and their values had enjoyed in Wilhelmine Germany. All this too Jung undoubtedly felt, if only vicariously. But he was cautious in the face of so much force . . . and sometimes uncautious.

Jung's own attitude toward the "New Germany," especially as reflected in his acts when the presidency of the International Society for Psychotherapy fell to him in 1933 upon the resignation of the anti-Nazi German president, Prof. Ernst Kretschmer, has been much debated. The strong German section, under intense pressure to attain *Gleichschaltung* (conformity) with the ideology of the new government, was being forced to purge itself of Jews. The section contained some Nazis sympathizers, one of whom was Prof. M. H. Göring, the Reichsmarschal's cousin and a Nazi, who would become head of the German section, and who came to share with Jung the editorship of the *Zentralblatt*, the German-language journal of the International

Society. During their editorship some articles appeared that were highly anti-Semitic and little more than Nazi propaganda. For this Jung as well as Göring have been faulted, and understandably so. Yet on such matters one must, regrettably, understand also the subtleties of writing and working in a totalitarian environment. There is also reason to think that Göring was able to use his Nazi credentials, the prima facie evidence of some sympathetic publications, and his exalted connections to shield not a few colleagues, Jews and others, who would otherwise have fallen foul of the Gestapo.[50] The section also included Jews and others unsympathetic to the German "revolution" who were in a desperately precarious position. The society was made international in order to contain the German maelstrom within a larger context.

Aniela Jaffé, herself a German-Jewish refugee and Jung's secretary after the war, has made a reasonably convincing case that, at least on his own conscious level, Jung had no sympathy for National Socialism as such, though at first, like others, he was perhaps naive about its full potential for evil. No doubt in Jung's mind some sense of confusing contradiction may have arisen between two of his principles: on the one hand, the Party was striving to get behind the alienation of modern mass man by returning to the "roots" and "soil" from which he was estranged; on the other, the German "revolution" was an egregious display of mass man's sheeplike instincts in operation. Afterward, Jung confessed:

> When Hitler seized power it became quite evident to me that a mass psychosis was boiling up in Germany. But I could not help telling myself this was after all Germany, a civilized European nation with a sense of morality and discipline. Hence the ultimate outcome of this unmistakable mass movement still seemed to me uncertain, much as the figure of the Führer at first struck me as being merely ambivalent. Like many of my contemporaries, I had my doubts.[51]

In any case, in his presidential role he was, Jaffé thought, trying to do the best he could as mediator in an extremely difficult situation. He also helped individual Jews in those terrible years, including his gifted disciple Erich Neumann.[52] In regard to the last, Laurens van der Post wrote: "[O]ne would be relieved forever of suspecting Jung of anti-Semitism by the reading of the letters he wrote in defence of Neumann, who had escaped from Germany and settled in Tel-Aviv. In these letters he shows such a profound understanding of the plight of the Jews in history, such compassion for all they have suffered from Christian projection of the Christian shadow onto them, such appreciation of their unique and indispensable contribution to the spirit of man, that one would shed the last traces of suspecting him as anti-Semitic."[53]

Yet questions remain. Jung wrote voluminously, often unguardedly, and sometimes inconsistently, leaving both critics and apologists much to quote selectively. Moreover, like many Europeans and others, he seemed quite capable of making a distinction between individual Jews like Neumann and "the Jews"; questions regarding his attitude toward them perhaps have more to do with the full political implications of Jung's system than with any specific actions of the well-meaning Swiss. Problematics center around a 1934 article of his translated as "The State of Psychotherapy Today," in which he expressed some hope for fruitful development in Germany out of National Socialism. This piece was clearly a descendent of "The Role of the Unconscious" (1918) and continues its study of generic "Aryan" and Jewish psychologies. The doctor of the soul opined that the "Aryan" unconscious contained creative tensions and, though now still possessed of a "youthfulness not yet fully weaned from barbarism," may hold the "seeds of a future yet to be born."[54] In the same essay, Jung expressed views of the Jewish psychological character which have given much offense, stating that "the Jew, who is something of a nomad, has never yet created a cultural form of his own ... since all his instincts and talents require a more or less civilized nation to act as a host for their development," and that Jews "have in common with women being physically weaker, they have to aim at chinks in the armor of their opponents ... having a civilization twice as old, they are vastly more conscious then we of human weaknesses. . . . But the Jew like the Chinese has a wider area of psychological consciousness than we. . . . In general [it is] less dangerous for the Jew to put a negative value on the unconscious ... The Aryan unconscious on the other hand, contains explosive fires."[55]

The lines on Jews are remarkably parallel to those expressed a few years before by Adolf Hitler in *Mein Kampf:* "Since the Jew—for reasons which will at once become apparent—was never in possession of a culture of his own, the foundations of his intellectual work were always provided by others. His intellect at all times developed through the cultural world surrounding him."[56]

Jung spent much of 1934 explaining in letters that this article was not meant to be anti-Semitic.[57] He said to one correspondent after another that merely to describe psychological differences between Jews and Christians is not to deprecate the former. Occasionally he permitted himself to be a bit testy about the "hypersensitivity" of Jews. It is clear also that Jung's conflict with Freud was still an open wound, for he referred to the Viennese doctor's alleged dogmatism and denial of his own Jewish roots, at the same time complaining that the conflict was oversimplified by "German" doctors into in issue of Christian versus Jewish psychotherapy. In a letter to Gerhard Adler, Jung spoke of the rootlessness of the "Jewish rationalist," but added, "So when I criticize Freud's Jewishness I am not criticizing the *Jews* but rather that damnable capacity of the Jew, as exemplified by Freud, to deny his own nature." He called on religious Jews to "summon up the courage to distinguish themselves clearly from Freud."[58]

The gross stereotyping of the original article, and that more or less unconsciously displayed in the apologetic letters, was perhaps slightly more acceptable in Jung's time than today, and one does not need to be a Nazi to at least raise the issue of the distinctive psychological qualities of different peoples, including Jews.[59] But two points stick in one's mind, even apart from the crudity and plain erroneousness of this particular example of comparative psychology. First, the appalling lack of moral judgment on Jung's part in choosing to write on racial psychology, including that of Jews, precisely at a time when such rhetoric could only fan the flames of racial fanaticism, and when the relative heat of such fanaticism could well be a matter of life or death for Jews.

Jung seemed to recognize something of this issue, though by no means the full consequences, in a letter of Abraham Aaron Roback of 19 December 1936: "Unfortunately the political events in Germany have made it quite impossible to say anything reasonable about the most interesting difference between Jewish and non-Jewish psychology." (The difference under discussion was the alleged Jewish ability, much greater than that of gentiles, to extend consciousness into the subconscious mind, which ability brought with it a "tendency of consciousness to autonomy with the risk of severing it almost entirely from its instinctive sources.")[60]

Second, the sweeping, unqualified manner in which Jung applied various attributes to Aryans and Jews as such suggests the truly breathtaking extent to which he was prepared to think only in terms of the collective unconscious when dealing with social and political matters, and not with individual differences. Closely connected to this capacity is Jung's obvious volkish predilection to think of a Jew—Freud or any other Jew—first and foremost only as a Jew, and so as Other, always profoundly different from "us." Like him or dislike him, one never loses awareness that the person is not just a person, but a Jew.

Richard Stein contends that despite his protestations Jung became identified with the image of the "mana personality," a condition that led to an inflation with the power and vitality of the Third Reich. Stein sees Jung's attitude toward Jews as a manifestation of his father complex, acted out both toward Freud and toward the God image of the Hebrew Bible. Ambivalent both toward the feminine and his own father, the son allegedly identified through the "mana personality" with the Reich as "Great Father."[61] This would explain, in terms of the recondite language of his own system, why Jung could write, from somewhere within himself, what he did about Aryans and Jews while maintaining outward independence. These observations are now chiefly of value insofar as they show how the system itself can support racist and (in a certain sense) reactionary mentalities while at the same time offering a powerful and valuable critique both of the anomie of modernity and the destructiveness of the National Socialist upsurge of irrationalism. After the fact, needless to say, Jung offered trenchant diagnoses of Germany's "epidemic insanity."[62] After "Wotan" and 1936 Jung curtailed all writing on race and Jews considerably. At the end of the war, he is reported to have said he "slipped up" in his first assessment of Nazism.[63]

It may be added that the Nazis themselves made cynical propaganda use of Jung, as they did of Nietzsche, Hegel, and others, citing those writings of Jung that appeared to endorse their regime, while banning books and articles from Zurich that did not. If one were only familiar with the Nazi-propaganda Jung, he would appear in a bad light indeed. Yet, as Frank McLynn has pointed out, in a sense he had only himself to blame. "He ran too much with the hare and the hounds, sometimes appearing to endorse 'the mighty phenomenon of National Socialism,' at other times mocking it."[64] Afterward, he did not clear the air as thoroughly and confessionally as he should have, instead seeking to ignore or even conceal his "slip-ups." The more sympathetic writer Laurens van der Post, in *Jung and the Story of Our Time*, concedes that "There was a brief moment at the beginning when this stirring of unconscious forces he saw in Germany seemed to him capable of a positive potential," but "within two years he had changed his mind. His warnings against events in Germany became more frequent, urgent, and unqualified, ending in such outright condemnation that when the war broke out his own books were banned in Germany and he himself was placed on the Nazi blacklist for liquidation at the first opportunity."[65]

Certainly by the beginning the war, Jung had no illusions whatsoever about the New Germany, if his letters of the time are to be regarded, though the pro-Allied unanimity of Switzerland may be questioned, as we shall see. In writing the distinguished British-American analytic psychologist Esther Harding on 28 September 1939, in his slightly idiosyncratic English, he declared:

> We naturally hope not to be implicated in the war, but there is only one conviction in Switzerland, that if it has to be, it will be on the side of the Allies. There is no doubt and no hesitation; the unanimous conviction in Switzerland is that Germany has lost her national honour to an unspeakable degree, and the Germans inasmuch as they still think know it too. I shouldn't wonder if the most curious things happened in Germany. The situation is completely opaque because of the inhuman terror the whole population is kept under by.[66]

In January of 1940 he wrote to Dr. Edward Lauchenauer, "What the public still doesn't know and can't get into its head is that the collective man is subhuman, nothing but a beast-man, as was clearly demonstrated by the exquisite bestiality of the young German fighters during the blitzkrieg in Poland. Any organization in which the voice of the individual is no longer heard is in danger of degenerating into a subhuman monster."[67] Though the "mass man" concept may have begun as an aristocratic condescension, in the end it fulfilled its own darkest potential.

To the enigma of C. G. Jung and National Socialist totalitarianism, honesty permits no simple answer. The issue is as complex and multisided as the man himself or, as we shall see, his native Switzerland. For every incriminating word or pose, its seems, a counterquote or deed can be presented; for every argument a counterargument. Probably the matter can be reduced no further; Jung was a man of many moods and personae who cannot be condensed to a simple essence. Morever, as a prolific writer and speaker he was far from consistent, and quite capable of unguarded remarks he must later have regretted. The best he has to give us is the Jungian perspective on the tumultuous times in which he lived.

The first half of the twentieth century, plus a dozen years past midpoint—Jung's days in the sun—were indeed awash with mysterious winds and submerged currents of the soul—Jung's realms of exploration—capable of roiling the surface waters up to storm force. The names differed: racial destiny, dialectical materialism, progress, the will of the people, the Freudian unconscious, the archetypes of the collective unconscious. Nothing that happened was what it seemed, either in individual life or the affairs of nations: invisible hands, of the sort best perceived by true modern gnostics, it was agreed on all sides, controlled, from deep within, the world of appearances of what nonetheless prided itself on being an age of sceince, reason, and democracy. The trouble was that those outward vehicles of modernity never were really large enough to guage fully all the vagaries of indvidual passion, or the fate of dynasties. There needed to be more, unplumbed depths teeming with depth charges, explaining why things were sometimes but not always as science, reason, or the democratic process expected them to be, and interpreting the world in terms acceptable to both modernity and the mystical tides behind modern history. To this endeavor Jung contributed generously.

## THE SOVEREIGNTY OF INDIVIDUATION

Paradoxically and significantly, in light of the immense German failure, the only solution Jung had to offer for the ills of mass man was individual—individuation, the harmonious rearrangement of the archetypes on an individual basis and within a modern individual. More and more this became apparent as Jung contemplated the Nazi disaster. As he confronted the land of blond beasts across the border, there was less than before in his ever-flowing writings about rootedness and lost communalism, and more about the reconstituted individual as the only hope. Mass man, always the bane of modernity to Jung, increasingly became only "mass psychosis." In "The Undiscovered Self" (1957), after showing that even the "religious forces," though in principle a possible focal point for resistance to totalitarianism, can be absorbed by the omnipotent state, Jung comes to his chief hope, the transformed individual. *"Resistance to the organized mass can be effected only by the*

*man who is as well organized in his individuality as the mass itself.*"[68] As
Hans Schaer has pointed out, if "modern man" cannot avail himself of
a universal symbol, the process must now set in which Jung called
individuation.[69] That will depend on discovering individual symbols,
for Jung put little stock in demythologizing, or the translations of
unconscious contents into the bloodless generic abstractions so beloved of a certain sort of modernist; concrete mythic images are the
real meat of the unconscious, and if the individual does not find his
or her own symbols in the carefully crafted ways of the best religions
or skilled analysis, one is more than likely to seek them out in debased
forms in the psychic epidemic or the battlefield.

Jung once spoke of three kinds of man: the good Christian, Catholic or Protestant, who lives unquestioningly in his faith and so does
not need psychology; "modern man" who is fully self-conscious, rational, extraverted, and unconnected with his past and so all too vul-
nerable to the unconscious; and finally "Jungian man," modern in
rejecting traditional Christianity but willing to reinterpret it in the
light of analytic psychology.[70] In this respect Jung's "cult" bears to the
modern world something like the status of Gnosticism over against
conventional Christianity in the ancient world, and Jung came to realize this.

Gnosticism was a presence in the intellectual world of Jung's
postwar years. The discovery of a new library of Gnostic texts at Nag
Hamadi in Egypt in 1945 had drawn fresh and exciting attention to
the ancient heresy. Carl Jung himself had an indirect part in making
this material available to the scholarly world and the public, at a time
when a turbulent political climate in Egypt caused severe difficulties.
The only portion of the remarkable find to leave Egypt in the 1950s
was a group of texts that came to be known as the "Jung Codex,"
purchased by the Jung Institute of Zurich in honor of the master's
eightieth birthday; the prestige of the great psychologist's name helped
pave the way for that acquisition.

In the first chapter we noted the use of the term *gnostic* by the
political scientist Eric Voegelin at around the same time in a negative
sense, to mean a presumed but in the end futile knowledge of the
secret laws of history and human nature. We observed that Jung shared
a similarly pessimistic view of the social order, though the labels might
well be reversed. What Voegelin called gnosticism was the political
expression of Jung's mass man and his psychic epidemics, under a

mana personality and the glamour of his ideology; Jung's gnosticism was the individual's way out of such a whirlpool world. He employed the term in a positive sense; gnostic was the name of those who escape from society by turning within. There is, however, the gnostic god Abraxas who was a significant figure in Jung's personal pantheon, and who can represent an attitude beyond good and evil, in the sense that this deity stood for recognition and assimilation of the Shadow archetype. To Jung's mind, however, what he once called "gnostic morality" was not necessarily unscriptural however it may confound conventional morality: it was God's command to Hosea that he marry a whore, or Jesus' parabolic commendation of the unjust steward.[71]

Actually, both Voegelin and Jung reshaped real gnosticism to their own ideological purposes. The ancient bearers of the name were not political in Voegelin's sense, but viewed all aspects of the outer world with deep suspicion, as the enslaving work of bent archons who did not wish humanity well. Jung, especially the later Jung, could so view the social order, but he was not as pessimistic as the gnostics in their metaphysical despair; he proposed not individuation out of the world but into it. Jung implicitly accepted the six characteristics of gnosticism described by Voegelin—dissatisfaction, belief that the cause of dissatisfaction is that the world is poorly organized, belief that salvation is possible, that the world can be changed by a historical process, that change can come about through human action, and that to accomplish it requires gnosis, true secret knowledge—as proper diagnostic criteria. But he more and more internalized them to the individual psyche rather than the social or political realm, substituting psyche for world. Once asked what one could do to help the world in its terrible condition, he reportedly responded, "Help yourself and you help the world."[72] He was, of course, always most interested in the psyche. He got into trouble with the notion that gnostic "salvation" was different for different races because of their differing collective unconsciousnesses. But it seems to have become clear to him in the end that this idea was a false gnosis. The true inward gnostic salvation requires nothing but free space. All it demands of the outer world is to be left alone so the therapeutic process can advance. One gains no positive inner salvation from any of the world's social or political movements.

Voegelin was, incidentally, not pleased with any sort of "self-salvation," and he may well have had Jungianism in mind along with other soteriological venues. "Self-salvation through knowledge has its own magic, and this magic is not harmless," for though understandable it runs away from the world at the cost of only increasing its disorder. Gnosticism did not solve the problems of the ancient world, Voegelin thought, but its deteriorating civilization was instead renewed "by that movement which strove through loving action to revive the practice of the 'serious play' (to use Plato's expression)—that is, by Christianity."[73] But Jung's individuation came out of the Nietzschean, late romantic rejection of both normative Christianity and Enlightenment clarity and reason. It favored the more convoluted and subterranean process of healing the world by healing the psyches that are the real makers of history, even if that healing required their withdrawal from the world to be reforged in a gnostic shop.

## THE PARADOXICAL POWER OF MYTH

So obviously all that can be done is to awaken mass men from their dreams by individuation, to be achieved through opening channels to the unconscious, including the archetypes and the collective. Myth and ritual can have a very important role in this awakening process, for they are able to penetrate mass man's amnesia and recall to some level of consciousness the archetypes and finally the mandala of full human/divine glory they embody when realized and in balanced harmony. Jungian works like *Archetypes and the Collective Unconscious* are full of studies of the Trickster, Kore, Fairy Tales, the Mother and Child archetypes, the last (as the marvelous child, the *puer aeternas*, the Christ Child) being the emblem of rebirth and new transformed selfhood.

Once awakened, the archetypes can then fairly contend for the soul of the persona and forge it as with hammer and anvil: "Between them," Jung said, "the patient iron is forged into an indestructible whole, an 'individual.' "[74] Iron must be heated to a burning red to be forged, and one can perhaps see why the upsurge of Wotan "like an extinct volcano" roaring back to fiery life in National Socialism could have given Jung a glimmer of hope, since at least connections were once more being made between conscious and unconscious. But it was quickly evident this effort had very badly misfired; it prematurely released nothing but raw and therefore destructive energies of the unconscious, with no truly conscious control at all, naught but that of the infantile dream state of mass man with a hysterical mana personality as psychopomp. It was no breakthrough, but the worst of both sides: semiconscious mass mind energized by the fires from below.

Jung was undoubtedly confirmed in this realization by his belief that the way out can only be individual; there is little hope in mass movements or political action, for they are generally part of the problem instead, annealing mass man more than healing him. Yet Jung nonetheless felt free to apply on an individual basis the same mythic potions that had been so disastrously potent when the intoxicants were quaffed by mass man and his mana-maniac leaders. They are indeed powerful draughts:

> One can perceive the specific energy of the archetypes when one experiences the peculiar feeling of numinosity that accompanies them— the fascination or spell that emanates from them. . . . The universal hero myth, for example, shows the picture of a powerful man or god-man who vanquishes evil in the form of dragons, serpents, monsters, demons, and enemies of all kinds, and who liberates his people from destruction and death. The narration or ritual repetition of sacred texts and ceremonies, and the worship of such a figure with dances music, hymns, prayers, and sacrifices, grip the audience with numinous emotions and exalt the participants to identification with the hero. If we contemplate such a situation with the eyes of a believer, we can understand how the ordinary man is gripped, freed from his impotence and misery, and raised to an almost superhuman status, at least for the time being.[75]

Obviously these exaltations could save or destroy.

## THE BURKEAN JUNGIAN STATE

Jung seemed able to hold out no hope that modern humanity could produce any satisfactory political solution it its dilemmas. Regarding his views of democracy, Volodymyr Walter Odajnyk wrote, in *Jung and Politics*:

> Jung does not espouse liberal democracy as a generally applicable, ideal form of government. Rather, he holds an organic view of the relationship between the individual, the society, and the state, so that, where there is no historical, social, and political basis for a democratic order, it is unwise to graft it on by decree. Moreover, given his opinion of the pernicious influence of sheer numbers, Jung would certainly argue that democracy is possible only on a small scale.[76]

Perhaps the small scale is reflected in Switzerland, for in 1928 he wrote of his democratic homeland as a "European center of gravity," despite its stolid and conservative citizens.[77] Again, after the war, he was able to say, "Living as we do in the middle of Europe, we Swiss feel comfortably far removed from the foul vapours that arise from the morass of German guilt."[78] He feared countries larger than Switzerland; here we see something of Jung's real character as a political man in the context of a real time and place: his own nation. The basic impression one gains from his "Swiss" writings is that Jung was conservative in a traditionalist, democratic sense, more instinctively than ideologically; it is better for a society to be, like Switzerland, open, democratic, stupid, frustrating, and changing only slowly, than to be carried away by psychic epidemics. For what such a small, isolated society could really mean is a society of individuals bound by natural and traditional orders, rather than the hollow idols of mass man, and one in which the only salvation was through the full individuation of the individual.

Perhaps Jung's claim that Switzerland escapes "the morass of German guilt" will strike many readers as excessively smug. Here arises another complexifying twist to the Jungian picture. Jung may have been right in saying that many Swiss, even German Swiss, disdained Nazidom and hoped for an Allied victory during the war. Yet widely publicized revelations have now demonstrated that Swiss banks profited from Nazi money, including moneys stolen from Jews who perished in the holocaust. More controversial charges have also alleged that anti-Semitic figures in the Swiss wartime government slowed the mountain nation's acceptance of Jewish refugees. None of this is very creditable to Switzerland, but serves to show that Jung no doubt shared the national attitude of most of his countrymen, who appeared to be convinced that Switzerland was basically good but, as a small state surrounded by far more powerful and often far more dubious powers, had no choice but to do business wherever it could and keep on reasonable terms with all sides. Jung's efforts at psychoanalytic statesmanship emanating from Switzerland may need to be seen partly in this light; he probably thought he was acting in the way most of his fellows would have thought was the only way one could act in such a situation.

Alan Morris Schom has found evidence, published in a report sponsored by the Simon Wiesenthal Center, that, contrary to Jung's assertion to the British Esther Harding, Nazi groups and sympathizers with the German cause were present in Swiss cities and towns, even villages, everywhere among the nearly 70 percent of the Swiss population that is German linguistically and culturally, the Switzerland of which Jung was a part.[79] There is even a photograph of parading, swastika-wearing Nazis in Zurich, Jung's city, in 1941. Germans volkish literature had broad distribution in Switzerland and anti-Semitism as well as fervent anti-communism was widespread. In a companion report, Schom has shown that not only was it exceedingly difficult for Jewish refugees from the Nazi terror to become Swiss citizens, conditions in Swiss refugee camps were often very harsh.[80] All this involved blatant discrimination between Jewish and non-Jewish immigrants and refugees, and was the result of policies set by high-ranking anti-Semitic Swiss officials. Moreover, although out-and-out pro-Nazis and activist (as compared to attitudinal) anti-Semitism may have represented only a minority, Switzerland was also bound economically to the Axis cause: by 1942, 97 percent of Swiss exports went to Germany, and there were also the Nazi arrangements with Swiss banks. All this, and many other indications of pro-German sympathies during the war years, have been since suppressed in Switzerland, Schom declares.[81]

On the other hand, Jung's own writings suggest it would not be correct to say that most Swiss endorsed the extremist, not to mention crazy and criminal, aspects of Nazidom, or actually hoped for a German victory—and Jung appears to have been about as typical a German Swiss as any on such matters; later we will see that Joseph Campbell's wife noted that when Jung moved conversationally into political and social issues, the less he was the brilliant world-class thinker, and the more an ordinary provincial German Swiss. Either the Schom reports are misleading, or German Swiss, and Jung among them, were capable of serious duplicity, or of possessing several contradictory levels of consciousness at the same time.

That is not impossible. German Swiss, like decent Germans in the fatherland, could well have been caught in the emotional bind of feeling on the one hand a natural patriotic and volkish, not to mention economic, identification with Germany, and at the same time a natural revulsion at some of its policies. It is also not clear that a real majority of Swiss would have actually wanted to trade Switzerland's peculiar but functional democracy for a führer-state.

Jung, with all his own immense subjective realms, was undoubtedly a microcosm of the Swiss perplex, and perhaps did not sort it out any better than his countrymen. Like them, he rescued Jews yet was capable of anti-Semitism; he felt volkishness in his blood yet could see how it led to national insanity. Like them, he was no doubt relieved when 1945 brought an end to the horrible tensions and contradictions. Perhaps the seeming contradictions of Jung's attitudes on Nazi Germany boil down to nothing more than this: politically he was not the brilliant intellectual, but an ordinary German Swiss with all the fears and prejudices and complications pertaining thereto. But though he felt this identity, he could also sometimes see through it; he was less than consistent.

It is striking, and no doubt significant, that Frank McLynn begins his massive biography of Jung with this perhaps unexpected declaration: "To understand Carl Gustav Jung one must first understand Switzerland, and this is no easy matter." Alluding to the complexities of a republic without a president and a confederation without direct power over its citizens, McLynn remarks that "Some observers have even suggested . . . that Jung could not have had the theories he had if he had been born elsewhere, since the Swiss constitution is itself 'Jungian,' " and adds, "Superstitious, xenophobic, conservative, earthbound, introverted, moneyminded—all these epithets have been used to describe Jung, and even more frequently to describe his native country."[82]

When he was dealing with Germany rather than his own multinational nation, however, Jung seemed instinctively to think more in volkish, racial, collective unconscious terms. (If little Switzerland has a distinctive national collective unconscious, Jung never really reveals what it is; however, there are no doubts about Germany's—from the unique vantage point of a German Swiss who was half under the heavy sway of that ominous unconsciousness and half an outside observer of it.) Andrew Samuels, in his important and balanced discussion of Jung and National Socialism, stresses that it is what we might call the corporate—the volkish, if one wishes—side of traditionalism that carried Jung close to disaster on that issue. "It was Jung's attempt to establish a psychology of nations that brought him into the same frame as Nazi anti-semitic ideology."[83] "In C. G. Jung, nationalism found its psychologist."[84] To Jung, especially the earlier Jung, national psychological identity was very important: hence the discussions of Germanness, and of the strange anomaly of the Jews as a people without a nation. Thus Samuels agrees there is something "in

Jung's habitual way of thinking that leads to anti-semitism."[85] It produces "ideograms" about nations, Jews and, leadership, that can move in dangerous convergence with Nazism.

I agree. But all this needs to be balanced with attention to the nonpolitical, or even antipolitical, significance of individuation. It also needs to be balanced with what might be called Jung's political "Swiss" side, with its commonsense if ambiguous aversion to extremism, and its regard for the small and the local—concerns also basic to the traditionalist mind. In addition to the anomaly of the Jews, there is the anomaly of the Swiss as a nation made up of fragments of three peoples, which has no particular Wotan of its own and little overt power in the world. Yet this incongruous state serves as a kind of counterweight to the ragings of the mighty, and was also able to provide Jung (and others) a privileged observation post in the eye of the storm. It is hard to believe he really ever intended to reject personally the political virtues of his own nation. Jung undoubtedly for himself affirmed civil-rights democracy in the conservative Swiss or Anglo-American style, for certainly a pioneering doctor of the soul needs adequate freedom to publish ideas and analyze patients without totalitarian interference.

In the end, Jung's apparent political philosophy seems comparable to that of Edmund Burke (1729–1797), the icon of modern democratic conservatism. Like the Burke of "On the Sublime and the Beautiful" (1756), Jung was a romantic rather than a classicist, holding that what is greatest and most beautiful is not clarity, but the infinite—the spacey realm of his "No. 2." Burke held that the sense of the infinite is heightened by obscurity: "It is our ignorance of things that causes all our admiration and chiefly excites our passions." Surely that sentiment is similar to the sense of numinous mystery aroused by Jung's unconscious, breaking into consciousness through the shadowy archetypes, which are only the conditioned forms taken by ultimate powers whose roots stretch virtually to infinity. Their potency was only enhanced by Jung's putative Kantianism, through which he considered that true reality cannot be known, for we can know only the projections of consciousness upon it; so its form is archetypal and its language is myth.

In politics, particularly in his famous *Reflections on the Revolution in France* (1790), Burke affirmed his belief in the wisdom of tradition. Even if they contain some evil, traditional institutions entail a covenant with the past not to be lightly broken, and to search for too great a purity in the political and social world is to invite fresh corruption. As a Christian, the British parliamentarian believed, like Voegelin, that the world and humanity are imperfect, and the quest for perfection in the social order spurious. The political obligation is to correct finite present ills and preserve established liberties, not to risk destroying the state in the hope of hypothetical large-scale improvement. Thus, as is well known, Burke favored the Irish and American rebellions, believing they were intended to preserve concrete liberties and bring about incremental change within the structures of established institutions, but opposed the French Revolution because it was supposed to produce a wholly new society based on rationalism. Undoubtedly it was the French republic's novel philosophical basis, founded on abstract and hypothetical belief in "atomistic" human liberty and equality, and no less its belief that a wholly new and irreversible human order could be commenced in historical time—exactly what Voegelin meant by political gnosis—which most deeply offended the conservative thinker.

Although Jung never referred to the British statesman, the latter's combination of romantic vision and cautious politics based on an appreciation of tradition resonates well with Jung's values. Tradition is, after all, where the myths and symbols which must embody the archetypes come from. The Burkean Jung also realized that the individual soul could often express itself in ways far removed from politics, and therefore politics was by its own nature a limited art. Throughout his life Jung was deeply suspicious of the social order. Adventures in the private worlds of childhood and early adolescence forced upon him an intense awareness of the irrevocable split between his inner self and the norms of the social order in which he had to live his outer life. He entered adulthood convinced that private experience took primacy over the paradigms offered by society.[86] He would therefore have been no very willing recruit to the subjugation of subjectivity itself that is the ultimate goal of any serious totalitarianism.

The deep No. 2 self cared nothing for politics at all, unless they could be experienced as some high wind of a rushing overwhelming force, powerful and blind, inevitable and final as birth or death. No. 1, though he might be awkward and ill at ease, knew he had to function somehow in the regular world, and as he did so No. 2 had to be kept discretely out of sight—and that applied to the politics of nations too, if they were to be run in such a way that No. 1 could find livelihood.

Then there was the strange, only half-explored terrain between 1 and 2, where the latter broke into the consciousness of 1 in the form of dream and inner adventure. This self was quite at odds with the social order, for it wanted nothing but freedom to explore its own realm. The requirements of the unconscious and preconscious "middle" self must take priority over those of the social order, religious or otherwise, for the fused 1 and 2 is the most authentic self known to us; on the spiritual scale its needs must be met first.

Ordinarily this self also would be most content with the politics of a minimalist state where it would be left alone. Yet the Burkean ideals of "prescription" or acceptance of traditions from the past, and the suspicion of excessive political rationalism, suit it, for these would best link it to what is left of "rootedness" and medieval glory. Moreover, once in a while, in the heat of a psychic epidemic, the middle realm might be fired by a tremendous Wotanlike archetype that called for political expression, or seemed to. But increasingly, after 1936, Jung recognized the inauthenticity of archetypal expression on that level. Instead myth must be the way out of political entrapment rather into it, and the Burkean kind of state ought to assure the context for such a move.

Though capable of adapting the volkish language of some of his fellow German speakers, in the end Jung possessed a sort of self-correcting pragmatism and decent respect for human values that put him, like many Swiss, more in the world of Burke than of Hitler. At the same time the covenant across the generations had to be kept alive for the sake of access to the outer forms of the archetypes encrypted in all the world's ancient myths and religions.

# 3

# MIRCEA ELIADE AND NOSTALGIA
# FOR THE SACRED

## A LIFE IN TWO PARTS

Mircea Eliade's life (1907–1986) divides neatly into two parts. The years until 1945 were lived in, or in relation to, his native Romania, where he emerged in the years between the wars as probably the best-known and most controversial of the passionate young Romanian intellectuals of his generation: a prolific and provocative newspaper columnist whose political and cultural views kindled fiery debate; a novelist whose works were praised extravagantly and denounced as pornographic; a dynamic lecturer at the University of Bucharest who virtually established history of religions and Indology as disciplines there; a political activist who was to be accused of fascism, and who suffered imprisonment for his loyalties under the royal dictatorship of King Carol II.

Then there was the second "life," when, in exile from his homeland after it fell behind the Iron Curtain, Eliade—now apparently nonpolitical[1] and noncontroversial unless on arcane scholarly levels—became the preeminent historian of religion of his time, widely known through such classics of that field as *The Sacred and the Profane, The Myth of the Eternal Return, Shamanism: Archaic Techniques of Ecstasy,* and *Yoga: Immortality and Freedom,* among many others. After 1945 he taught first at the Sorbonne in Paris, and then from 1956 at the University of Chicago.

Until recently little was widely known in the West about Eliade's prewar and wartime life. When I was a graduate student at Chicago, only a few rumors—some of them wildly inaccurate, it turned out—floated about among his docents. The professor himself talked about his past very little, and though kindness and graciousness itself in his relationship to students, he was not the sort of person into whose life one pried freely. But now it has been reconstructed, first through Eliade's own two-volume *Autobiography,*[2] supplemented by postwar journals.[3] Second, Mac Linscott Ricketts, the splendid translator of the autobiographies and other Romanian works of Eliade, has compiled a massive and definitive documentary portrait of the years up to 1945, based on countless hours of digging in Romanian archives and libraries, and with the help of Professor Eliade himself up until his death.[4] On top of this, a controversial literature about Eliade in the thirties and forties has emerged in several languages and several countries.[5]

The son of a career officer in the Romanian army, Eliade spent his childhood in various towns where his father was stationed before retiring to Bucharest. In that capital city Eliade emerged in his lycée years as something of a teenage prodigy, reading assiduously, learning languages, writing articles for popular young people's magazines. He kept well-packed journals and even penned an autobiographical novel, *Romanul adolescentului miop* [The Novel of a Near-Sighted Adolescent; composed 1924].[6] Eliade thought that it was the first novel about adolescence by an adolescent. He had more than a hundred published articles to his credit by his eighteenth birthday. Commencing a struggle against time, a battle which came to have metaphysical as well as psychological dimensions, the near-sighted student systematically reduced his hours of sleep to allow time for reading and writing, as well as socializing and Boy Scout activities. Mac Ricketts remarks: "And *about* all these things—his readings, his intellectual discoveries, his friends, his scouting adventures, his biological field trips, his recurring bouts of melancholy, his running battles with his lycée teachers, and even his innermost thoughts, struggles and ambitions—he *wrote.* Probably there are few adolescences so thoroughly documented as that of Mircea Eliade."[7]

Beginning studies at the University of Bucharest in 1925, he kept up the frenetic pace, attending lectures less often than educating himself, trying to do everything all at once under the compulsion of an overwhelming sense that there was not and would never be enough time. He received his degree in philosophy only three years later. During those undergraduate days he had become a regular columnist for a daily newspaper, and was recognized as the "leader" of the younger generation, full of bold and provocative thoughts on literature and the regeneration of Romanian culture.

Mircea Eliade emerged from the university with two great interests for continuing study—Renaissance thought and Indian philosophy. He was able to spend three months in Rome in 1928 pursuing the former. At the same time he noted, in a book by the distinguished historian of Indian philosophy Surendranath Dasgupta, an acknowledgment of the patronage of the Maharaja of Kassimbazar, the tribute even giving that potentate's address. Impulsively, the young Eliade wrote the Maharaja, expressing his own interest in India. Three months later he received a reply inviting him to come and study at the ruler's expense. Arrangements were made for him to live in the Dasgupta home in Calcutta. In late November 1928 Eliade set sail for India, where he remained until 1931.

The budding historian of religion kept busy in several spheres. He did research that laid the foundation for his 1933 Bucharest Ph.D. thesis on Yoga.[8] He sent letters and articles back to Romania excoriating the brutality of British rule in India and expressing his admiration for Gandhi's nonviolent, spiritual revolution against it. He also found time for an indiscreet romantic relationship with Dasgupta's young daughter, Maitreyi, which led to his being abruptly expelled from the home—but which also provided grist for his ultraromantic short novel of intercultural love, *Maitreyi* (1933).[9] Exile from Calcutta enabled him to spend several months at the famous city of yogis, Rishikesh, so the disgrace was not a complete loss. He was compelled to return to Romania in 1931 for army service, but the duty was not arduous, affording him time to complete his doctorate and establish himself anew as a journalist and writer. He also quickly became a dynamic young lecturer at the university as assistant to his mentor, the existentialist philosopher and later extreme nationalist Nae Ionescu.

Like Ionescu, Eliade, for all his world-spanning intellectual interests, was intensely conscious of being a Romanian at a critical moment in his country's cultural history. Long provincialized but now much enlarged territorially by its World War I victory, Romania was wondering if it was ready to find a place on the world stage. Some young Romanians, including the playwright Eugene Ionesco and the sculptor Constantin Brancusi, had migrated to Paris to become major figures in the European avant garde of the 1920s and 1930s. They had already became role models for young Romanians. Eliade now saw himself in a position to do the same at home in Bucharest, assuring his nation's intellectual youth that their country had an important role in addressing both Eastern mysticism and Western rationalism. Romania was, he and others believed, in a unique situation between East and West, on the traditional frontier between Latin civilization and the Byzantine, Islamic, or "mystical" East. Ted Anton has commented of those days that "Of all the radicals of that generation, though, it was the young, handsome, adventurous, bearded Mircea Eliade who captivated them most."[10]

However, his sort of cultural cosmopolitanism was not the only enthusiasm of Romanian youth between the wars. A more nationalistic army of the spirit was also marching in the streets under the aegis of an archangel, and Eliade after some resistance was caught up in that iron enchantment. This brings us to the problematic story of Eliade's relationship to the Legion of the Archangel Michael, a political/spiritual movement with fascist and anti-Semitic leanings powerful in Romania during the thirties. The Legion came to be better known as the pro-Nazi and virulently anti-Semitic Iron Guard influential in Romania's tilt toward the Axis powers in 1940 to 1941, and associated with numerous atrocities of that period. (Technically, the Iron Guard was originally the military arm of the Legion, consisting of all male members between eighteen and thirty). Eliade suffered four months imprisonment for his alleged connection with the Legion when the royal dictatorship of King Carol II turned against it in 1938. He was then enabled to escape the worst of the disasters that swept through his country by serving as its cultural attaché in London and Lisbon. In 1945 he began a new life as a scholar in exile in Paris and finally Chicago, but the shadow of his frenetic and passionate youth must have continually haunted him from within, even if the world sometimes forgot.

It was difficult to associate the graying and rather detached scholar living near the shores of Lake Michigan after 1955 with the tumultuous youth of the Romanian thirties, sleepless, wanting to know and experience everything, willing to undertake political adventure even in perverse form, somehow naive and pure in the midst of it all. However, the record is there. But once burned, twice cautious; when I knew him in the sixties he had nothing to do with the passionate politics of that era in the United States apart from a few caustic comments; reportedly he never read newspapers and was not always even aware of what was transpiring outside his study.

MESSIANIC NATIONALISM

The Legion of the Archangel Michael with which Eliade has been linked was founded in 1927 by Corneliu Z. Codreanu, as a movement dedicated to the cultural and national renewal of the Romanian people by appeal to their spiritual roots.[11] Deeply concerned about the endemic poverty and demoralization of the Romanian countryside, young legionnaires went out to share the life of peasants and help them in practical ways, while Legion literature unsparingly denounced the corruption and complacency of the ruling class. Romanian youth who came of age after World War I—Eliade's generation—like their counterparts elsewhere, were eager to lay the foundations of a new and better world. They were also likely to be deeply nationalistic, partly in response to the benediction the course of that conflict had seemingly given to affirmations of national identity. In the twenties, after self-determination had been much publicized as a part of Woodrow Wilson's hopeful Fourteen Points, and after so many peoples, including the Romanians of Transylvania, had been released from bondage to dying empires, nationalism had all the appearance of a pure, innocent, and idealistic commitment. Out of combined passions for uplift, nation, and spiritual renewal, together with the natural yearning of the young for commitment and solidarity, many Romanian youths of the twenties and thirties were drawn to Legionary dreams. Young people like a living ideal, and in Codreanu they had a leader widely regarded as heroic and saintly. For Eliade, the rich spirituality the Legion espoused, encapsulated in Condreau's talk of "national resurrection" and the creation of a "new man," was an added lure. Unlike comparable fascist-type movements in Italy and Germany, the Legion was explicitly Christian, linked to Romania's Eastern Orthodox religious tradition.

But the Legion was also capable of violence and raw anti-Semitism. In 1933 three Legionnaires, who claimed to be acting independently, assassinated the prime minister, I. G. Duca; Codreanu was arrested but later released. The latter, together with promising redistribution of land to the peasants, pledged also that he would solve the "problem of the yids." Legionary rhetoric continually identified Jews with godless Bolsheviks as well as with unpopular financiers and foreign intruders; the movement circulated such hoary anti-Semitic texts as the "Protocols of the Elders of Zion," and worked for restrictions on Jewish admission to universities and participation in government.[12] The roots and ongoing enthusiasm of the Legionary movement for violence and anti-Semitism is well documented and beyond question.[13]

This side of the movement obviously gave pause to Eliade as the young journalist and intellectual took up his Romanian career after returning from India in 1931. Although Eliade had always been a cultural nationalist who liked to speak of Romanian "messianism," meaning that the country had a cultural heritage to redeem and a special destiny to fulfill, these views usually were relatively nonpolitical at first. They constituted "Romanianism"; Eliade wrote columns of a "Romania for the Romanians" sort, suggesting that the influence of the country's numerous minorities—Jews, Hungarians, and others— was excessive and needed to be curbed.[14] In the context of the times he was not the most chauvinistic of his countrymen. His memoirs, as well as articles and correspondence, indicate that despite the notorious anti-Semitism of his homeland, he prided himself on his friendship with a Jewish novelist like Mihail Sebastian, and took a relatively moderate public position on the "Jewish question." His journalistic assaults on Jewish influence in Romanian life, distasteful as they are, seem to single out Jews for resentment little more than Hungarians, Bulgarians, and other of the many peoples now resident within the "Greater Romania" created by World War I. In the eyes of partisans of Romanianism, those minorities appeared prepared to usurp the prerogatives of the ethnic majority.

There were several intellectual influences on the young Eliade. Ivan Strenski, in his valuable discussion in the section on Eliade in *Four Theories of Myth*, has emphasized the role of his friend Lucien Blaga, a Romanian mythologist and folklorist who "saw his own hermeneutic work as a hybrid form of depth psychology and ontology."[15] Eliade also carried his understanding of religious psychology, especially of the sacred and its primordial symbols, virtually—but I believe not entirely—to metaphysical lengths.

But no one was more influential for the young Eliade than the charismatic, fascist-leaning philosopher Nae Ionescu (1890–1940). Ionescu inculcated mysticism, political activism, and a sort of pre-existentialist questioning, risk-taking irrationalism. Eliade entered the academic world as assistant to this holder of a chair of philosophy at Bucharest. Ionescu wrote little; Eliade himself edited his one collection of essays in 1936. But Ionescu's charm and Socratic method of teaching led many of his acolytes to follow him into dangerous political realms. At one time he was a sympathetic student of Jewish thought and mysticism. But as the influence he had once had at the court of King Carol II waned, by 1933 he was a supporter of the Legion. Eliade was his admirer and protégé; undoubtedly much of the responsibility for Eliade's own rightist involvement must be laid at Ionescu's feet. Nonetheless, in a significant 1934 event, Eliade rebuked Ionescu over an appalling preface the latter had written to a novel by their Jewish friend Mihail Sebastian: Ionescu, by then an Eastern Orthodox rather than cabalistic mystic, had said, amid much else, that the Jew suffers "because he ought to suffer," having refused to recognize Jesus Christ as the Messiah. This controversy led to an exchange in the press over whether Jews can be saved; against more rigid theologians as well as Ionescu, Eliade argued that they indeed can.[16]

Jews were certainly suffering to the northwest in newly Nazi Germany. In early 1934 Eliade could write: "How can we imitate Hitlerism which persecutes Christianity or Communism which burns cathedrals? The Communist arsonists of churches are hooligans—and so are the Fascist persecutors of the Jews. Both of them trample down humaneness and personal faith—which are the freedoms of every individual."[17] For that matter, he went on to anticipate another evil consequent upon the victory of totalitarianism either of the right or of the left: the division of the people into two groups, one "good" and one "bad"—based on race in the case of Nazism, on social class under communism. Only those of the "right" category would be permitted to live in "freedom." But this, Eliade perceived, was nothing more than a reversion to primitive tribalism, wherein only those who knew the correct totem were free to "eat and couple at will."[18] Talk of *political* revolution—so much a part of thirties life on both the right and the left, did not impress him, and he doubted if others were impressed either: "I don't believe there's a conscious young person in this country who hasn't been soured by so much Karl Marx, so much Mussolini, so much Communism, Corporatism, and who knows what else?" The true revolution, he insisted, would have to be inward, a revolution of "soul," on the level of the "permanent revolution" brought by the Son of Man, who taught "revolution against the old economy" to bring in a "new economy of charity, hope, and love."[19] He believed that such a revolution was possible, even on the political plane. In India, he had been much impressed with Mohandas K. Gandhi and his nonviolent, spirituality-based movement for Indian independence and renewal. In December 1935 he told a Romanian radio audience:

> Gandhi's nationalist movement is not a political movement but primarily a mysticism, that is, a spiritual revolution addressed to the soul, aiming at the purification of man, the reformation of social values, and ultimately the salvation of the soul. Paradoxical as it may seem, the only spiritual revolution in the Christian spirit which exists in the world today—is Gandhi's non-violent movement.[20]

In the same spirit, in those years the "Romanianism" he fervently promoted was described as a "higher," nonpolitical nationalism, embracing enthusiasm for all that was sublime in the Romanian heritage. Indeed, Eliade went on with some justice to contrast the renaissance then underway in Romanian art and letters with the sorry state of the nation's political life. "Romanianism," he contended, "is realized fully on the artistic plane, but is trivialized on the political plane."[21]

But the consequent though highly unfortunate result of awareness of this gross dichotomy was Eliade's growing disillusionment with democracy: not only with what passed for democracy in his homeland, but with the idea generally. As his thought developed in this ominous direction, political and "mystical" dimensions of revolution became more and more mixed, and while Eliade always professed to esteem nonviolent, truly "spiritual" methods of combat and renewal both individually and nationally, it became increasingly easy for him to overlook lapses on this point by those he believed genuinely dedicated to the right goals. In 1936 he wrote admiringly of Mussolini for the first time, while noting that "democracy has not made modern

Romania a powerful state." He contrasted democracy's process of "slow, larval evolution," which had only brought poor Romania to the point of being a laughingstock, with a "violent, risk-filled revolution" that would restore a people's pride and faith.[22]

It was then but a small step further for him openly to extend his favor toward the Legion, the only visible prospective agent of such a revolution in Romania. He seems to have been directly inspired by the death in battle of two Romanian legionnaires who volunteered to fight in the Spanish civil war on Franco's anticommunist side, and whom he, like many of his countrymen, regarded as Christian martyrs. (One of the two martyrs, Ion Mota, had been a fervent Jew-basher and Romanian translator of that notorious anti-Semitic forgery, *The Protocols of the Elders of Zion*.)

In his memoirs Eliade dilates almost ironically on the Legion's "cult of death" in those same years, 1937 to 1938.[23] But, though he does not mention it, he must have been aware that a cult of violence in the Legion paralleled its cult of death. Indeed, Codreanu's exaltation of both was extreme even by fascist standards. Not only was violent struggle on behalf of the country lauded, not only was "martyrdom" for its sake the worthiest and most holy of all deaths, but to forfeit one's eternal salvation for the sake of Romania, by committing on its behalf acts that were necessary but so terrible they would cast the doer of them into hell, was to display a nobility beyond praise. By espousing such bizarre sentiments the Legion revealed, however perversely, its "Christian" foundation, in contrast to the paganism of most other fascisms.[24]

Eliade said nothing about this, but he did catch the spirit of the Legion's goal of "national resurrection." In 1939 he wrote of the "new aristocracy" of the Legion: "Legionarism has reintroduced to Romania the joy and the pedagogy of the honest, open struggle. . . . It has created the awareness of an historic mission, the feeling that we were born in order to carry out a unique revolution in the history of the nation . . . in this new, Legionary aristocracy. . . ."[25] In "Why I Believe in the Triumph of the Legionary Movement," Eliade is made to say that its affirmation was because "I believe in the destiny of our nation, I believe in the Christian revolution of the new man, I believe in freedom, personality, and love." (This article appeared in the Guardist paper *Buna vestire* over Eliade's name, although according to Mac Ricketts, Eliade, in 1981, denied writing it. Ricketts states, however, that in any case it was based on paraphrases of articles Eliade had written, and probably contained nothing with which he would not have agreed at that time.)[26] What appealed to him most about that militant movement was its "spirituality," the dedication of its young cadres who went into the villages to help peasants, and the movement's own ostensible dedication to social rebirth and the creation of the "new man"—a goal which seems very clearly to exemplify what Eric Voegelin meant by political gnosticism.

Though perhaps with distaste, Eliade seemed willing to accept the Legion's violence and anti-Semitism as a price that had to be paid for national resurrection. While he clearly seemed to view the Legion as something comparable to Gandhi's spiritual, nonviolent movement for the liberation of India, it must be noted that even many years later he accepted violence as also acceptable in India's case. In his 1978 interview with the French journalist Claude-Henri Rocquet, he said that it was in India that he became "politically aware," in seeing the repression of Indians by their British rulers.

> I said to myself: "How right the Indians are!" It was their country; all they were asking for was a kind of autonomy, and their demonstrations were completely peaceful. They weren't attacking anyone, just demanding their rights. And the police repression was pointlessly violent. So it was in Calcutta that I became aware of political injustice and at the same time realized the spiritual possibilities of Gandhi's political activity: the spiritual discipline that made it possible to stand up to blows without hitting back. It was like Christ; it was Tolstoi's dream.
>
> [Rocquet said] So you were won over, heart and soul, to the cause of nonviolence. . . .
>
> [Eliade] And of violence too! For example, one day I heard an extremist talking, and I had to admit he was right. I understood perfectly well that there had to be some violent protesters too.[27]

In reference to Gandhi's handling of the volatile Indian situation, Eliade once remarked that "in a political movement, the only leaders with a chance of success are those who know how to satisfy (or to Chloroform) the extremists."[28]

At the same time, it must be noted that Eliade's public Legionism extended only for little more than the year 1937—a year of phenomenal growth for the movement—though the question of his sympathies during years of service to rightist Romanian governments allied with Hitler until 1944 cannot be overlooked. But he claimed never to have joined the Legion, and actually wrote very few pieces explicitly praising it. However, his sometime friend, the Jewish writer Mihail Sebastian, whom as we have seen he befriended in the affair of the preface, penned in his journals at the time that in private Eliade was capable of expressing euphoric enthusiasm for the Legion, even its violent acts, and also for its anti-Semitic outbursts. Needless to say, Sebastian was deeply distressed, commenting, "He's not joking, nor is he demented. He's only naive. But there is such a thing as catastrophic naiveté!"[29] Sebastian also had much to say about the "Guardist conversion" among young intellectuals spearheaded by Nae Ionescu and the newspaper, *Cuvantul*, which Ionescu edited, a swelling tide that reached its climax in 1937 and 1938, the years of Eliade's adherence.[30]

Though nothing can excuse Eliade's enthusiasms today, two factors may at least help us to understand: first, the abysmal corruption and incompetence of the nominally democratic monarchy that ruled Romania in those days; and second, the natural attraction of the Legion's romantic, spiritual, and mythic rhetoric for one of Eliade's susceptibilities. The way in which all fascist movements appealed to deep instinctual yearnings for communal solidarity, spiritual rebirth, and enacting deeds of mythic dimension—feelings not far removed from the religious—is not to be underestimated.

During most of the thirties, the king had tacitly encouraged the Legion and its nationalism. But in 1938 Carol II, alarmed at the Legion's rapid growth and electoral triumphs, established a royal dictatorship and turned against the Legion, seeing it as a rival source of power. Codreanu was arrested in April and finally executed "while trying to escape" on November 30, 1938. Eliade, along with his beloved teacher Nae Ionescu and many others of supposed Legion sympathies, was imprisoned; Eliade for refusing to sign a document dissociating himself from the Legion. He said, first, that he had never joined so could not leave it; and, second, that he did associate himself with many of its aims. Eliade never criticized Codreanu, the movement's founder and leader. In memoirs written shortly before his own death, he wrote:

> I don't know how Corneliu Codreanu will be judged by history. . . . For him, the Legionary movement did not constitute a political phenomenon but was, in its essence, ethical and religious. He repeated time and again that he was not interested in the acquisition of power but in the creation

of a "new man." . . . [He] believed in the necessity of sacrifice; he considered that every new persecution could only purify and strengthen the
Legionary movement, and he believed, furthermore, in his own destiny
and in the protection of the Archangel Michael. . . . A good part of the
Legionary activity consisted in worship services, offices for the dead,
strict fasts, and prayers.[31]

Eliade, who emphasized in his own autobiography the exten-
siveness and seriousness of religious life among the incarcerated legionnaires, was released after four months and, in 1940, enabled by
well-placed patrons to depart his increasingly desperate country to
become its cultural attaché in London, where he endured the Blitz,
and then, just before Britain declared war on Romania in 1941, in
neutral Lisbon, Portugal, until 1945.

During the latter years Eliade (who had never completely endorsed
the Mussolini or Hitler regimes) found time to compose a book in
praise of Portugal's "benevolent" dictator António Salazar, a fellow
professor raised to a position of power, whose administration he recommended as an example to his countrymen. (The book, he earnestly
says in the introduction, was written to answer a question: "Is a [na-
tional] spiritual revolution possible?" The answer, he now found, is
Yes! Salazar has "achieved a miracle"; "a totalitarian and Christian
state, built not on abstractions, but on the living realities of the nation
and its tradition.)"[32]

At the same time, we must note that, according to his memoirs,
Eliade was aware of Legion atrocities, though apparently only those
occurring after the 1938 death of Codreanu. While the Legion had
always been anti-Semitic and protofascist in character, the 1938 persecution and the replacement of Codreanu by the extremist Horia Sima
as leader still further darkened the character of the Iron Guard, as it
was increasingly called. Then, as loyalties shifted and events moved
with bewildering speed, in 1940 the legion came to power in alliance
with the king and the pro-Nazi military dictator Ion Antonescu to
create a "National Legionnaire State." Eliade was clearly shocked by
a series of assassinations of prominent political enemies enacted soon
after by the Legionnaire State on November 30, 1940.[33] Then, in January 1941, according to his autobiography, he further "learned of the
excesses and crimes of the Legionnaires (examples were cited of po-
groms: in particular, one at Iasi)."[34] At the same time, Antonescu turned

against the Legion and the Legionnaire State, though not the outrages, came to an end. In fact, these horrors and later Romanian anti-Semitic atrocities were exceeded only by the Nazi holocaust in numbers and brutality, leaving scores of desecrated synagogues and thousands of mutilated corpses.[35] It is not evident that Eliade saw any relationship between these "excesses" and the central ideology of the spiritual nationalism, with its anti-Semitism, that he had once admired, perhaps to the point of rapture.

In 1978, Eliade was to write to Ioan Culianu, a fellow Romanian and protégé who had questioned him about his involvement:

> I don't think it is possible to write an objective history of the Legionary Movement nor a portrait of C.Z.C. [Codreanu]. The documents at hand are insufficient; moreover, an objective attitude can be fatal for the author. . . . After Büchenwald and Auschwitz even honest people cannot afford being "objective."[36]

What he seems to be saying, in effect, is that what the Legion meant forty years before to a young, starry-eyed, and instinctively spiritual person like himself, capable of being fired up by mythological archetypes and with no awareness of the evil that was to be unleashed, is a reality locked in a past that, after the gates of time have been slammed shut on it, can never be recovered, much less communicated to one who was not there, without hopeless misunderstanding. Undoubtedly in his youthful idealism he had sided with the Legion because he saw them as persecuted righteous mystics and idealists. Responding to their high-flown Christian and spiritual rhetoric, he doubtless believed the Legionnaires were at heart peaceful friends of the peasantry, though prepared to struggle and die for their cause. But who could say or hear such things now without a cynical snicker? Better simply to say nothing.

What is to be made of a case like this? After the war, Eliade definitely condemned the evils of the Nazi regime, usually in parallelism with those of the Marxist states, just as he had in the early thirties. In *Myths, Dreams, and Mysteries*, talking about the mythological character of Marxist communism, he says that

> it is clear that the author of the Communist Manifesto takes up and carries on one of the great eschatological myths of the Middle Eastern and

Mediterranean world, namely: the redemptive part to be played by the Just (the "elect," the "anointed," the "innocent," the "missioners," in our own days by the proletariat), whose sufferings are invoked to change the ontological status of the world. In fact, Marx's classless society, and the consequent disappearance of all historical tensions, find their most exact precedent in the myth of the Golden Age which, according to a number of traditions, lies at the beginning and the end of History. Marx has enriched this venerable myth with a truly messianic Judaeo-Christian ideology; on the one hand, by the prophetic and soteriological function he ascribes to the proletariat; and, on he other, by the final struggle between Good and Evil, which may well be compared with the apocalyptic conflict between Christ and the Antichrist, ending in the decisive victory of the former.

He here implicitly recognizes communism as Jungian inflation or as gnostic in Voegelin's sense. (In a journal entry for November 3, 1960, Eliade reports that Eric Voegelin visited him, and he was "surprised by the affinity of our positions," and concerning his perception of modern gnosticism, Eliade said the political thinker "can't get over the fact that no one has ever seen these things up to now")[37] Regarding the other totalitarian ideology, Eliade in the same passage is in fact less generous:

In comparison with the grandeur and the vigorous optimism of the communist myth, the mythology propagated by the national socialists seems peculiarly inept; and this not only because of the limitations of the racial myth (how could one imagine that the rest of Europe would voluntarily accept submission to the master-race?), but above all because of the fundamental pessimism of the Germanic mythology. . . . for the eschaton prophesied and expected by the ancient Germans was the ragnorök—that is, a catastrophic end of the world.[38]

However, apart from the few allusions in the memoirs like those cited above, both the mythology and the atrocities of the Legion are passed over in silence, almost as though he expected few of his worldwide readers to know or care anything about the dark-stained history of one small country.

Defenders of Eliade like Bryan Rennie point out that Eliade's relatively few published statements on behalf of the Legion in his one year of public association were, given the context of time and place, quite moderate. He did not, Rennie states, single out Jews apart from other minorities for condemnation, much less utter words that could have incited the anti-Semitic terrorism that came after Codreanu's death and the brief tenure of the Legionnaire state. In the most notorious case, an article castigating Jews for their "intransigence," Eliade actually placed the real blame on "Christian history" and its tragic influence on Jews under its shadow.

In *Reconstructing Eliade* Rennie analyzes the allegations of four of the major critics of Eliade's political activities in the thirties—Ivan Strenski, Adriana Berger, Leon Volovici, and Daniel Dubuisson—and makes substantial, often convincing countercriticisms. He leaves us, as does Ricketts, with a picture of a young man who was not personally anti-Semitic or fascist, though nationalistic and strongly under the illusion that the Legion was a spiritual and nonviolent activity something like Gandhi's movement for the independence of India. Rennie concludes his chapter on Eliade's political involvement with these words: "[I]t has to be said that there is to date no evidence of actual membership, of active services rendered, or of any real involvement with any fascist or totalitarian movements or ideals. Nor is there any evidence of continued support for nationalist separatist ideals after their inherently violent nature was revealed, nor of the imprint of such ideals in Eliade's scholarship." Scholars who have made such allegations, he contends, "have pursued their own agendas with little regard for the integrity of their textual sources."[39]

Certainly other Romanian intellectuals of the thirties, as Volovici amply illustrates, were far more blatantly fascist and anti-Semitic than Eliade. One need mention only Eliade's "Mephistopheles," as he has been called, Nae Ionescu, or the insufferable Emil Cioran, who acquired a measure of postwar fame as an existentialist philosopher in Paris. Perhaps Eliade was also the victim of too much fame too soon, a brilliant but still immature figure who may have felt compelled by his position as "leader of the young" to take public stands he might privately have preferred to avoid. Many of us, including myself, would not care twenty or thirty years later to be held accountable for everything we said or believed about religion or politics at age thirty-one. It is also fair to point out that the Legion experience of the thirties was only part of what shaped the mature Eliade who emerged after the war, as if from a difficult and prolonged near-sighted adolescence: there was also India, the classical literature of several languages, existentialist philosophy, the ideas of the renaissance. In a striking journal entry for January 3, 1961, Eliade wrote:

Today, coming home from the university, in the vicinity of the Oriental Institute, I suddenly experienced my life's *duration*. Impossible to find
just the right word. I suddenly felt, not older, but extraordinarily rich and
full; expanded—bringing together in me, concomitantly, both the Indian,
Portuguese, and Parisian "time" and the memories of my Bucharest childhood and youth. As if I had acquired a new dimension of depth. I was
"larger," "rounder." An immense inner domain—where, not so long ago,
I was penetrating only fragmentarily by trying to relive such-and-such an
event—was revealed in its totality: I'm able to see it from end to end and,
at the same time, in all its depth.

A vigorous, strong feeling. Historical human life suddenly takes on
meaning and significance. Optimism.[40]

Nonetheless, on the political side, Eliade was old enough and experienced enough in the thirties to know what he was doing, or should
have been. Perhaps he was "catastrophically naive," but that also is a
failing which needs to be addressed. There is no need to doubt the
sincerity of his scattered denunciations of fascist or Nazi ideology and
practice, both prewar and postwar, including of atrocities against Jews,
or to cavil at his also scattered, respectful treatment of Jewish scholars,
such as Gershom Scholem, and of religious Judaism.[41]

But what has bothered many critics was Eliade's subsequent inability to renounce or even discuss seriously the Legion aspect of his own
life, beyond the still apologetic and naive-sounding references cited above
in the posthumous volume two of his autobiography. He would say
little more than he did, for example, in response to denunciations by an
Italian scholar in 1950 of his "alleged 'fascist' activity before the war."
Eliade thought the allegations ultimately emanated from the then-
communist Romanian embassy in Rome; his only comment was the
remark that they were "a timely reminder that my imprudent acts and
errors committed in youth constituted a series of malentendus [misun-
derstandings, mistakes] that would follow me all my life."[42]

Yet it is statements like this that have only caused doubts to fester.
Ion Culianu, a brilliant young historian of religion, a protégé of Eliade
and his literary executor, put his finger on the problem in a review of
Eliade's autobiography when he said of 1936 to 1938: "Why insist at
such length on a relatively short episode in a long life? Because the
rest of that life is relatively well known and transparent, whereas it is
precisely this episode that the second volume of the autobiography
reveals in a detached tone."[43]

Culianu was himself murdered at the University of Chicago on May 21, 1991, perhaps at the hands of Guardist elements still lingering in the murky world of Romanian politics. As a Romanian, though born and raised in the communist era, he must have had some insights into Eliade's mentality and the political culture of their homeland less accessible to outsiders than to a native. After reading "the whole coveted file concerning Eliade's political sympathies in 1938–1940," he wrote Mac Ricketts, "my position is still the same. Mr. Eliade has never been an anti-Semite, a member of the Iron Guard, or a pro-Nazi. But I understand anyway that he was closer to the IG [Iron Guard] than I liked to think." He also raised the problem, important to our own discussion of three mythologists, of reading the words and thoughts of one era through the lens of another, after horrible events that were once still in the future had become terrors of history.[44] How much can we excuse a mythologist or historian of religion for, like most humans, not possessing absolute precognition, while still blaming them for not reading aright the signs of the times? How could sentiments that in the end led to unspeakable horrors have been at one time fairly "normal," though not blameless?

Culianu quoted Seymour Cain, "a penetrating reader of the Autobiography":

> Eliade never directly forswears his ideological association with the Legionary movement, and sees its decline and fall as a Romanian tragedy, the inevitable result of its political naiveté, rather than a good thing. He is more like the fellow-travelers of Soviet communism who gave up their association but never repudiated the ideology to which they had given their youthful devotion.[45]

One can only regret that the mature Eliade never found the time or the courage to address open and fully those errors of his youth, subjecting them to the acute analysis of spiritual consciousness of which he was capable in examining the initiatory ordeals of others. It seems more than likely that he was one of those intellectuals so innocent and naive, and so entranced by the pull of a spiritual drama that raised one above the pale cast of thought, that he as youthful "mythologist" saw the myths he wanted to see enacted by the Legion, and blinded himself to its ugly side. Throughout the twentieth century the likes of the young Eliade have embraced fascism and Marxism, feeling only the same righteousness and joy. Quite nonviolent by nature himself, fundamentally more aesthetic than political (or, for that matter, than scholarly in the most rigorous sense of the term), he exalted the Legion's own martyrs but, incredibly given its martial tone and its propaganda, was surprised by its kills.

Had he talked about all this as the light of common day overtook his fantasies after 1945, he would have raised his own stature in the end, and we would have known more about the mid-twentieth century, that era of unprecedented opulence and terror, of myth and science, through which he made his pilgrimage. Culianu, after mentioning Eliade's reference in the autobiography to his taking a "dangerous turn," at that point in his life, adds, "How much we wish he had said: a *wrong* one!"[46] But he did not.

The apocalyptic year 1945 was a time of radical disjuncture in Eliade's pilgrimage, a season of moving from one life to another. The late thirties and early forties had been a time of death in his personal world, as they had been for so many millions in the world at large. Codreanu was executed in 1938, Nae Ionescu died prematurely of a heart attack in 1940, Sebastian was hit by a truck and killed in 1945, Eliade's first wife Nina died of cancer in 1944.

After 1945 death changed to new life. He met his second wife, Christinel, in Paris where they were both postwar exiles from Romania. For Eliade was in exile in a strange new postwar world, a world shaped by atomic bombs, the revelations of Auschwitz, communist triumph in eastern Europe, elsewhere the victory of British and U.S. values. In such a world the less said about the past the better, of course. But it must quite honestly have also seemed to Eliade that 1945 afforded an opportunity such as is rarely given a human being to reconstruct himself thoroughly and begin anew, despite the possibility that a few ghostly "malentendus" would still waft out of the now-remote past. During the final months of the war, still in Lisbon, he sensed a profound change overtaking him. He suffered severe insomnia:

> But I did not resort to sleeping pills. Instead, I reread and meditated on the Gospels, trying to discover the direction to take to get out of the labyrinth. It had seemed to me for a long time that I had been wandering in a labyrinth, and as time passed I became more and more convinced that it was yet another initiatory ordeal, as many crises in the past several years had been. All the despair, depression, and suffering had a meaning: I must understand them as so many "initiatory tortures" preparing me for the symbolic death and spiritual resurrection toward which I was

heading. I knew that I could not remain indefinitely in my present state: I was no longer the man I had been in the first year of the war, but still I had not attained another mode of being. I was in an obscure phase, a transition period . . . [even as] the whole world was in the process of being transformed.[47]

Many lives are divided into definite parts, but in not all of them is there such a clear wall as in the case of Mircea Eliade, exiling one at a definite point from one set of days that are no more, and from a place to which one can never return physically. Inevitably there will be a sense of loss and gain, of regret and of opportunity. But also one will be achingly aware there is something in one's past which no one who had not lived in that now-forbidden space and time could ever truly understand. Undoubtedly the experience only enhanced an inborn gnosticlike sense important to Eliade that exile is among the profoundest metaphors for all human life.

It is not the purpose of the present study to sort out Eliade's guilt or innocence, or combination of both, in respect to Romanian fascism, beyond what has already been said. He was a man of assorted secrets, and some of them probably he took with him in death. We must now turn to the larger question of the meaning of Eliade's past to the scholar's history of religions work—and to the implicit political themes therein.

In pursuance of these answers, we shall, I think, learn three things:

1. That the fundamental motif of Eliade's life, certainly after 1945, but really all the way through, was the theme of exile. He felt himself, after adolescence, an exile from his own childhood and youth. Before long that feeling was extrapolated into regarding himself as something of a gnostic exile from eternity. Even his passion for Romanianism was really the groping of a wandering soul for solid ground, more than the sort of gritty political commitment it may have been for others.

2. That there is reason to think the disastrous experience with Romanianism and the Legion led him to pluralize and universalize the experience of the Sacred, while at the same time bringing home forcefully the terror of history. As experiencer of totalitarianism and as exile, he could well have been led to perceive totalitarianism's opposite and exile's opportunity, radical pluralism, as a positive good. Bryan Rennie does not hesitate to say: "I would suggest that Eliade's brush with totalitarian ideologies in the 30s influenced his theoretical position as expressed in his later books as a reaction against such tendencies; that his perilous attraction to the extreme right in his

younger years led to a far more mature position; that, in its own way, his later works were a repudiation of the exlusivism and ethnic superiority of the later Iron Guard."[48] The most important question, however, is not whether Eliade made serious political misjudgments at particular times, which he certainly did, but—as in the case of Jung—what relation those judgments have to his lifework as mythologist and historian of religion.

3. That in all this he was not a traditionalist but a sometime political and then a scholarly modernist in the most rarefied sense of the word, who saw tradition as material to be studied, perhaps used for political or other ends, but not to be believed or personally adopted. For the essence of what informs sacred tradition is often under secular camouflage in a secular age, and if it is discovered at all will be found under new and often secular wrappings.

But first let us consider Eliade the exile.

## EXILE FROM ETERNITY

Mircea Eliade has recorded this striking memory from his early childhood:

> I remember especially a summer afternoon when the whole household was sleeping. I left the room my brother and I shared, creeping so as not to make any noise, and headed toward the drawing room. . . . It was as if I had entered a fairy-tale palace. The roller blinds and the heavy curtains of green velvet were drawn. The room was pervaded by an eerie irides-cent light. It was as though I were suddenly enclosed within a huge grape.
>
> I never told anyone about this discovery. Actually, I think I should not have known what to tell. Had I been able to use adult vocabulary, I might have said that I had discovered a mystery. . . . I could later evoke at will that green fairyland. When I did so I would remain motionless, almost not daring to breathe, and I would rediscover that beatitude all over again; I would relive with the same intensity the moment when I had stumbled into that paradise of incomparable light. I practiced for many years this exercise of recapturing the epiphanic moment, and I would always find again the same plenitude. I would slip into it as into a fragment of time devoid of duration—without beginning and without end. During my last years of lycée, when I struggled with prolonged attacks of melancholy, I still succeeded at times in returning to the golden green light of that afternoon. . . . But even though the beatitude was the same, it was now impossible to bear because it aggravated my sadness too much. By this time I knew the world to which the drawing room

belonged—with the green velvet curtain, the carpet on which I had crept on hands and knees, and the matchless light—was a world forever lost.[49]

In a real sense, this scene as remembered struck the template of a life governed by nostalgia: for childhood, for historical times past, for cosmic religion, for paradise. Like any real historian, he loved the past just because it was past, but he also saw in the gulf between the human present and its past an icon of the rupture between time and eternity. At the same time, he was aware also that the human condition is to live in tension between one's present state and the objects of nostalgia: they can never be fully recovered; perhaps they are always partly a dream. In *Myths, Dreams and Mysteries* he is careful to point out that primal peoples "were also aware of having lost a primitive paradise."[50] They did not believe they lived in mythological time; their myths too were set in an indeterminate past, severed from their present by a mythological "fall." For Eliade no more than for Jung was "the primitive" idealized; it was merely different, in some ways embodying a consciousness better able to understand, and thereby to yearn for, the primal paradises of myth.

Eliade was fundamentally a structuralist who began with an ideal type, *homo religiosus*, religious man, and then analyzed the structures of the world as seen by this person. His religious cosmos is first of all not "homogeneous" but divided into the sacred and the profane, sacred space and time, like the green room, the space of temples and the like, the time of rite and festival, over against their "ordinary," nonsacred counterparts. The sacred ultimately cannot be contrived but only discovered through "hierophany," communicated by means of myth and preserved in rites whose "gestures" symbolically repeat those of the mythical time, *illud tempus*.

All this was best realized by archaic peoples who still lived in the world of "cosmic religion," in the "paradise of archetypes" before time has been "allowed to become 'history'" through discovery of the "irreversibility of events"; in those days of innocence its corrosive effects could be periodically reversed and evil expelled through rites of renewal.[51] Postarchaic man has fallen into historical time and hence into the dolorous "terror of history," a place of nightmares and *ignes fatui* in which "Modern man's boasted freedom to make history is illusory for nearly the whole of the human race."[52] But shadowy relics of the old cosmic sacred still abide on the fringes of consciousness, and can be evoked. Why should one call them up? In a word, to be free. In contrast to the false freedom of which moderns boast, which is really slavery to history, and to "leaders" who promise freedom only to take it away,

> the man of the archaic civilizations can be proud of his mode of existence, which allows him to be free and to create. He is free to be no longer what he was, free to annul his own history through periodic abolition of time and collective regeneration.... [T]he archaic and traditional societies granted freedom each year to begin a new, a "pure" existence, with virgin possibilities.[53]

This is an interesting issue in view of Eliade's own political history. Fascism, as its historians have increasingly noted, was a paradoxical mix of tribal, romantic, and historical consciousness; in a word, a mix of cosmos and history. Fascism was not really reactionary; as Stanley G. Payne has pointed out, a large part of Hitler's National Socialism—and, I would add, of fascism generally, even that of the Iron Guard—had roots as much in the Enlightenment, and subsequent popular ideas of the "modern" and the "progressive," as in romantic reactions against the Enlightenment: the revolt against traditional culture in the name of a revolutionary secularism and racial or social "science" (or a revolutionary "Christianity" in the Romanian case), the idea of progress, emphasis on the "people" and the nation, in accordance with the Rousseauian notion of the "general will."[54]

But what is distinctive about fascist history is that it does not want to work through rational democratic "larval" progress, depending on the occasional reform that survives the tedious compromising course of politics as usual, and their incremental human implementation. It demands instead sudden and magical history, charged by the sovereign power of will. This history is more akin to the strange freedom Eliade saw in cosmic man than what the terror of history was likely to bring. It is a recovery of the radical enlightenment dream of a new Eden, which after 1789 not a few thought could be refounded by revolutionary violence. Never mind that the cosmic religion freedom espied by Eliade barely corresponds to the reality of primal societies, which by modern standards are in fact burdened with conformity, repetitions, and exceedingly slow rates of change. The apparent freedom of new beginnings suggested by primal myths of eternal renewal implied to this modern observer magical revolution, the Guardist idea of national resurrection. The point now is, though, that after 1945 Eliade looked at the primal magic all in the mode of the modern scholar/observer, not participant/observer. Whether in repentance or victory, Eliade emerges as a thoroughly modern man, a historian of religion.

And at the same time he was a slave of history, which role he had lived to the full. As all from the World War II generation know, that mighty conflict taught the lesson well. As Stefan, in Eliade's major and in large part autobiographical novel *The Forbidden Forest*, put it:

> Today the master of all of us is the war. . . . It has confiscated the whole of contemporary history, the time in which we are fated to live. All Europe's behaving like a monstrous robot set in motion by the news being released every minute from hundreds of radio stations, from special editions of the newspapers, from conversation among friends. Even when we're alone we think about the war all the time. That is, we're slaves of History.

And he adds, in what undoubtedly are Eliade's own words:

> Against the terror of History there are only two possibilities of defense: action or contemplation.[55]

He had once, diffidently and out of character, tried the former. The postwar years gave opportunity for the latter.

No doubt in later years Eliade felt about his own Romanian past as did primal folk about mythic time. He was drawn back to it, yet he knew he could not live there, and that all was not well with it. Even then, however, there were nostalgias upon richer nostalgias. In the thirties he published *Intoarcerea din Rai* (*Return from Paradise*, 1934), a novel of the "young generation," which dealt with the "loss of the beatitude, illusions, and optimism that had dominated the first twenty years of 'Greater Romania.'" He had, he said, lived his adolescence in an atmosphere of euphoria and faith that already lay behind him and his cohorts. "We had lost it before becoming aware of it. Ours had been, in fact, the first and only generation which could enjoy the 'paradise' established in 1919–1920"—a spiritual and not political paradise, he hastens to add, and one already gone.[56] "I knew that I had lost the paradise I had known in adolescence and early youth: *disponibilité*, the absolute freedom to think and create. That was why I had produced so much, so fast; I knew that the leisure history had allowed us was limited."[57]

Then there is Eliade the Platonist, who knew that on some still deeper level the timeless world and the world running down in time coexist, the days of time being eternity's mirrors. This meant that the sacred, the illud tempus or mythic time at the beginnings, all the initiations of shamans and heroes' quests, all the hierophanies, must be as real now as ever. Insofar as that side of reality is no longer visible in its traditional forms, it must be in deep camouflage. The sacred things are in fact universals, like Jungian archetypes (though Eliade insists, not identical with them), protean and capable of taking many shapes in many cultures.

The "camouflage of the sacred" is a major theme of the reflective side of Eliade's work. Probably the two Eliadean themes that have most influenced the intellectual world outside religious studies are the notion of modern camouflages of the sacred and the interpretation of shamanism in *Shamanism: Archaic Techniques of Ecstasy*,[58] with its vivid portrayals of the shaman's call, "initiatory psychopathology" and marvelous flight. A generation of critics, playwrights, and psychiatrists found in those constructs abundant tools for their craft. At the very end of *The Sacred and the Profane*, Eliade alludes to various "camouflages" of the sacred in the modern: in the veiled mythologies recapitulated by the cinematic "dream factory," in the yearning for the Golden Age in Marxism, in the "nostalgia for Eden" of nudism and yearning for complete sexual freedom.[59]

In *Cosmos and History*, Eliade compares eternal return time, the time of "cosmic religion," with the time of history. The latter term embraces all that is creative and destructive in time as we, beings conditioned by history and historicism, know it: the "terror of history." But historical creativity is actually limited by the paths the past has preset, and so the present is really determinate though it seems free. Primal man, on the other hand, re-created the world each year and so is truly free. Christianity, with its promise of freedom but its rootedness in specific conditioning time and place is the supreme historical religion.

Those implications can be read in a way that harks back to the first significant book about Eliade, Thomas J. J. Altizer's *Mircea Eliade and the Dialectic of the Sacred*.[60] Altizer, famous as one of the "Death of God" theologians of the 1960s, argues that the ultimate fulfillment of

Eliade's vision would be a *coincidentia oppositorum* in which the sacred and the profane become one in a world after the death of the God who is separate from the world and "other." Certainly Eliade seems often on the verge of saying this, as he speaks of even the primal *deus otiosus* as a first Nietzschean death of God, of paradise as being a mere object of nostalgia, and of the increasing camouflage of the sacred in the modern world. But one never finds in Eliade the celebration of the sacred-secular symbiosis extolled by Altizer; rather, there is a sense of wistfulness for lost days when the twain were well defined. In reference to Altizer, whom he knew fairly well in the days of his 1957–1969 journals, Eliade remarked in early 1963: "I am continuing my discussions with Tom Altizer. . . . I reply: All these famous authors that Tom admires so are *Westerners*. . . . My dialogue has other interlocutors than those of Freud or James Joyce: I'm trying to understand a Paleolithic hunter, a yogi or a shaman, a peasant from Indonesia, an African, etc., and to communicate with each one."[61]

Certainly there is an element of nostalgia in Eliade's treatment of cosmic religion times when the sacred was strong and the terror of history had barely raised its head. But such rear-view-mirror sentiments must come up against the phenomenologist and structuralist side of Eliade's work, in which *sehnsucht*-laden feelings are of little account and the observer's cold eye can see the forms, at least, of the sacred in the secular. Even whether or not a thing is called religion does not matter, so long as the structure and the forms that appear image the ancient guises of the sacred. Thus Superman is Indra or Hercules reborn, and Aphrodite enchants again as Marilyn Monroe.

Charming as these comparisons are, though, one may well ask if the hero or the goddess was really functionally the same in the two very different cultures. Where, for the modern deities, are the classic temples, the smoking altars, the paeans by civic leaders in what were community as well as private devotions? Can one find Eliadean sacred space on the silver screen or, more recently, the internet?

These are not frivolous questions; Catholic indulgences have been given via televised masses, and Neopagan rituals have been enacted in cyberspace. We cannot here sort out all the issues; suffice it to note that these developments only confirm the persistence of religion, its ability to take an astounding variety of forms, and to adapt to virtually any new worlds technology and social change may bring. This Eliade would hardly deny, and this openness to the flexibility of the sacred must be taken into account in any comprehensive view of the political implications of Eliade's mythology.

## NONHOMOGENEOUS WORLDS

Indeed, something of the primal vision can be recovered, though perhaps only individually and vicariously, through the history of religions. Eliade was excited about the contemporary cultural importance of his discipline as "a new humanism," ultimately I believe because he saw it as offering the prospect of transcending the tyranny of history. Not only does modern history transcend the past, but the study of the history of religion can lead to self-transcendence. He wrote that "the history of religions is destined to play an important role in contemporary cultural life . . . especially because, by attempting to understand the existential situations expressed by the documents he is studying, the historian of religions will inevitably attain to a deeper knowledge of man . . . [because] by studying the religious expressions of a culture, the scholar approaches it from within."[62]

But let us return to the observation that Eliade began with an ideal type, the concept of homo religiosus. What this ought to mean, of course, is not that all persons, or all conventionally religious persons, always think and act like homo religiosus. But when they are acting religiously they "become" homo religiosus, and the homo religiosus way of viewing and being in the world is what their ritual or other religious behavior says through its own language the world is like, regardless of the extent to which conscious belief is attuned to it. Like Jung speaking of mass man and collective unconsciousness, however, Eliade's phenomenology tends to slide over that last qualification, and to assume that subjectivity follows ritual action.

Being Eliade-trained, I am adamant myself that religion should not be reduced to inward belief—the Protestant temptation—and that it is very important to listen to the languages of the ritual, art, and other nonverbal signs of any religious community. But it is equally important not to presuppose that the subjectivity behind such "gestures" is necessarily holistic and homogeneous throughout the community. To return to the political case and, for examples, to the National Socialist era, in the postwar interview published as *Ordeal by Labyrinth* Eliade responded to a question by the French journalist Claude-Henri Rocquet about religious murder, such as that of the Aztec sacrifices. Rocquet had inquired, "What criterion enables us to decide that the Aztecs lived out a justified illusion whereas the Nazi storm troopers didn't? What is the difference between ordinary murder and sacred murder?"

In reply, Eliade said, "For the SS, the annihilation of millions of people in the concentration camps also had a meaning, and even an eschatological one. They believed that they represented Good versus Evil. . . . We know what Good was for Nazism: fair-haired, Nordic man, what they called the pure Aryan. And the rest were incarnations of Evil, of the devil. It was almost a form of Manicheanism: the struggle of Good against Evil."[63]

The point is not that Eliade was justifying the Nazis. He was not. Later in the same discourse he spoke of them as "those sick men, or zealots, or fanatics—those modern Manicheans" who "saw Evil as being embodied in certain races: the Jews, the Gypsies," and so for them, "sacrificing them by the millions was thus not a crime." It is rather that, first, he never really answered Rocquet's question as to how one can tell the difference between Aztec ritual murder (if one make the questionable assumption that it was a "justified" religious "illusion") and the Nazi crimes; and second that, in a peculiar reflection of the Nazis' own mentality, he saw the Nazis themselves collectively rather than singly, an ideal type like the Aztecs performing roles (or rather one role) in their own myth.

In fact not all storm troopers liquidating their millions saw themselves consistently and homogeneously as acting out a "Manichean" Aryan myth of Good versus Evil. Some were sickened but fearful of resisting orders, some were numbed, some were just ordinary sadists, a few did resist in various covert ways, some probably were True Believers. While Eliade's mythology may help us to understand the message of the grim overall pattern, it is these individual nuances that one misses: for him the individual becomes his/her role in myths and rituals that are essentially social. For Eliade the phenomenologist, unlike Jung the physician, there is not even talk of individuation out of those roles—unless through a still-mythologized transformative process like that of the shaman or the yogi, or unless that is attained in the privileged position of the "new humanist," the modern scholarly observer like Eliade himself!

The historian of religion was well aware of this tendency on the part of Marxists, as he made clear in a journal comment:

I've extracted, somewhat haphazardly, from the vocabulary of Communist trials: Titoist, Trotskyite, assassin, agent of imperialism. These are
categories, characters, archetypes which do not correspond to human,
historical personalities, One has the impression that in Soviet trials it is
not men, not individuals, who appear, but types, archetypes, characters.
Exactly as in the ahistorical horizons of archaic societies. (cf. *The Myth of
the Eternal Return*)

And again:

Marxism doesn't reflect the objective, scientific sprit (not even the
spirit of positivism)—but rather the tension and aggressivity of prophetic
theologies. Marx and the Marxists write just as aggressively and polemi-
cally as the theologians of the Reformation and Counter-Reformation.[64]

Eliade therefore went on to talk to Rocquet similarly of the "myth"
then afflicting his homeland:

Exactly the same can be said about the Gulags and the apocalyptic
eschatology of the great Communist 'liberation': it sees itself as confronted
by enemies that represent Evil, that constitute an obstacle to the triumph
of Good, the triumph of liberty, of man, and so on. All this can be compared with the Aztecs.[65]

Although after 1945 Eliade no longer much committed himself
publicly to any political or other myths, there is a deep-level continuity to his work. He saw the world as the arena of, in his term, the
"dialectic of the sacred," or, to put it another way, as an arena of myth
against myth and ritual against ritual, for in such a world even the
profane is still part of the myth. This is a view that is reactionary, if the
word may now be used in a neutral descriptive sense, because it implies
that the archaic world is needed to interpret the modern. The modern
world really acts out myths as much as ever, including those sodden
with blood sacrifice, but knows not what it does. By returning to the
archaic world, which lived much more consciously by myth and ritual,
we can understand how we too are homo religiosus behind the secular
masks. In doing so we may find the rather rarefied salvation offered
by Eliade's New Humanism, and spice it with the humane excitement
he found in scholarly exploration.

This is not, however, fully to agree with Ivan Strenski's contention
the "the Romanian right, the 'new generation' and Ionescu's irratio-

nalist traditionalism provide the context essential to an 'external' understanding of Eliade's thought in general, and his thought about myth in particular." Strenski holds that Eliade's thinking about myth is a species of right-wing political thinking, "though for some time now it has been given to us in a universalised and at least avowedly apolitical form," but nonetheless offers a rightist sort of "sweeping ontological judgement upon the material, secular, modern world" based on a "volkish" sort of nostalgia for the "archaic, cosmic and telluric."[66] The Romanian right is certainly one context in which Eliade's thought emerged, but Strenski, writing before Mac Rickett's two-volume work on Eliade's Romanian roots or the published journals (apart from *No Souvenirs*) were available, was perhaps not fully able to take into account the diversity of the historian of religion's experiences and attitudes, which apart from one or two years have been more complex than anything that could simply be pigeonholed as "rightist" or "archaic" in either religion or politics. Most significant on the other side of the argument is the way Eliade does not fully embrace archaism or "cosmic religion" as a monolithic value, but portrays significant human life as in continuous dialectic between history, together with modernity, and the "cosmic."

Strenski rightly criticizes Eliade's phenomenology and structuralism for its lack of "falsifiability,"[67] and on the grounds of selective and apparently "essentialist" categories. Like Jung and Campbell, or Sir James Frazer in *The Golden Bough*, Eliade draws an overwhelming wealth of examples from a range of sources and cultural contexts, treating them all uncritically as equal. Obvious selectivity obtains in favor of the point to be made, and perhaps on the grounds of the great scholar's vast but ultimately finite learning. There is, for example, very little if any use in his phenomenological books of Protestant Christianity, of which he seems to have had little comprehension despite his many years on the faculty of a traditionally liberal Protestant divinity school. (Nevertheless, among earlier modern thinkers it is probably the father of liberal Protestantism, the romantic theologian Friedrich Schleiermacher, who most closely resembles Eliade's approach to religion on a deep level. Eliade was indebted to the French school of Emile Durkheim, Roger Caillois, L. Lévi-Bruhl, and their dialectic of the sacred and the profane, but in Scheiermacher and Eliade alike the fundamental means of access to religion is feeling, or homo religiosus' sense of the sacred, and without feeling, both the Romanian and the German concur, religion will never be understood aright.)

Eliade's accumulation of examples without full contextual analysis or admission of falsifiable evidence fails to prove that homo religiosus lurks behind every cult and culture. Yet in the end a valid aperture into the nature of religious experience and religious constructions of reality remains. What it does prove is that homo religiosus has left his mark on countless minds, from those of at least some archaic men and women to those of the travelers and anthropologists who recorded them, to those of the savants in their studies who theorized about them. They may not be everywhere, but the sacred and the profane, and cosmos and history, are out there, as categories of perception, whether one see them reflexively in one's own spiritual life or, as is more likely, impute them to someone else. Recall that, for Eliade too, the real sacred was always somewhere else, in some age already past or some fanciful land over the horizon; our own examples are but types and shadows.

These images, though they may have reality mainly in the mind, attain vividness as they are reinforced over and over. Thus the Indian sovereign attempts to reconstruct in his capital the mythical cities of the Age of Gold; the palace-fortress of Sirigiya in Ceylon, for example, being modeled after the celestial city Alakananda, though that made it "hard of ascent for human beings."[68] Or, in an unforgettable but apparently now discredited story—one of a number of instances in which detailed knowledge reveals weak links in Eliade's superficially imposing marshaling of examples in support of his theories—the sad case of the Australian Achilpa tribe who constantly carried a sacred pole with them which represented the cosmic axis, and who determined the direction they would move by the way the pole bent after they had set it up in the center of their camp. It was a splendid example of the Eliadean Axis Mundi. But on one occasion the pole broke; the devastated people then wandered around aimless until finally they lay down and waited for death to overtake them.[69]

On attaining vividness, the examples then serve as catalysts for further thoughts, insights, into the realm of the sacred; these are more on the level of metaphor, poetic conceit, or philosophical fancy than of "hard" facticity. One might muse that psychoanalysis is the modern shaman's initiation, or that Mount Rushmore is American sacred space. One may see ways in which even the most unprepossessing Protestant churches have their sacred space and time, the open Bible on the altar, the moment of a preacher's call for converts. Eliade would not at all have been displeased by these cultural hermeneutics. He was really far more modern than reactionary and traditional, and he knew it. As a cultural critic, and to be that was his only real reason to be a historian of religion, he was most interested in new vestments for old gods. In "A New Humanism" he states that the history of religion will play an important role in contemporary cultural life, not only because of the cultural dialogue it facilitates, not only because of what it teaches about human nature generally by revealing it in all its varieties and extremes, but even more through the powerful stimulus to new and unexpected cultural creativity that "meeting with the 'others'—with human beings belonging to various types of archaic and exotic societies" inevitably brings.[70]

To say Eliade was an "essentialist," who believed that the sacred has a special objective ontological status or even special status as a heuristic or empirical category, is a misunderstanding. He knew well enough that the sacred was in the eye of the beholder: "an element in the structure of consciousness."[71] Why otherwise pile up so many examples of its thousand different forms? He did believe that the sacred was a category of perception common to the minds of many, "indissolubly linked to the effort made by man to construct a meaningful world,"[72] and this was worth noting. But to him the sacred was really a phenomenological entity; calling something like the Achilpa's pole sacred was shorthand for saying they regarded it as sacred, in broadly the same way other poles, in other times and places, have been regarded as sacred elsewhere. That presupposes, of course, that the similarities of such objects, times, and places across time and space exceeds their specific differences. That is probably an intuitive matter, and can be debated endlessly. I can only say that I find it more useful than not, with certain cautions suggested by, among other things, a religion like Protestantism, but this matter is not really germane to the present argument.

In the same way, to draw the conclusion from Eliade's repeated contention that religion is sui generis, of its own type of being and irreducible to anything else, that this aspect of human life has, in his eyes, special ontological status would be unwarranted. He may have thought so; but sui generis of itself need only mean that religion as some point needs to be interpreted out of its own categories, which

Eliade believed he had isolated in such referents as sacred space and sacred time. Religion requires self-interpretation no more or less than, say, political science, economics, sociology, or psychology. Only a crude ideologue would say there is nothing at all in the political world that cannot be explained solely in terms of money, or on the other side that the vagaries of finance are subject only to political or spiritual considerations. Eliade was concerned that the study of religion likewise not be merely subordinated to politics, economics, sociology, or psychology. But religion is no more sui generis that politics, economics, sociology, or psychology—each major sphere of human life has its own irreducible core of necessary interpretive categories and "laws," as well as vast areas that are best understood in dialogue with the other human disciplines. The same is true of art, and he was ever more of an artist, or at least an aesthetician of religion, than a scholar. Eliade wrote:

> Works of art, like "religious data," have a mode of being that is peculiar to themselves; *they exist on their own plane of reference*, in their particular universe. . . . A work of art reveals its meaning only insofar as it is regarded as an autonomous creation; that is, insofar as we accept its mode of being—*that of an artistic creation*—and do not reduce it to one of its constituent elements (in the case of a poem, sound, vocabulary, linguistic structure, etc.) or to one of its subsequent uses (a poem which carries a political message or which can serve as a document for sociology, ethnography, etc.)[73]

Note that Eliade's idea of religion as sui generis, irreducible to any other interpretation, could as well be applied to nationalism and political commitment generally. If strong feeling associated with and focused on a particular clear and distinct symbol or idea is sufficiently intense, the sui generis argument seems to be saying, then that symbol and its associated circles of feelings and believers is a unique, self-validating entity, not to be explained in terms of academic categories that are less intense, more generic and abstract. An example can, to be sure, be judged a good or bad case of nationalism on moral grounds; after 1945 Eliade was apparently prepared to make a moral judgment about the quasi-religious nationalism of the storm troopers. Perhaps if pressed he would make similar judgments about religions as good or bad, though he was usually unwilling to do so.

However, this is not the last word on Eliade. There is also the way in which his recognition of the intrinsic, sui generis similarity of commitment and experience in the many mansions of religion, and perhaps of quasi-religious movements as well, opens up a world of benign pluralism. This is itself a good, for the comparative method enables one to experience vicariously the passions of other faiths as well as one's own, so leading to that enrichment of total human experience that is the fertile ground of the new humanism.

As we have already noted, critics of Eliade raise charges of "essentialism"—currently a very bad word in some academic circles, as is its opposite, "reductionism," in the Eliadean camp—based on a particular reading of Eliade's concept of religion as sui generis. They also point to the Romanian's political past and its supposed connection with his history of religion project, implying that the fascist essentialism of race or nation is of a piece with Eliade's universal essence of religion. Needless to say, those for whom religion is a priori understood to be a quest for an ahistorical essence (of humanity? of the universe?), which will never be found because it is not there, will probably never be pleased with Eliade. The temptation to throw in Eliade's political past as an additional proof is then hard to resist, though to me the connection seems rather tortured, in the end amounting to little more than an ad hominem argument which attempts to tar Eliade's entire work with the ill-repute all decent people feel for storm troopers and the Iron Guard. In fact, it would seem that Eliade's religious universalism, right or wrong, "essentialist" or not, is ontologically and morally very different indeed from the racism or nationalism in which the fascist found his essences. It may be added that some of these same scholars who criticize Eliade on political grounds cite marxist and marxist-tinged sources without imputing to them all the sins of Stalinism and the gulags.

For persons like myself, instinctively religious but caught up in modernity's pluralism of space and time, Eliade's work performed an interesting function. It enabled one to use the sense of reality felt in one religious context to intuit the same in another, while undercutting clashes of theology through paying attention instead to the props by which religion forms its various realities, making them nonhomogeneous with the stream of profane life. For me, if not for everyone, Eliade's talk of "the sacred" in various times and places, even sometimes under deep camouflage, was neither mere reification of abstract categories nor covert theology. Perhaps it was a combination of Schleiermacher's religion as feeling with the social constructs of Durkheim's social

effervescence. It was quieter and subtler than Otto's *Das Heilege*, yet
more objective than Jung's archetypes. Words about it were a kind of
language a little different from anything philosophy or theology could
speak of coherently. Those who could not get it might be, as Max
Weber said of himself, "religiously unmusical."

The appeal as well as the weakness of Eliadeanism lay in such a
combination of vagueness and an evocative romantic style. The style
depended on calling forth a mighty army of images from the distant
and the past, freighted with the frisson of significance those "musical"
to this approach are likely to give that which comes across great gulfs
of space and time. The romantic ear considers such feelings cognitive
and exemplary.

Thus the importance one felt in Eliade's books depended more
than anything else on the stylistic and imagistic calling forth of a
romantic sense of wonder associated with archaic religion. Yet it may
well be that only with the aid of that sense could moderns intuit at all
the subjective meaning of religions past, or compare them meaning-
fully with religion or quasi religion present. For while the romantic
feeling may not be exactly the same as the archaic religious feeling, it
is at least a feeling about transcendent realities, and perhaps as close
as most of us will get to the subjective experience of religions of other
times and places. It can evoke, as Eliade once remarked, "the Platonic
structure of Australian spirituality," in which, as for the Greek, "to
know means to remember."[74] Those to whom such feelings are inaccessible, or unimportant, can only be regarded as "unmusical" in this
particular respect, perhaps the better to analyze the mathematics of
the notes.

Equally important is the issue of universalism versus the particular. In the late twentieth century the sort of discovery of universal
themes so characteristic of Jung, Eliade, and Campbell, as of Frazer
earlier, has been much denigrated. In the wake of "postcolonial" back-
lash against the intellectual "imperialism" and "Orientalism" of practitioners of the universalist art, any idea that the mythic themes of a
given cultural context could be taken out of that setting to display
universal, archetypal meanings was considered not only inevitably to
distort the myth, but to be demeaning of the particular culture. It
implied that the known meaning of the myth in the culture had to be
subordinated to a more universal "real" meaning assigned by an outsider. Yet, as Wendy Doniger, Mircea Eliade Distinguished Service

Professor of the History of Religions at the University of Chicago, has pointed out, extreme particularism ends up with absurdities every bit as awkward as those of the universalist extreme.

Taken to its own ultimate absurdity, the sensible observation that myths have a culture-specific message that cannot be detached from that setting would imply that myths can have no meaning except for the individual who creates or tells them. "For where extreme universalism means that the other is exactly like you, extreme nominalism [particularism] means the other may not be human at all." Moreover, we may find that members of the "context" group may themselves approach the story differently. Achilpas and Algonquins are not entirely alike, but neither is any one Alchipa or Algonquin exactly like everyone else of the same tribe. One might indeed be more similar to a person of another culture than not, and just as some non-English understand Shakespeare better than do not a few Englishmen, so some Alchipa or Algonquin myths may be as well or better understood and appreciated by twentieth-century persons of European decent as by some of their own tribe; to deny this possibility would also be to demean the humanity of their creators.

> Rather, every telling is different, and a telling from one country is as likely to share something with a telling from another as with a telling from elsewhere in the same country. The focus upon individual insight leads us to a kind of second naivete: it leads us to posit a "sameness" based not on any quasi-Jungian universalism but on a kind of pointillism, formed from the individual points of individual authors whose insights transcend their particular moment and speak to us across time and space. . . . By searching for our individual artists not merely in the bastions of the western canon but in the neglected byways of oral traditions and rejected heresies . . . one is arguing not for a narrow range of cultural excellence but, on the contrary, for a wider construction of cross-cultural inspiration.[75]

Eliade had in fact said the same thing earlier:

> The principal objection made against me: I "idealize" the primitives, I exaggerate the importance of their myths, instead of "demystifying" them and emphasizing their dependence on historical events (colonialism, acculturation, pagan-Christian syncretism, etc.) But . . . it is precisely because it has been emphasized too much and because what seems to me essential is thus neglected: the hermeneutic of religious creations. . . . A

Bantu or Indonesian critic will only be able to wonder: How were the
Westerners able to write thousands of volumes on the "beauty" and the
"eternal values" of *The Divine Comedy*, the work of a political exile, and
see in our mythologies and our messianic symbols only a protest of oppressed peoples? Indeed, why am I suspected of "idealism" each time I
try to analyze these primitive and archaic creations with the same care
and the same sympathy that we bring to commenting on Dante or Meister
Eckhart?[76]

## THE POLITICS OF PARADISE

The political philosophy of Eliade's mature—post-1945—work is
only implicit. That in itself is significant, for it tells us there is a clear
break from the mercurial young man with opinions on everything,
including rulers at home and abroad, from India to Italy. The silence
says as loudly as could any words that not only does he himself no
longer have interest in the political world, but he also rejects commitment to particular political causes and ideologies as the way to construct the new humanism.

That is evident, first in the explicit deconstruction of political
mythologies such as those of Marxism and Nazism we have examined. Those postwar Eliadean reductions of once-potent ideologies to
age-old but never realized eschatological motifs would clearly reveal
their futility to all but hopeless true believers. Those passages put
Eliade back to where he was before 1936, before the Codreanu or
Salazar years, when he denounced the barbarians of Berlin and Moscow more or less evenhandedly.

There is this difference, though: now nothing appears about contemporary political parties or movements, unless it be by implication
the present rulers of Romania; there is only harking back to the passions of the thirties. If those fascist-era ideologies are mentioned, it is
to place them, as he does the Marxism then gripping his homeland, in
the timeless mythological matrix to which he clearly thinks all such
schemes belong, and from which they should never have escaped. In
this respect they are all of the nature of *illud tempus*, bespeaking though
with forked tongue the paradise for which we humans are all nostalgic. But even primal peoples are estranged from paradise; it can never
be more than a dream and a set of symbols here in profane time. As
the gnostics well knew, creation and the fall are one. Totalistic ideologies are politics of nostalgia for paradise, and therein lies their appeal

and their deceptiveness. But how much else in this post-Eden world is nostalgia for paradise as well!

Therefore even totalistic ideologies also are parts of the radical pluralism of the world as it is today. Radical pluralism militates against absolutizing any one myth. The danger of absolutizing Eliade had no doubt learned from his thirties and forties experience, though again he chose to say so only indirectly. Yet any multiplicity of myths and venues of the sacred clearly must hold, for one who is aware of it, the political consequence of mandating either freedom of choice or arbitrary totalitarian imposition of a single ideological myth. Since 1945, Eliade certainly never proposed the latter, and lived and talked in a way wholly consistent with abiding in a world of mythological freedom. That would be a world in which the sacred is real but under all sorts of camouflages; the state presumably ought to let a great array of them flourish, so that they may be freely and individually discerned by those able to see their hierophanies. As an exile, Eliade knew the soul-saving value of choiceless seeing, observing, and understanding in a world of which one was not, and could never be, completely a part.

In *Ordeal by Labyrinth* Eliade emphasized that, although he was deeply concerned about the tragic state of Romania in 1945 and after, he did not believe that overt political activity was what was of most importance. "Of course, one can always sign a manifesto, protest in the press. That is rarely what is really needed." Instead, he and a circle of Romanian intellectual exiles formed a circle to "maintain the culture of a free Romania and, above all, to publish texts that had become unpublishable in Romania itself." The essential liberating work, in other words, was not political but intellectual and cultural. It is the intellectual, we are told, who is regarded as "enemy number one" by tyrants, and "making culture" is the "only efficacious form of politics open to exiles." There is nothing is this dialogue about Eliade's prewar life; whether the premise about culture over politics is universally true or not, the discussion gives a significant clue to the postwar identity he assigned himself.[77]

There is something more here than the Burkean affirmation of existing tradition as necessary and good for the well-being of society that we marked in discussing Jung. Here is a more radical thrust. Despite Altizer's claim that the historian of religion was too backward-looking, in reading Eliade we sense that new tradition can always be revealed by new hierophanies, that the sacred can be found at any time in radical new forms and in some way the primordial chaos of creation creatively revisited. In *Ordeal by Labyrinth* we read:

> What I am sure of is that any future forms of religious experience will be quite different from those we are familiar with in Christianity, Judaism, or Islam, all of which are fossilized, outmoded, drained of meaning. I am sure that new forms, new expressions, will come. What will they be? I cannot say. The great surprise is always the freedom of the human spirit, its creativity.[78]

Eliade had no interest himself in making or even selecting myths for contemporary purposes; he was content to let myths fend for themselves in a free marketplace of ideas. He had no desire for the role of the mythmaker or propagandist, much less to be the founder of a new religion. Indeed, the post-1945 Eliade insisted that the sacred *cannot* be made intentionally, by an act of the will; it can only be *discovered*, albeit perhaps in new venues.

This is a very important point. It gives the lie to those fascist and other pseudo religions that presume to manufacture their own sacralities, while it permits the sacred to be *found* in any number of unlikely and unexpected corners of the modern world. The possibility of new discoveries of the sacred meant that one always had the freedom to make new beginnings, it may be alone. This was a freedom very important to an exile whose life and world had been sorely ruptured.

The freedom to make new beginnings: this is the real sense of being free from the terror of history. Here Eliade appears to move into the postmodernism of liberation from the "metanarratives" of progress and universal knowledge, which also meant bondage to the terror of history. For, to the modernist, history with all its terrors was the necessary vehicle of anything modernism could understand as progress or the increase of knowledge. Now, back before history, Eliade has discovered another possibility: the return to the near memory, at least, of illud tempus, and the nonreactionary re-creation of the world.

But the abolition of historical time stands in equal relation, in principle, to all points in time. It therefore comes at the end of history—the eschaton—as well as at the beginning. Moreover, it can be enacted, at least symbolically, at any point in time; we can become primal man, not by regress but by egress, moving out of history to gain, as far as possible, the vantage of one who is unconditioned, merely human before the universe. Eliade perceptively saw that the modern quest for the "origin" of religion, so earnestly engaged in by an earlier generation of anthropologists and historians, was in fact futile since an absolute and singular beginning could never be reached. The search was really little more than a scholarly version of the mythical quest for origins.[79] One can only try: Eliade once said, "My essential preoccupation is precisely the means of escaping History, of saving myself through symbol, myth, rite, archetypes."[80]

How is egress to be done? It can only be approximated, of course. Primal man can only hear of illud tempus and yearn for it, or recover it symbolically at the turn of the year, never actually. So one leaves history only, so to speak, in one's spiritual body. One way—the modern way—is through attaining a level of scholarship so sublime that one is able to gaze panoramically over the world with serene and untouchable understanding, the modern "privileged position." This was a way which Eliade himself strove as arduously, and as successfully, to master as anyone in the twentieth century. It represents, in fact, his contribution to culture-creation as the sublimest of politics.

In the end he felt he could only chronicle the escape from history of others. Eliade once said in my hearing that the highest human being was the mystic, since he could actually perceive and experience ultimate timeless reality; the second highest was the poet, who could at least express what the mystic saw in adequate language; the third was the historian of religion like himself, who could only record the seeings and the words of the mystic and his poet. But as their scholarly chronicler, one could perhaps make the best political contribution, for the mystic and the poet with their words that draw lightning are dangerous mediators in that realm, as he doubtless well knew though did not say. For by such a mystic out of time Eliade did not necessarily mean only a cloistered monk or a yogi in a cave. Judging from his novels, especially *The Forbidden Forest*, the idea was important to him that in the midst of active life, even of wartime flight across Europe, one could know moments when time stopped and began anew. Perhaps while becoming a full-time historian in 1945, Eliade attained an Altizerian radical *coincidentia oppositorum* of the sacred and the profane, and of time and timelessness.

If he did not, it was because he tended spiritually to privilege archaism over the contemporary world, and to hold that we can no longer quite experience reality as fully as our ancestors. It was only in the archaic world, before history, that one could fully face reality unmediated and without terror. To Eliade, the primitive was not unconscious and "buried in nature," as Hegel claimed. Rather, it is important to realize that the primal cosmos is "open," a realm where transformation is possible, so the sacred is not automatic in the real world, but is an existentialist possibility.[81] Thus, we are told in *Patterns in Comparative Religion*, the inauguration of a new king or chief is like a new creation of the world.[82] This merely symbolizes the perennial yearning for primordial return, which is not a return to the "primitive," but to the chaos of completeness, when male and female are equal, and all are embraced within the divinity.[83] History is a fall, a rupture, from that primordial unity.

The loss of this state goes back to the beginning, to cosmic religion, as does its memory. The *deus otiosus* could be called "the first example of the 'death of God'" of Nietzsche,[84] but gods do not so much die as change, taking camouflaged forms in a diversity of myths. Perhaps more could be said than Eliade did about the living sacred in contemporary religion. For whatever the case with God, religion certainly lives and is vibrantly experienced, no doubt as much now as ever.

But Eliade, afflicted by the secularization myth like most intellectuals of his time, and also by his own nostalgic temperament, often affected a yearning attitude toward the sacred past while acknowledging its metamorphosed forms in the present. In so doing he did no more than distill the attitude of most modern people, who generally assume religion past to have been stronger than religion present. No myth of religion is more powerful, even among scholars of religion, not to mention among the pious, than the myth of the pious past. Like all myths of loss, it is laden with guilt.

The crime is there: the death or murder of God cannot be forgotten; that would be the supreme sacrilege. So we have a modern world in which the memory of God remains, but the divine is camouflaged and hidden in an infinite variety of disguises. Eliade said that the sacred is camouflaged in the profane in a reverse of the way Freud and Marx had claimed the profane is hidden in the supposedly sacred! To find it in such places as modern works of literature one needs a sort of "demystification in reverse."[85]

What can be done? Origins and eschaton tell us there is hope available, that we do not need to be tied to a guilty past or historical terror. Eschatology, the new beginning, is in the future but starts now. In *Cosmos and History* Eliade often referred to the futurology of Joachim of Flora, whom he like Campbell and Voegelin saw as a paradigmatic visionary of modernism and beyond. Hope requires a founding myth. Once it was Codreanu's idea of national resurrection and a "new man." Eliade never apologized for this faith or wished to proclaim it again. But what if the new world could come about in an entirely novel and surprising way, nonrevolutionary and only marginally political?

Eliade was clearly not interested in writing a postwar political philosophy, and it would be presumptuous to read too much into mere asides or discussions whose main focus was elsewhere. He wanted, if his remarks in *Labyrinth* are to be taken seriously, to affect politics, above all the liberation of Romania, through his work as a culture-creating scholar—a typical Eliadean "camouflage." But what kind of politics does his scholarship teach? It is clear he was not, at heart, a traditionalist either in politics or religion. He was interested in tradition, to be sure, *but* as "other" to the modern world to which he was always aware he belonged. He was, indeed, virtually an archetype of the modern scholar, much derided by postmodernists, secure in his privileged position at the highest pinnacle of human progress, from there able to survey the earth and the ages, bringing them all to terms with his universal categories.

Moreover, he was a radical modernist: "I feel myself wholly contemporary with all the great political and social reforms or revolutions."[86] Those who see Eliade's fascination with the primordial as merely reactionary in the ordinary political or religious sense of the word do not understand the mature Eliade in a sufficiently radical way. He knew very well the uses of tradition, of course; as propaganda and, better, as affording vicarious experiences that complete the humanity of moderns by giving them entry into all that is and has been human. But tradition was not for him exactly Burkean "prescription" or sacred trust to be kept alive generation after generation, for Eliade was fully aware that tradition, like men and nations, lives only by changing and even occultation. The tack is not to try fruitlessly to keep it unchanging, but to discover where it is hiding. The past can help by offering paradigms, but it cannot fully make the present. It is appropriate to feel nostalgia for particular powerful or beautiful examples of the housings of the sacred locked into the centuries, but it must be understood that Eliade did not mean to suggest by such nostalgia that they should be appropriated wholesale into the modern world. He was in fact perhaps unnecessarily harsh in his scorn of attempts to do so by what he called the "little religions . . . the pseudo-occult, neospiritualistic, or so-called hermetic churches that almost always present the aberrant aspect of pseudomorphs."[87]

Nor did he, in his own life, live as a traditionalist Eastern Orthodox Christian or anything else. His own sacred was much more personal than traditional, comprised of images of wonder from his travel and inward explorations, and increasingly he knew it had to be that way for moderns. The corporate sacred of the Legion, for instance, was worse than futile. He may have come to sense that its excessive and morbid fascination with martyrdom and death indicated some deep subconscious realization that, for all its faith and passion, Legionism could never really long prevail in a modern world that had left its kind behind. It was as though only in death, not in long life, could such an ideal as the resurrection of a nation and creation of a new man be achieved in the twentieth century.

What was consistent for Eliade was both exile and eschatology, walking through the world seeing the sacred on every hand but unattached to any single form of it, nostalgic for the beginning but also hopeful for a better end when the scholar and the believer would no longer be at odds. The past was not the sole creator of the sacred because the sacred could morph into new forms continuously, some seemingly secular, and it can be fueled by revolution—though Eliade was torn between the idea of the "new man" of enlightenment gnosticism and awareness of human finitude. In the end the revolution became intellectual—the "new man" became the "new humanism"—rather than political. It was interiorized, and if it was to have political form it would have to be in the passive role of merely allowing the new man to emerge, a minimal rather than a maximalist state.

## ELIADE AS AMERICAN

This is implicit in Eliade's appropriation of the principal land of his exile—a nation with a political heritage quite different from his homeland's—the United States of America. In response to the concerns of his American students, whom he perceived as being surprisingly concerned with "methodology," he made a remarkably sweeping statement about his adopted land of exile:

Often a student would ask me, solemnly and yet with strong feeling: "What's the best method of study to understand the history of religions?" It seemed to me I recognized the descendants of the first waves of pioneers, embarked on the conquest and cultivation of the enormous space that lay beyond the frontier. It was the same fundamental conviction: if we have the best tools possible, we can make a paradise of this land; if we have the best method available, we will understand the history of religions in all its complexity, and we will be in a position to make discoveries unsuspected by anyone before.[88]

He was no less impressed by the pluralism of the University of Chicago Divinity School faculty, with its Protestant, Roman Catholic, Jewish, Buddhist, and agnostic members, "hard to imagine in a European faculty of theology."[89] All this suggested that the United States was a quite different model for the organization of ideology, academic life, and society as a whole than what he had known in the old Romania, or even Salazar's Portugal.

The one article Eliade wrote that focuses largely on America is "Paradise and Utopia: Mythical Geography and Eschatology,"[90] a study of the considerable volume of literature, from the age of exploration almost down to the present, that made the new world of America an existing paradise, or at least a place where humankind, leaving behind the burdens of the past, could make an entirely new beginning. While largely a celebration of America's isolation and intentional innocence, Eliade recognizes that the legacy of the "city on a hill" has affected U.S. foreign policy and made for an eagerness to spread its "way of life" around the world. In his journals for 1961, Eliade noted that "One can understand nothing of American life, culture, and politics if one doesn't realize that the United States has its roots in theology." The nation's strengths and weaknesses alike stem from its religious origins; it is a democracy but not yet a secularized one.[91] Yet the ambiance of "Paradise and Utopia" indicate how ambiguous that religious democracy can be. First published in 1966, that paper is contemporaneous with a similar neoeschatological interest in America by the "death of God" theologians, Thomas Altizer and his colleague William Hamilton. Altizer was drawn to William Blake's mystical vision of America as the place where the apocalyptic freedom of the Christian would finally be experienced, and Hamilton, in "Thursday's Child," spoke of America as "the place that has traveled farthest along the road from the cloister. . . . We are the most profane, the most banal, the most utterly worldly of place"—and therefore the place where the radically profane yet sacred future will be realized.[92]

Only eschatology perhaps can handle such paradoxes, and Eliade notes also that in America there has also been a tradition of affirming that here is a unique chance to begin history again, to do right this time what was done wrong before, and in this connection he quotes a series of writers of the stamp of Jefferson, Hawthorne, Thoreau, and Whitman, suggested by his reading of R. W. B. Lewis's *The American Adam*, on America's rejection of the past and belief in America's unique opportunity to *begin history over*—an idea that had always fascinated Eliade. Undoubtedly it had overtones of his own almost unique opportunity to begin over again in 1945. He naturally saw in this notion the revival of the age-old hope for periodical regeneration of cosmos and society. Indeed, he associated this idea with the primordial "archaic" eternal return mentality that stood before the dismal discovery of the terror of history.[93] Was the archaic ahistorical paradise really coming back in American guise? Eliade does not say that he necessarily accepts this notion, or endorses any political commitment it might entail. Eliade also noted, in connection with a supposed American enthusiasm for the historical thought of Jacob Burkhardt, that a minority of Americans prefer that writer's pessimistic European view of history.[94]

The Americanism of Eliade's last years, unlike the earlier Romanianism, was not chauvinist and presumably included room for all the country's many minorities, including exiles like himself. On the other hand, he called for no national resurrection or creation of a "new man"; it is as though this was somehow already accomplished or unnecessary, as though paradise was already in place and eschatology realized as much as it could be in the grimy world of current American democracy. He was disappointingly indifferent to the civil rights movement in full spate during his first American decade.

His journals reveal that while he was intrigued by the "hippies" and the sixties counterculture with its frenetic rediscoveries of the sacred past and present, he was less favorably impressed by the "new left" of the same decade, though he was still willing to experiment mentally with even the most extreme political openness. In his journal entry for December 3, 1968, he muses on the way one window of the university bookstore was filled with books against the war in Vietnam and American crimes there, while another window boasts the translated works of Mao Tse-tung. Earlier in his journals he had set down accounts, brought to him by escapees from the homeland he clearly believed reliable, of unspeakable tortures to which priests and others had been subjected in Romania by its current Marxist regime; in the absence of any corresponding university bookstore exhibit on those horrors he undoubtedly considered the young American aficionados of Mao and the Vietcong hopelessly naive and biased. He commented: "Naturally, all this seems difficult to believe in Europe. But I wonder what sign is to be seen in this excess of tolerance: strength, self-confidence, and confidence in American destiny, or indifference, fatigue, the first symptoms of decadence? To what limits can tolerance be stretched, politically speaking?"[95]

He looked at the campus upheavals of the late sixties, such as those at Chicago and Columbia in 1968, with European eyes, as the work of well-trained agitators and propagandists like the fascists of thirty years before. All that lay between the two: "several million dead."[96] More important than such "ravaging in the name of democracy" was the existing democratic space for pluralism and, if one wish, for a nonpolitical life, or rather one in which the political goal of tolerant pluralism can be advanced by the camouflaged means of scholarship.

One cannot make a strong case for it, because he did not, but I would suggest that while he may not have known much about Thomas Jefferson beyond what he read in Lewis's *American Adam*, perhaps in the end Eliade would have enjoyed a conversation on political matters (as well as the many other matters on which both polymaths were eminently well informed) with the sage of Monticello as much as with anyone else who comes to mind. Both did not hide their disdain for manipulative and dim-witted kings under whose rule they suffered, both had deeply conservative instincts on such things as affection for traditional rural life and its virtues, both loved a world where travel and intellectual discovery were possible. At the same time, both believed religious and political institutions could and should be renewed, that it was possible to return, in some essential way, to the point of creation and start a *novus ordo seclorum*. Like Eliade, Jefferson was fascinated by the ideal of a pristine paradise, when humans lived together in simplicity and harmony before the coming of feudal oppression, which could be the model of a new age. Both were intrigued with the idea, at least, of total liberation from history and the past, and an entirely new human beginning. The new beginning required, above all, careful attention to methodology, and at the same time a paradisal vision of the future as well as of the past.

In passing, the thought occurs to one that Eliade and Jefferson had more than a little in common in character and destiny as well. Both have known periods of adulation in popular and scholarly esteem; both have come down a bit as both have been accused of more show than depth in their encyclopedic learning, of less than originality in their core ideas, and of serious inconsistency in their social and political attitudes. But there is more: both were also incredibly complex and elusive personalities who, whenever it seems one has pinned them down, display another side that undercuts a premature assumption. Jefferson had a remarkable ability to avoid seeing unpleasant realities, as for example his artful disguising the nature of his slave quarters, manifesting what Joseph Ellis has called "the deep deviousness only possible in the dedicated idealist"[97]—a characterization that could well cover significant aspects of Eliade's life, particularly the relationship with the Legion of the Archangel. Yet in the case of both men it would be quite unfair to let a life of rich, varied, and shifting interests and experiences be swallowed up by any one of them, including the political.

Eliade was not at heart a scholar, much less a politician or social scientist, but a litterateur, a writer and literary critic—though it may be a critic of myths rather than current bestsellers. His *oeuvre* must finally be received and assessed in that light. So he was at the beginning, and so at the end. If he was not always accurate or consistent in terms of social scientific canons, neither are not a few other writers of works nonetheless admired for elegant style and evocative quality. He claims that Freud once "had the courage to admit: 'I am not really a man of science. . . . I am by temperament nothing but a conquistador . . . with the curiosity, the boldness, and the tenacity that belong to that type of person.' "[98] Mircea Eliade likewise could not be contained in a single discipline, but used lamps stored in one corner of the academy to cast light around several rooms and out into the street. The scholar endeavors to distance himself and his passions from the material; Eliade, the man of letters, was concerned like any literary writer to invoke moods and feelings by transmitting his own experience and that of his generation through his shamans and cosmogonic myths. More than anything else he yearned to create mirrors of words that would reflect back and forth between the aeons, and give humanity an accurate portrait of itself comprised of them all. He would really rather have been known as a great novelist than historian of religion.

Finally, returning to politics, let us make Eliade a little more radical, as would Altizer. What kind of politics would come out of the radical conflation of sacred and profane? And is this what Eliade really wanted, or did he allow a role for tension between the two in safeguarding freedom on all inner and outer levels? One senses a move toward the Jeffersonian values of his adoptive society, the United States, as he saw around him a land thankfully pluralistic and pragmatic, though one which also had a disconcerting way of identifying itself with the primal or the eschatological paradise, and thus outside the terrors of history. The latter was a view which, though innocent by European standards of identifying the homeland with paradise, nonetheless could have policy and cultural significance. The American way of combining the illusion and reality of innocence in the midst of a sinful world was described in a forceful and disturbing book by Eliade's contemporary Reinhold Niebuhr, *The Irony of American History* (1952). However, Eliade himself was careful not to identify America with paradise, though he appreciated the value of the vision of a new Eden if it was properly optional.

At least the Romanian was not so incautious in America as to call for uniting sacred and profane there in an immediate eschatology that would legitimate demands for a national resurrection and new man here and now. Altizer, in criticizing Eliade's backward-looking reverse eschatology, seems not to appreciate how much eschatology realized is not only revolutionary but also totalitarian. Eliade knew well enough that the appeal of eternity actually depends on the experience of history, that, of itself, eternity would be so absolute as to be oppressive. In *The Forbidden Forest*, in the midst of the wartime terror of history, Anisie argues eloquently and at length that all we can hope for is "the annihilation of our civilization" and the closing of the present cycle, which will allow "the other type of humanity to reappear, a humanity that does not live as we do in historic time but dwells only in the moment—that is, in eternity."

But Stefan, who more than anyone speaks for the author himself, answers: "I too dream of escaping from time, from history, someday. . . . But not at the price of the catastrophe you forecast. Human existence would seem vain to me if it were reduced solely to mythical categories. Even that ahistoric paradise of which you speak would be hard for me to endure if it didn't have the hell of history accompanying it. I believe—I even hope—that an exit from time is possible even in our historic world. Eternity is always accessible to us."[99] But clearly what makes real human life worth living is the dialectic between the two.

If Eliade ends up with any political philosophy, it is in offering the ideal of a way to do this, by means of a politics of radical sacred-in-the-secular pluralism, where nothing is touched that would disturb the sacred's fragile and fascinating diversity, since it is only from a hierophany here, and a lost parable there, that real humanism is learned. Here is where the radical polarity of Eliadean religious universalism from fascist totalitarianism becomes clear. The capacity for the sacred to take new shapes needs to be preserved. But it can only exhibit its wonderful diversity and take new shapes in the matrix of a world which contains at least the *apparent* nonsacred, even the terror of history, against which the sacred stands in bold relief and above which it shines like the heavens.

Any apocalypse that would melt it all down to a single glory must be indefinitely postponed. No doubt in practice this would mean voting for moderate candidates who support higher education and are willing to live and let live so far as religion and "values" are concerned. To be otherwise nonpolitical and do one's work well is the best way for an exiled intellectual, artist, poet, or scholar to effect real change.

# 4

# JOSEPH CAMPBELL AND THE NEW QUEST FOR THE HOLY GRAIL

## "THE SAVANT AS REACTIONARY"

Joseph Campbell (1904–1987) was probably the best known of all interpreters of myth to late twentieth-century Americans, thanks to a series of learned but highly readable books, assiduous lecture-hall performances, and above all his posthumous PBS appearances with Bill Moyers. The response to that series of six interviews was remarkable. As Mary R. Lefkowitz put it: "On television Joseph Campbell was the embodiment of the ideal academic: gentle, fatherly, informative, reassuring, unworldly, spiritual, and articulate without being incomprehensible. He was knowledgeable about what we didn't have time (or inclination) to discover for ourselves, pleasantly remote, and (unlike most of nontelevision professors) entertaining. Campbell could tell a good story."[1]

But perhaps Campbell's greatest triumph of all, though an indirect one, was in the overwhelmingly successful series of *Star Wars* movies, commenced in 1977 and directed by George Lucas. Together with that other science-fiction classic the *Star Trek* series, these films have created out of science fiction what seems to be the dominant living imaginative mythology of our time, comparable to the role of Arthurian fantasy in Victorian England or Wagner's heroes in Wilhelmine Germany. The sacred atmosphere of the Wagnerian Bayreuth festival in its golden age was reproduced on the opening nights of the Star Wars "Phantom Menace" in 1999, when crowds across the country cheered deafeningly, then settled into reverential stillness save for appropriate hisses and acclamations as the epic ground forward. While of course Campbell cannot be given full credit for this modern myth cycle, George Lucas freely acknowledges the influence of reading that savant's *The Hero with a Thousand Faces* and *The Masks of God*. Later, beginning in 1983, the relationship developed into a personal friendship over the last three years of Campbell's life.[2]

In the older *Star Trek,* cooperation among a diverse crew was the key to success in saving the galaxy. But in *Star Wars* the emphasis was more on individual heroism, a theme dear to Joseph Campbell's heart. Those films wonderfully combine ultra "high tech" computers and spaceships with gunfights and combat in one-man fighters reminiscent of a generation of matinee westerns or of World War II dogfights. Then, on a still deeper level of meaning, there came the swordplay of Jedi knights and the solitary quests of dedicated heroes like Luke Skywalker. The fundamental cultural message was that a great society is founded upon great individuals. One should be oneself, fighting for oneself and one's friends and comrades alone, except when freely joining a band of like-minded heroes to lose, or rather transcend, individual separateness in the mystique of a noble cause—which will be the cause of individualism against tyranny. Moreover, many subordinate themes of traditional mythology and folklore, often also themes made famous by Joseph Campbell, appear in the *Star Wars* cycle : the hero who is of noble blood but doesn't know it (Luke Skywalker), the intelligent robots in the role of the companion animal or faithful "sidekick" like Don Quixote's Sancho Panza.

Furthermore, an almost indefinable quality in *Star Wars* from the experience of the title frame on makes it like walking into a dream, above all if the film is experienced in the cavernous womb of a great theater with a wide screen. The unforgettable images of huge ships, archetypal monsters and heroes, and otherworldly planets loom into consciousness like denizens of the night. It is as though, along with wanting to make the world safe for individuals, Campbell/Lucas wanted to make it safe for dreams. The association of myth and dreamlike mood in Campbell is no accident for, following Jung but if possible even more so, he thought myth and dream, as well as truly great literature, all came from the same place. His storytelling skill told us as much, for like an ancient bard he had the ability to bring the reader or hearer into the world of the myths he retold as into the secret places of one's own dreams, so that for the time the narration was the receiver's subjective as well as outer reality.

The heroic notes in *Star Wars* are not really about conquest, no more than are those in the Arthurian and Wagnerian cycles of myths. All three epics showed the ultimate futility of grasping for power. Rather, these stories make their way into subjective consciousness because they are about deep-level psychic identities—above all, one's own. Of that deepset individual identity the adventurous individual heroes of all great stories are symbolic vehicles. So Campbell profoundly believed. His message supreme above all was that all myths are really about oneself, one's profoundest identity, the innermost self still waiting to be found and realized. Campbell's conviction was that myths are not past but present, embodying the eternal essence of life.

Something in Campbell's message clearly resonated with the yearnings of the Reagan, Bush, and Clinton years. Certainly the appeal of Campbell was rooted in a quality more fundamental than entertainment. When Moyers asked if myths "are stories of our search through the ages for truth, for meaning, for significance," Campbell replied:

> People say that what we're all seeking is a meaning for life. I don't think that's what we're really seeking. I think that what we're seeking is an experience of being alive, so that our life experiences on the purely physical plane will have resonances within our own innermost being and reality, so that we actually feel the rapture of being alive. That's what it's all finally about, and that's what these clues help us to find within ourselves.[3]

Campbell could make others believe with him that myths were important because they are vivid and timeless voices of the rapture of life, and clues to the identity of the enraptured self. People respond to people with passionate convictions about human life, and Campbell manifestly cared about human life and about myth—perhaps in that order.

For despite his academic credentials as a professor at Sarah Lawrence College, and though remarkably widely read in mythology,

Campbell exhibited limited interest of the usual academic sort in his subject matter. He evinced little concern about mythic variants or philological issues, or even about the cultural or ritual context of his material. He was not really a folklorist, much less an anthropologist; he had started his scholarly career in literature and cultural studies, and always basically approached myth through the eyes of a cultural critic.

For him a myth seemed to be a rather disembodied, timeless story of eternal human significance. It might happen to come from here or there, but in the final analysis all myths are equal and interchange- able—with the possible exception of those of "the Yahweh cult" upon which the Judaic-Christian-Islamic tradition is based, and which Campbell clearly disliked. Otherwise, what myths all say, finally, is that behind all forms there is a Brahmanlike Oneness, and that in moving toward its realization one should "follow one's own bliss"— a saying no doubt capable of interpretation on several levels.

Despite the exoticism of many of Campbell's myths, the impor- tance they gave to the inner experience of a pure and authentic self fitted with that American gnostic strand Harold Bloom detected in the national soul. We have noted Harold Bloom's provocative thesis that American religion is fundamentally gnostic in character; if that is so, this must also help explain Campbell's wide appeal in a culture so formed. Karen L. King in fact earlier had written of Campbell's "Ameri- can Romanticism," which held that truth lay in authentic experience of the often alienated but genuine inner self; a view which, she holds, was shared by the ancient gnostics and helped explain Campbell's interest in both the gnostic and romantic traditions.[4]

Robert A. Segal, probably Campbell's most measured and percep- tive critic, confirmed that Campbell's draw lay in the "unashamed romanticism" of his theory of myth. Romanticism, along with Enlight- enment post-Christianity, was the seedbed of modern mythology, and moreover was a significant strand in that "gnostic" Americanism of political individualism and individual salvation to which Campbell ministered. But Campbell was, if conceivable, even more romantic in spirit than Jung or Eliade. Disdaining any of the pretense to medical or historical science that remained with the two Europeans, he built firmly on the foundation of literary romanticism his equation of feel- ing-inflected consciousness and cosmic meaning.

For Campbell, a myth was an eternal, not merely a primitive, narrative. Nothing could supersede it, because it is not about protoscientific explanation but about the human condition, which in the last analysis is always expressed metaphorically, and always has to be spoken. Thus for Campbell, according to Segal, myth is indispensable, and the primitives who first bespoke it were really wiser than moderns because they knew implicitly that the metaphors of story tell human things better than the abstractions of science, and they constructed a worldview centered on their stories.[5]

Elsewhere the same commentator, Segal, remarked that actually Campbell "is oddly not much interested in myth—as myth. He is much more interested in human nature, which he simply finds revealed in myths. He sees myths as a repository of the experiences and beliefs of mankind. He is far more concerned with the information myths contain than with myths themselves."[6] But while it is easy for academics to disparage such an attitude, this is in fact no more than the approach that most predicants, more concerned with saving the world than with footnotes, take toward their scriptural and other sources, and no doubt represents one legitimate level of hermeneutics.

What of Campbell's social and political views? Although, unlike Jung and Eliade, he never expressed himself fully and explicitly in print on such matters, they were known to acquaintances, and posthumously created something of a furor. The ruckus was essentially started in a 1989 article in the *New York Review of Books* by Brendan Gill, who claimed to have known Campbell well. Gill complains that, though one might have expected a person given to a lifelong study of the world's diversity of cultures to accept a variety of points of view in his own culture, this Campbell was never able to do—toward minorities, toward feminists, or toward liberal social programs. The mythologist was reportedly anti-Semitic, anti-Black, and in 1940 unable to grasp the threat represented by Hitler. Needless to say, the sixties did not meet with his approval at all, despite his frequent lectures at one of the decade's most celebrated shrines, the Esalen Institute. Brendan Gill commented: "So far was Campbell from applying the wisdom of the ages to the social, political, and sexual turbulence that he found himself increasingly surrounded by that he might have been a member of the Republican Party somewhere to the right of William F. Buckley. He embodied a paradox that I was never able to resolve in his lifetime and that I have been striving to resolve ever since: the savant as reactionary."[7] Gill advanced several scraps of evidence, largely anecdotal and hearsay, to support Campbell's reactionism.

As to why Campbell's Moyers interviews were so well received, Gill opined that most viewers assumed his was a liberal message—religiously liberal, at least, with its relativistic openness toward the myths and faiths of many cultures. But, Gill claims, the covert message of the tag-line, "Follow your bliss"—whatever makes you happy—is none other than the philosophy of "Wall Street yuppies, junk-bond dealers," or of an Ayn Rand type of elitist individualist with no discernible social conscience.

Gill's article was followed by an orgy of letters-to-the-editor activity. Further anecdotal support was given the legend of Campbell's rightist biases. He was called a "romantic fascist" and virulent anticommunist, was said to have objected to admitting Blacks to Sarah Lawrence, and at the time of the Moon landing in 1969 to have remarked that the earth's satellite would be a good place to send all the Jews. One woman recounted that she had been in a class of his at the height of the sixties campus upheavals; Campbell had said he would flunk any student who took part in political activism—and when she did, he made good on his threat

Other correspondents rose as vehemently to the mythologist's defense. One contended that his position at Sarah Lawrence had to be understood in light of the fact that he had fallen foul of a faculty "Marxist clique"—the same academic politics satirized in Mary McCarthy's *Groves of Academe*. Others argued that "Follow your bliss" has nothing to do with Ayn Rand individualism, much less materialistic selfishness, but the opposite—follow your own way to spiritual liberation.

Admittedly, it is hard to connect the Campbell of the bigot stereotype with a man who for nearly forty years was an immensely popular teacher at Sarah Lawrence, until recently a women's college and one which has long had a reputation as a liberal bastion with a large Jewish enrollment. Yet, if even some of the anecdotes are true, there does appear to be a paradox, the paradox of what Gill called "the savant as reactionary"—in this case, not so much a sophisticated intellectual reactionary, a de Maistre or even a Jung or Eliade, as a smooth articulate nonpolitical mythologist who, off the record, dropped remarks one might have more readily expected to hear from a country club Bourbon. One almost senses a double life.

That perception would not, however, be correct; there were relationships between the mythologist and the political reactionary, and Campbell's political views, though strongly held and on occasion forcefully expressed, were more subtle than might appear on the surface. Campbell loved a good argument, often taking "contrarian" positions at polar opposite to those of his circle or his interlocutors perhaps as much to spark lively debate as anything else. Yet he expressed himself with such charm and contagious intellectual enthusiasm that even many who disagreed strongly with his views remained friends and fans.

At the same time, he held deeply to political and social opinions usually identified as conservative. In his way of thinking, they stemmed from the passionate belief in individual intellectual and artistic liberty that had always been important to him. Thus, in the early fifties, he saw liberty as far more threatened by communism than by the transitory phenomenon of McCarthyism and said so, appalling his more liberal colleagues. In the sixties, despite a long infatuation with pacifism, he supported the Vietnam War on the same antitotalitarian grounds against a hostile intellectual atmosphere. Yet in 1940 and 1941 he had not been able to muster a similar opposition to Hitler, then holding instead to a very high view of the artist's and intellectual's need to remain an independent observer above the political passions of the moment.

## WANDERING AND WONDERING

One can begin to understand Joseph Campbell by looking at his life. He was born in 1904 of Irish-American parents, who moved frequently but always in or around New York. Both his grandfathers arrived in the United States as poor immigrants escaping the Irish potato famine, but Joseph's father, Charles W. Campbell, was a successful salesman who raised his family to upper-middle-class status with all the advantages pertaining thereto: travel, entertainment, good private schools. They were a lively bunch, the parents always ready to give Joseph and his younger brother and sister exposure to the art and culture of the world. They went to concerts, plays, and museums, and traveled at home and abroad. Practicing Catholics without excessive piety, his family and Catholic schools doubtless bestowed on Joseph an innate sense of religion and its symbolism, and at the same time presented him with an experience of religious institutionalism he was later to rebel against. The well-rounded family also loved sports, and Joseph had ample opportunity to develop his natural skill as an athlete. The children all made something of themselves: Joseph's brother, Charles Jr., became an actor; his sister, Alice, a sculptor.

Like Eliade, Joseph was both an avid Boy Scout and a precocious reader. While still in grade school, particularly after being taken by his father to Buffalo Bill's Wild West show, he cultivated a strong interest in American Indians. He admired the Native Americans both for their simple way of life and their heroic though futile resistance to the Whites. He imitated Indian practices on camping trips, and by the time he was ten or eleven was reading the voluminous reports of the Bureau of American Ethnography.

After attending Canterbury, an upscale Catholic boarding school, Joseph enrolled as a freshman at Dartmouth in 1921, soon transferring to Columbia. He took English, comparative literature, and languages, and listened to lectures in anthropology by the distinguished Franz Boas. He combined an outstanding academic career with national-class, and some thought potentially Olympic, dash and middle distance running, a sport of course emphasizing individual strength and competitiveness. Handsome and outgoing, he was socially popular as well. In 1923 Joseph and the family returned to the east coast from a trip to California by ship, passing through the Panama Canal and visiting points in Mexico, Central America, and the Caribbean en route. Campbell's letters and journals indicate he was mainly impressed by the heat, dirt, and flies of that impoverished part of the world, a "culture shock" he was much later to experience again in India, and one much in contrast with the experience Europe was to be for him the following year and later.[8] But Campbell never really resolved a deep-level conflict between love at a distance for the culture and myths of exotic places, and a virtually physical revulsion at their characteristic lack of order and cleanliness when confronted first-hand.

In 1924, between his junior and senior years, Joseph traveled to Europe with his family, in part to attend the Olympic Games held in Paris that year. As it happened he was on the same ship with the young spiritual teacher Jiddu Krishnamurti and a small coterie of supporters. Although Krishnamurti was then being advanced by many in the Theosophical Society as the "vehicle" of a coming World Teacher, Campbell encountered him chiefly as an attractive youth full of unpretentious but deep wisdom. The American toured England with this group, and through his new friends and their circle enjoyed his first real encounter with oriental spirituality. Rosalind Williams, later Rosalind Rajagopal, one of the young "messiah's" youthful companions, gave Edwin Arnold's *The Light of Asia* to Campbell to read on shipboard; he was enthralled by this poetic story of the Buddha's quest for the greatest treasure of all, supreme enlightenment.

Joseph's undergraduate career at Columbia was followed by graduate studies in medieval literature at the same institution. He took an M.A., writing a dissertation on the Grail legend, a theme to which he was to return throughout life. In 1927 Campbell received a munificent grant through Columbia enabling him to spend two years in Europe studying Old French and Provençal in preparation for the Ph.D. he later received from the Sorbonne. Like any intelligent young man abroad he studied many other things as well. He read the Parisian publication of James Joyce's *Ulysses* while that controversial novel was still banned in the U.S. He kept in touch with Krishnamurti, visiting him at Eerde in Holland, a center for the Krishnamurti movement. It was after hearing Krishnamurti lecture in Paris in 1928 on rejecting all dependence on external authority that Campbell stopped attending mass; he remained free of formal religious attachments for the rest of his life.

He was soon to find philosophical and mythological grounds for his own subjective deinstitutionalization of religion. Traveling on to Germany, he found himself deeply drawn to German language and culture. During this time he read Freud and Jung and, no less significantly, the novelist Thomas Mann. A little later, though undoubtedly on the basis of the love of Germany and German scholarship acquired on this trip, he also delved deeply into the work of the historian of the West's decline, Oswald Spengler, and that of the anthropologists Adolf Bastian and Leo Frobenius.

Joyce, Freud, Jung, Mann, Spengler, Bastian, Frobenius . . . these are the names, whether in fashion or not, which recurred by far the most frequently in Campbell's writing up until the very end of his life. It is indeed remarkable the extent to which Campbell's intellectual life from then on was set in grooves cut in those two wonderful wandering years in the gay but tormented Europe of just after the Great War, the Europe of giddy futurism and reactionary pessimism, of Weimar Germany and the Paris of the "lost generation."

Except perhaps Freud, the Germans who so deeply influenced Campbell were then parts of an antimodern reaction that set against Weimar's democratic ideals the romantic organic view of society to which we have already alluded, a perspective often associated with "volkish" thought, and with mythology, in that era. (Mann was, to Campbell's distress, later to renounce much of this credo.) The position also entailed what Spengler and Frobenius called "cultural morphology," the idea that societies possess distinctive and interlocking cultural patterns in all areas of expression, a concept important to Campbell to be discussed later.

First an even more significant Campbellian issue initially derived from the cultural pessmimism side of Weimar Germany. Although differing in many particulars, these three—Mann, Spengler, and Frobenius—also agreed that it was important to look at the calamitous events of recent history from the perspective of a larger screen on which whole cultures and epochs flourish and decline like biological units. And they believed in standing back from the screen. Facing this stupendous panorama, the true artist and scholar maintains personal autonomy, observing and interpreting, but disdaining both fatuous optimism and the soiled passion of practical politics.

For Campbell, such artistic independence was certainly associated with an advanced view of artistic freedom, like that of Joyce publishing in Paris despite censorship in the United States, not to mention in his Catholic Irish homeland. Something of the Parisian and, above all, late twenties German, intellectual worlds found an abiding home in Joseph Campbell. (The apparent dissonance between cultural morphology, with its implication of cultural and historical determinism, and Campbell's fierce individualism might seem to be another contradiction in the man, although he tried to deal with it by claiming, with Frobenius, that a new era of individualism was what the cycles of history had scheduled for the world now emerging.)

After returning to the United States as the great depression began, Campbell spent several unsettled but immensely valuable years continuing life as a sort of intellectual pilgrim. He lived among writers and artists in the Catskills 1930 to 1931, sampling the life and times of the avant garde. In 1931 to 1932 he was with John Steinbeck, Robert Jeffries, and their circle in Monterey, California. In the summer of 1932 he shipped with a biological expedition to Alaska, where he made observations of Native American culture. He taught briefly at his old school, Canterbury. During all this time he was also attempting a career as a writer, and he sold a few short stories. In the early thirties, like many intellectuals of those desperate years, Campbell harbored a sympathetic and hopeful interest in communism and the Russian "experiment," though he was never politically active. Then, in 1934, he joined the faculty of Sarah Lawrence College in Bronxville, New York, where he was to spend the remainder of his academic career.

Campbell thus had the opportunities to absorb two brief but fabulous cultural eras of the twenties that have since passed into legend: the Paris of the famous expatriates, of Hemingway, Fitzgerald, Picasso, Joyce, and the rest; and the raucous, "decadent," yet desperately and brilliantly creative Weimar Germany of its purple twilight years before night fell. With his bright curiosity and his knack for meeting the right people and being in the right place at the right time, the young visitor from overseas returned with an abundant hoard of memories and stories of a Europe all too soon to be forever gone. Upon his return to gritty depression-era America he managed to add to his repertoire of experience another hardly less extraordinary culture circle: the California writers around Miller and Jeffries. And he added to his pack yet another experience of a sort that helped credential not a few American writers: a year of Jack Londonlike labor with the sailors and loggers of the great Pacific northwest, and up the coast to Alaska. Amid all these encounters with various worlds within the world, he went through a common early thirties infatuation with the Soviet venture and flirtation with the radical left, before settling down to the kind of comfortable academic life in which such halcyon days as these could be recalled at leisure—though his work was not over and the skies outside continued to darken.

## War and Peace

The environment at Sarah Lawrence changed Campbell politically and ideologically. The first course he taught, on "Backgrounds to Literature," was based on "Spenglerian morphology." In his third year he taught a course on Thomas Mann and the influence of Kant, Schopenhauer, and Nietzsche on that writer. By now the Germany he loved was under the Nazi boot. His German interests brought him in close contact with another faculty member, the artist Kurt Roesch, a refugee from Hitler who was antimarxist as well. Campbell came to realize that a maverick individualist like himself would not fare well in a dictatorship of either left or right, nor would the values of inner-directed free expression in the arts that were almost a religion to him. By the late 1930s he claimed to be nonpolitical, and his interests were moving in the direction of mythology under the influence of cultural morphology.

The tormented thirties ended with the opening shots of the greatest war in history. Campbell, who knew more intimately than most Americans the intellectual Europe in which its demons had gestated, was now safely on the western side of the Atlantic. But the miasma of a world sorely divided did not escape him, no more than it did the United States generally. Campbell was eminently affected in two ways: through a controversial lecture on values in time of war he gave on December 10, 1940, to which Thomas Mann responded; and through his association with two distinguished refugees from Germany, the indologist Heinrich Zimmer, and the publisher Kurt Wolff, who was to found the Pantheon Press.

The talk, "Permanent Human Values," was given at Sarah Lawrence in days that were dark indeed for the Western alliance, just after the fall of France and the Battle of Britain. Britain and its empire stood alone against the tyrants of Berlin and Rome, and the United States was still an island of peace in a world of war. Campbell clearly wished it to remain so, and he wished moreover to maintain an attitude of even-handedness toward the belligerents. He made such statements as, "Permanent things . . . are not possessed exclusively by the democracies; not exclusively even by the Western world. My theme, therefore, forbids me to be partial to the war-cries of the day." In light of "the duties of objective intelligence in the face of sensational propaganda," "no educated gentleman can possibly believe that the British Empire or the French Empire or the American Empire was unselfishly founded in 'kindly helpfulness,' without gunpowder or without perfectly obscene brutality." After speaking of the original sin in all and the admonition of Christ to "Judge not, that ye be not judged," he added, in his most inflammatory statement, that "We are all groping in this valley of tears, and if a Mr. Hitler collides with a Mr. Churchill, we are not in conscience bound to believe that a devil has collided with a saint.—*Keep those transcendent terms out of your political thinking*—do not donate the things of God to Caesar—and you will go a long way toward keeping a sane head."

As for the permanent values at risk in time of war, they included capacity for critical objectivity, the apparently useless diligence of the disinterested scientist and historian, the work of the literary man and the artist, education as human beings rather than as patriots, the preaching of religion free of those "always ready to deliver God into the hands of their king or their president." ("We hear of it already—this arm-in-arm blood brotherhood of democracy and Christianity.")[9]

Much of this is of course unexceptionable on one level. Few sober observers can deny that the evil which is war has its ways of corrupting participants on all sides, that the first casualty of war is often truth, and that the best means of maintaining some degree of sanity amid war's horror is to keep in contact with permanent values forever above and beyond the battlefield. But in 1940 the apparent moral equivalency which Campbell, unnecessarily, kept positing between the democracies and their totalitarian adversaries, as though no more was involved than a personal quarrel between "Mr. Churchill" and "Mr. Hitler," or as though Britain, for all its faults, was on the same abysmal moral level as the Nazi regime, was more than many then or since could swallow. One critic was his one-time idol Thomas Mann, who by now had fled to America. In his Weimar period Campbell had been much influenced by Mann's 1918 *Betrachtungen eines Unpolitischen* ("Reflections of a Nonpolitical Man,") a disillusioned statement from the end of World War I. In that tract for the times the great novelist wrote with disdain of the one-sided tendentiousness of every political achievement, and celebrated instead the balanced and full-blooded portrayals of the human condition accessible to the artist and poet. That transcendent vision, Campbell thought, Mann had achieved in his own many-layered and luminous novels. But by 1940 Mann had undergone a considerable awakening to the profound evil of which politics was capable, and the danger of viewing evil in the Hitlerian degree with aloof neutrality.

Campbell had sent to Mann a copy of the "Permanent Human Values" talk at the suggestion of Mrs. Eugene Meyers, an older student who knew both the professor and the German exile. Campbell had earlier met the novelist through her mediation. Even then, Campbell had been disturbed by Mann's 1938 book *The Coming Victory of Democracy*, in which the refugee from the land of concentration camps had simply identified the good with democracy and evil with fascism. The once "Great Master of Objectivity," as Campbell called him, who had started out as the supreme advocate of seeing both sides of every question, was now so far in the partialities of the temporal world as to see God, or the timeless Absolute, as on the side of the "democracies."

Then, in a letter of January 6, 1941, in response to the talk, Mann pointedly asked Campbell what would become of the five "permanent values" of which he spoke if Hitler triumphed. "It is strange," the novelist declared, "you are a friend of my books, which therefore in your opinion probably have something to do with Permanent Human Values. Well, those books are banned in Germany and in all countries which Germany rules today. And whoever reads them, whoever sells them, whoever would even publicly praise my name, would end up in a concentration camp, and his teeth would be beaten in and his kidneys smashed."[10]

Campbell replied to Mann equivocally enough, but to his journals he confided his disappointment: "The letter which I received from Thomas Mann in reply was one of the most astonishing revelations to me: it signified for me the man's practical retraction of all his beautiful phrases about the timelessly human which no force can destroy, and about the power of love over death and about the Eternal altogether. It exhibited a finally temporal-political orientation, and not only that, but a fairly trivial and personal view of even the temporal-political."[11]

Here as elsewhere in his journals, he set against the evils ascribed to the fascist side the British role in Ireland and India, the American conquest of the continent and its native population, and the situation of "Negroes" in the South, together with all the graft and hypocrisy of which democracy was capable. It would be unjust to say Campbell was then or ever pronazi or profascist; he several times expresses his distaste for the crudeness, brutality, and anti-Semitism of Germany's present masters. But against all that, he put his freely admitted love for Germany as a country and a culture, and also the passion of hatreds closer to home. He possessed an Irishman's bitterness toward the British Empire, and he was the sort of American intellectual who despised many of his countrymen's shallow patriotism and self-satisfied complacency with the vitriol of an H. L. Mencken, whom he read. Unfortunately, it was perhaps his yearning for transcendent, mythical purity of thought, together with a lack of such actual experience as Mann had had, that kept him from willingness to admit any degree of proportionality in the political evils of the world, or any absolute moral obligation to oppose as well as transcend the worst of them.

Moreover, not only did Campbell like to see himself as an Olympian above the fray, as we have seen he also liked a good argument and had a tendency, which more than once got him into trouble, to argue for the opposite point of view from that prevailing among the company he was keeping. As American public opinion moved more and more decisively toward Britain, whose claims to superior virtue left Campbell quite unimpressed, he remained blind to anything but equivalency and a deeply felt pacifism. When the United States entered the war on December 8, 1941, Campbell wrestled with his conscience, reading among other things pacifist literature from the Fellowship of Reconciliation, for nearly three months before finally registering for the draft. He soon found, to his immense relief, that he was just past the age limit for being called up to active service.

Refugees from the other side, however, kept coming into his life. And while it is clear that Campbell had long felt deep inner currents flowing in the direction of mythological interests, the new contacts during World War II seem to have moved him decisively in that direction. Both connections were with Germans who, like Mann, were in the United States because of Hitler. Heinrich Zimmer, an Indologist whose wife was part Jewish, and who was a friend of both Mann and Jung, had fled Nazi Germany in 1938. After teaching at Oxford for two years, he had come to New York and Columbia University in 1941. There Campbell was among his first pupils. He had first met Zimmer through Swami Nikhilananda of the Vedanta Society. When Zimmer died prematurely in 1943, Campbell received the responsibility for editing his manuscripts for publication.

That was through the agency of the other new contract, Kurt Wolff, a half-Jewish German publisher who, after a few years in Italy, also arrived in New York in 1941. There, initially on a shoestring, he established the Pantheon Press, dedicated to books of intellectual and spiritual significance. Among its first projects was the Bollingen Series, a Jungian-tinged (it was of course named after Jung's hideaway) set of volumes on myth and world religion funded by Paul and Mary Mellon. At Zimmer's suggestion Campbell was named first editor of the series. An early work was Maude Oakes, *Where the Two Came to Their Father: A Navajo War Ceremonial*. Zimmer, knowing of Campbell's lifelong interest in American Indian lore, recommended that the Sarah Lawrence professor write the scholarly commentary on that text. After 1943, Campbell continued to prepare Zimmer's works for posthumous publication in the Bollingen series, sometimes slipping in his own writing when the older scholar's notes were disconnected or incoherent. The results were such classics of Indology under Zimmer's name as *Myths and Symbols in Indian Art and Civilization* (1946), *The King and the Corpse* (1948), the magisterial *Philosophies of India* (1941), and the two-volume *Art of Indian Asia* (1955). Though it required putting aside his own work for a time, the Zimmer efforts undoubtedly laid a very solid foundation for a mythological career.

The Zimmer and Wolff connections enabled Campbell to become attached to the famous Eranos conferences held at the villa of Frau Froebe-Kaptayn in Ascona, Switzerland, overlooking the deep blue waters of Lake Maggiore. These more or less annual conferences brought together the cream of the world's mythology and history of religions scholars: persons of the rank of Eliade, Gershom Scholem who had revived the study of Jewish kabbalah, the student of Gnosticism Giles Quispel, Henri Corbin of Iranian mysticism, D. T. Suzuki the apostle of Zen, and many others, including he who was by now the grand old man of them all, Carl Jung. Campbell had been set to work in 1946 by Pantheon preparing selections from seventeen previous *Jahrbücher* (Annuals) of the Eranos conferences for English publication in the Bollingen series. In 1953, 1957, and 1959 Campbell attended the legendary conclaves himself, presenting papers at the last two. After the 1953 event, he and his wife Jean had the rare privilege of an invitation from Jung to visit him at his medieval tower retreat, Bollingen, outside Zurich. The conversation moved over many topics; Jean noted that when speaking of psychology and mythology, the great man was brilliant and wide ranging, but on social or political issues, "he became more parochial, sort of like a small-town Swiss."[12]

In the meantime, Campbell's own writing was continuing apace. His first book, written with Henry Morton Robinson (later author of the best-selling novel, *The Cardinal*), was on James Joyce. *A Skeleton Key to Finnegan's Wake* (1944) consummated his daring discovery of Joyce in the Paris of the twenties.

The big event, however, which truly transformed Joseph Campbell into a major figure in the world of mythology and of midcentury culture generally, was the publication in 1949 of his own Bollingen series book, *The Hero with a Thousand Faces*.[13] This sweeping and engrossing study of the hero myth was Campbell's first single-authored work. It had a definite influence on a generation of literary critics and historians of religion.

Campbell's two-page preface splendidly defined the context and mission of the book in short space. He began, significantly, with a few lines from Sigmund Freud's *The Future of an Illusion*: "The truth contained in religious doctrines are after all so distorted and systematically disguised, that the mass of mankind cannot recognize them as truth." Campbell wrote, of course, in the heyday of Freudian psychoanalysis as an intellectual vogue, and the Freudian Campbell behind the Jungian version must never be forgotten. Yet the lines bespeak Campbell even more than the Viennese doctor. They are Campbell's way of saying that the whole mythological enterprise must be understood not as mere antiquarianism, but an important intellectual venture conducted in the midst of the modern world, with full awareness of its thought currents and its needs. Campbell's mythology readily concedes all that modern skepticism claims, and still argues for the discipline's contemporary importance.

Campbell then proceeded to explain what he was doing in his own words: "It is the purpose of the present book to uncover some of the truths disguised for us under the figures of religion and mythology by bringing together a multitude of not-too-difficult examples and letting the ancient meaning become apparent of itself." When this is done, using psychoanalysis as a tool, "the parallels will be immediately apparent; and these will develop a vast and amazingly constant statement of the basic truths by which man has lived throughout the millenniums of his residence on the planet." This unified story he called, after James Joyce in *Finnegan's Wake*, the "monomyth." That was the account of the hero's adventure from departure through initiation to return, where he underwent along the way such intriguingly named experiences as "The Crossing of the First Threshold," "The Belly of the Whale," "The Meeting with the Goddess," and "Atonement with the Father," after which he becomes "Master of Two Worlds." A second part of the book, "The Cosmogonic Cycle," discusses such related themes as the Virgin Birth and various forms of the hero: warrior, lover, emperor, redeemer, saint. In all, the book has Campbell doing what he does best: he tells stories and tells them well, bringing them together with profound-seeming undergirdings of timeless meaning, and says it is all very important for our lives today.

The basic monomyth informs us that the mythological hero, setting out from an everyday home, is lured or is carried away or proceeds to the threshold of adventure. He defeats a shadowy presence that guards the gateway, enters a dark passageway or even death, meets many unfamiliar forces, some of which give him threatening "tests," some of which offer magical aid. At the climax of the quest he undergoes a supreme ordeal and gains his reward: sacred marriage or sexual union with the goddess of the world, reconciliation with the father, his own divinization, or a mighty gift to bring back to the world. He then undertakes the final work of return, in which, transformed, he reenters the place from whence he set out.[14]

*Hero* resonated with its times. The Bollingen aura was in the air. In some circles, the midcentury intellectual mood was saturated with myths, dreams, mysticism, psychoanalysis, and archetypes. Stanley Edgar Hyman, reviewing *Hero* in the *Kenyon Review*, remarked that "Myth is the new intellectual fashion, apparently." He was not fully impressed, however. Agreeing that myths can tell "basic truths," he found Campbell a bit too general and "mystical." One can say "yes" to the notion that myths have meaning, but still ask "when, and to whom?" "The study of myth continues to be the least rational of the humanities. Joseph Campbell . . . now comes forward with an amiably befuddled volume the purpose of which is to discover the 'secret' truths concealed in the myths and to apply these truths to our desperate modern situation." Hyman also pertinently noted that Campbell was still fundamentally literary; folk tales were to him inferior, "undeveloped or degenerate" in relation to the "great mythologies" of the higher civilizations.[15] The distinguished folklorist Richard Dorson also later observed that Campbell emphasized the universal, dreamlike quality of myth, calling attention to the fact that he was actually a "professor of literature."[16]

Significantly, *Hero*, like most of Campbell's work, went down better with literary and drama critics, and the literate public, than with professional folklorists or anthropologists. Campbell, basking in his popular success, came to take this phenomenon in stride. The issues were larger, in his mind, than whether a particular volume was "amiably befuddled." They were no doubt also larger than the later com-

plaint of a Soviet critic who, laboring under the terminology of doc-
trinaire marxism, complained that *Hero* completely divorced myth from
"the real actuality in which it arises and develops" as it overlooks "the
social role of a given work, its specific national traits, its artistic imag-
ery and ideological peculiarities."[17] The universalizing and psychoanalytic study of myth in the Campbell mode would, from this
perspective, undoubtedly represent its appropriation by bourgeois consciousness; the latter, in marxist eyes, tends to subjectivize and
aestheticize myths and stories that had their real roots in social alienation and economic deprivation.

Campbell's own socioeconomic setting, at the time of *Hero*, was
the unprecedented affluence of postwar America and the coldest years
of the Cold War. Schools, colleges, and adult education programs were,
like churches, growing briskly as veterans enrolled under the GI bill.
More families had money for college than ever before, and schools
and businesses prepared for the new world of the baby boomers now
beginning to see the light of day. Mythology was not a major part of
postwar education, but it was not an entirely insignificant factor either. To recapitulate themes from our introductory chapter, we may
recall that literary discourse in the New Criticism style was serious
then, and Campbell's elegant, lightly psychoanalytic and literary-critical
style of mythology fitted in well. Its appeal was enhanced by the
postwar yearning to retrieve the best of the premodern past, articulated in generalized mythology as well as in Vedanta, Trappist monas-
ticism, Zen, and the Thomism of Catholic campuses. A big issue that
obsessed the early fifties was the individual versus "mass society."
The existentialists and social critics like David Riesman of *The Lonely
Crowd* approached it in their own ways; Campbell did it by making
the hero the central figure in myth and showing that, therefore, only
in the individual is there true glory.

## THE MATURE MYTHOLOGIST

Campbell was very much a part of this world; but as usual everything was a little different for him. In the McCarthy days his problem
was not to avoid blacklisting, as it was for many professors, Hollywood figures, and others; it was rather the disdain that come in such
circles to one perceived as being on the other side. But Harold Taylor,
president of Sarah Lawrence at the time and a friend of Campbell's,

said of him that "Campbell's view was always more complex than could be easily grasped by most people."

> One of the things Joe really didn't like was Communists. . . . [But] he didn't think we should, as a college, be just one thing; each person who came in should be given legroom to move in whatever direction his legs took him. . . . He was a man of strong, independent views. . . . He was very fond of the college and a lot of the people in it, but he was annoyed by the politics of the habitual liberals on the faculty.[18]

Campbell got to know Alan Watts around this time. They were two of a kind, lively, sensual, still youngish lovers of spiritual traditions who also knew how to enjoy good food, drink, and all-night parties. In his autobiography, *In My Own Way*, Watts described Campbell in this manner, ". . . his attitude to life is Tantric: an almost fearsomely joyous acceptance of all the aspects of being, such that whenever I am with him his spirit spills over into me."[19]

Like Watts, Campbell was part of a movement to bring the wisdom of the East into the classrooms and living rooms of the West. But for him this process was a bit more complicated than simple praise and appropriation. For one thing, he was never quite sure just how much he liked the East. Confronting it, he could swing from fulsome accolade to acerbic impatience; he loved the mythology and philosophy he had explored in the Zimmer years, and even as far back as the meeting with Krishnamurti. But the social and political reality of Asia today could be something else, above all when they seemed at right angles to the mythologist's proud individualism and staunch political opinions. In the end, he fell back on one of his first loves: the pagan or quasi-pagan myths of the West, from the Odyssey to the Grail to James Joyce.

The issue was exacerbated in 1954 and 1955, when Campbell took an extended tour of India, a country he had of course studied intensively by virtue of his work on the Zimmer manuscripts. He was accompanied by Swami Nikhilananda and a couple of prominent members of the New York Ramakrishna-Vivekananda Center. The Ramakrishna Mission had arranged lectures and opened doors for him. But his opinions and observations, recorded in an engrossing journal, were his own.[20] Neither he nor Zimmer had actually been to the land whose rich art and thought had so influenced them, and of which they had undoubtedly constructed a half-fantasy land of wonder. India on the ground was an experience that left Campbell shaken by no small degree of culture shock.

Campbell admitted in a letter to his wife, Jean, that nothing in the real India "was quite as good as the India I invented" in New York before the trip.[21] The religion, the temples, the gurus, the mythological background of course was there. But all was interfused with the heat, the poverty, the dirt, the beggars, and the chauvinism of the newly independent state. The repressive qualities of the ancient civilization were also more than evident, in the evils of caste and the hopeless drudgery of those on its lower rungs. For one whose ideal was obviously the cleanliness and order of Germany, India with its filth and chaos clearly left much to be desired, just as had the Central America of an earlier trip. A few scenes approached the Germanic ideal. Of the state of Orissa the visitor was able to say that it was "the best thing so far in India: lovely air, beautiful skies, fertile flatland by the sea, and, after Calcutta, clean and orderly looking people."[22]

But much of India was highly unsuitable to one of Campbell's values and temperament. Most infuriating to him were the ubiquitous and persistent con-men and self-appointed guides and attendants, all clamorous for baksheesh. On top of that, he had to deal with the officious but inefficient bureaucracy, and to listen to tirades from intellectuals claiming that the United States—not even Britain—was somehow responsible for India's problems. At the same time India was, at this moment, enamored with socialist visions and the idea of friendship with the Soviet Union and the communist bloc. All this definitely hit a sore spot in the devoutly anticommunist mythologist.

He found himself becoming more patriotically American than ever, and more promodern as well. Once, in response to a comment by Swami Nikhilananda that "there is no progress, only change," Campbell replied, "I used to think that too, Swamiji, but since coming to India I have changed my mind. I think there is progress, and I think India will begin to experience progress too, pretty soon."[23] Even Gandhi did not enjoy from Campbell the whole-hearted admiration he received from Eliade; the American called him and his disciple Vinoba "primitivists," whose "alienation from the inevitables of modern life makes for a kind of romantic escapism."[24]

Campbell also learned something about himself and his own alienation in India. In a telling remark in his journals, he said, "In the

Orient I am for the West; in the West for the Orient. In Honolulu I am for the 'liberals,' in New York for big business. In the temple I am for the University, in the University for the temple. The blood, apparently, is Irish."[25] That sort of independent, contrarian individualism was what he missed in modern India.

After *The Hero with a Thousand Faces* and the journey to India came the four-volume series of collected and annotated mythologies called *The Masks of God: Primitive Mythology* (1959), *Oriental Mythology* (1962), *Occidental Mythology* (1964), and *Creative Mythology* (1968).[26] In this series the attitude toward East versus West was gradually changing, though often wavering back and forth. In *Hero* Campbell had, despite the individualistic theme, praised the East for its mythological subtlety, and so did he in the Oriental volume of *Masks*. But by the time he got to the Occidental volume, and in *Creative Mythology*, he was increasingly hostile to the East for its suppression of the individual.

Like most of Campbell's work the *Masks* series impressed literate laity more than specialists. Writing from the latter side about *Occidental Mythology*, Stephen P. Dunn vividly declared in the *American Anthropologist* that

> Campbell's book is in a sense a throwback to an earlier heroic age of anthropology, when the air was dark with flying hypotheses and comparisons rained down like acorns in autumn. Reading it, the case-hardened social scientist derives the same sort of nostalgic half-shamefaced pleasure as the ordinary adult would from reading G. A. Henty or Robin Hood to his children. Campbell uses the traditional equipment and methods of the literary critic, for whom comparison and analogy are tantamount to proof and fact. He writes in a curiously archaic style—full of rhetorical questions, exclamations of wonder and delight, and expostulations directed at the reader, or perhaps at the author's other self—which is charming about a third of the time and rather annoying the rest.[27]

Like Eliade, Campbell was not really a social scientist, and those in the latter camp could tell. Dunn felt that Campbell did not distinguish sufficiently between great and little traditions of religion; none of the latter, so far as he was aware, really embraced the mysticism or pantheism that he saw behind all myth. Nor were his views on Hebrew or Greek religion particularly novel. But a poet, as Campbell was at heart, can see what he wants in the lives and beliefs of nonpoetic folk, and in so doing make their lives sing.

An interesting document of Campbell's East-West wobbling is a 1967 paper, "The Secularization of the Sacred."[28] This curious essay has the feel of something transitional. It commenced with rather standard remonstrances against the "anthropomorphic" God of the West, at first exalting Eastern religions over the Western for their ability to see the divine in everything rather than in a particular place, and because the East seems to point beyond the image rather than limiting God to the literal and the particular.

But then Campbell came to the theology of love and the transformation of human to divine love, of eros to agape, kama to prema. (His study of this process is one of his more significant contributions to comparative religion.) He saw this exchange as an important sector of several spiritual traditions. In bhakti, love for the particular form becomes love for the universal divine. In Christianity it becomes a relationship in which love for the human beloved is more and more replaced by the love of God for divine lovers like Saint Francis and Saint Bonaventure. But, in a move Campbell loudly applauded, in the West pagan love was then surreptitiously revived in stories like Tristan and Isolde or Parsifal, in which the heroes and heroines remain separate and earthly in all their glory.

In making this point, "The Secularization of the Sacred" became an affirmation of something early in Celto-Germanic and Greco-Roman culture, which was subsequently weakened by Christianity with its "Semitic" absolutizing of the particular sacred. "It is my thought, that the wealth and glory of the western world, and of the modern world as well (insofar as it is still in spirit, western) is a function of this respect for the individual, not as a member of some sanctified consensus through which he is given worth."[29]

Those words were written at about the same time as turmoil over the great trauma of the late sixties, Vietnam, raged through the United States. Regarding the war, Campbell's contrarian instincts were to rile up. In fact, as Campbell's biographers, Stephen and Robin Larsen, point out, his position in 1967 had similarities as well as differences with that taken in the 1940 "Permanent Human Values" speech. During World War II he favored nonintervention. But in the sixties, while he continued to loathe war, he seemed to believe that communism represented such a mind-enslaving system that violent opposition to it was justified. However his main concern at Sarah Lawrence was, as in 1940, that students should be students, concerned with more permanent values than those of day-to-day politics, or the activism associated with the decade. With perhaps a touch of self-deception, he saw himself as a nonpolitical classroom professor, and insisted he was there to teach, and students on campus there to learn what he had to teach and for no other reason.

The Larsens state that, contrary to what was sometimes alleged, Campbell did not actually fail students for political activism as such, but did hold them responsible for material presented in class even during strikes and demonstrations. They describe the late sixties atmosphere at Sarah Lawrence vividly, evoking the highly visible posters of Mao, the Vietcong flags, and the student strikes, which so inflamed the conservative mythologist, though he himself had been infatuated with communism in the early thirties.[30] The Larsens were friends of Campbell and their biography is generally sympathetic, though they acknowledge that in the Vietnam era they "leaned to the left" and often disputed Campbell's prowar Republicanism with him, trying to get him to see such sixties dramas as the march on the Pentagon sympathetically as contemporary events of mythic dimension. They attribute his then-unpopular (at least in the circles in which he and they generally moved) stance to his visceral anticommunism, his idealization of American individualism, and his stubborn independence. They point out that later he also had problems with the Republicanism of the eighties on three important points: its alliance with Christian fundamentalism (he believed strongly in separation of church and state, and did not care for either Catholic or Protestant authoritarianism), its opposition to abortion (perhaps because of his radical individualism, he believed in a woman's right to choice), and the GOP's inadequate stand on ecology (a great lover of nature, Campbell supported strong measures for its protection). As the decade advanced, he claimed he was so disillusioned with all parties that he might not vote at all.

It might also be added that Campbell enjoyed friendship with, and influenced, a number of prominent figures of the sixties and seventies who did not necessarily share his political views but appreciated his creative intellect and who applied his mythic vision to their art or social role. In addition to the filmmaker George Lucas, these included Bob Dylan, The Grateful Dead, the psychologist Joan Halifax, and California governor Jerry Brown.

How did Campbell come by the conservatism that set him apart from what otherwise ought to have been a very congenial decade for one of his vision? One view is presented in Toby Johnson's *The Myth of the Great Secret,* an interesting account of the author's personal movement away from conventional Roman Catholicism under the aegis of Campbell's perception of myth. Johnson, who did not and does not share Campbell's politics, reports he was quite taken aback when, unaware of Campbell's views, he first met him in 1971, during the years of upheaval over Vietnam, and found that his mentor identified himself as a Republican and a supporter of Nixon and the war. (Johnson had, in fact, steeled himself to oppose the war through the power of certain lines about the hero's resolve in Campbell's 1949 classic, *The Hero With a Thousand Faces.*) He found also that Campbell was opposed to sixties-style sexual and psychedelic drug experimentation, and "sounded like he'd been listening to too much Art Linkletter."[31]

In further conversations, Johnson came to understand Campbell better. The mythologist called himself a "classical conservative," citing the story of the Grail Quest as an example of the staunch individualism on which that position is allegedly based: the knights agree among themselves that they will not follow in another's footsteps, but that each should pursue his own path to the holy object, beginning at that place in the forest that was darkest and most alone. Campbell, in fact, according to Johnson prided himself on not really being part of the modern world. He never watched television and had no interest in popular culture. (Eliade too, incidentally, during the Chicago years when I knew him, never read newspapers or sat in front of a TV and had virtually no awareness of what was happening in the outer world.)

In Campbell then we see, in this context, an extreme and obviously idealized individualism—the assumption that the knights of capitalism would voluntarily all start equally distant from the prize—combined perhaps with something of the puritanism of his Irish Catholic background, were the dominant constituents of Campbell's social views. He explained to Toby Johnson that the real danger in modern society was the threat of swamping personal freedom with concern for collective needs, which would lead the government to meddle in people's lives and cater to pressure groups.

By the time the *Masks* series had been completed, Joseph Campbell was famous. He had reached several audiences who believed that what he had to say about myth and contemporary civilization was worth hearing. *The Hero with a Thousand Faces* had fascinated a quorum of writers and literary critics like himself, and together with the rest of the postwar myth-mood had helped launch the "myth criticism" of scholars like Northrop Frye. The Bollingen Series work, especially the edited Eranos Yearbooks, had made him a familiar name in the large professional and lay circles interested in comparative religion, Jungianism, and related inquiries. Now the *Masks* series hit the nation's bookshops and coffee tables in another decade, the sixties, much taken with recovering the wisdom behind myths and symbols from out the race's occult past. Their impact was abetted by active lecturing and media appearances on the part of an author who looked so much the Hollywood image of the popular, winsome yet wise professor. There were critics, but few of them had royalties to match Campbell's.

The next book, *Myths To Live By* (1972), reworked lectures given over many years at the Cooper Union in New York.[32] Emmett Wilson, Jr., in the *Saturday Review* called it "badly written," retaining "the cloying chatter of a rather unstructured lecturer talking to an undemanding audience."[33] The book did, however, continue something of a new departure for the mythologist begun in *Creative Mythology*: writing directly and centrally concerned with the contemporary need for new myths in a time of what he called "pathology of the symbol," when religions based on outdated views of the cosmos have been losing their force, but the new gods have not yet arrived. In *Creative Mythology* he had become very concerned with the role of mythology in social stability:

> For those in whom a local mythology still works, there is an experience both of accord with the social order, and of harmony with the universe. For those, however, in whom the authorized signs no longer work. . . . there follows inevitably a sense both of dissociation from the local social nexus and of quest, within and without, for life, which the brain will take to be for 'meaning.' "[34]

In *Myths To Live By* Campbell returned to Spengler and Frobenius for ways of understanding the current critical eschatological situation, and talked of finding new mythologies in Outer Space. J. A. Appleyard, writing in *Commonweal*, was disconcerted by Campbell's "*we*-know-better" attitude toward the wisdom of the past, but others, like Peden

Creighton in the *Journal of Religious Thought* recognized that the present symbol situation was schizophrenic, and whether or not Campbell had all the answers he was at least asking the questions.[35]

There were other books by the mature mythologist: *The Flight of the Wild Gander*, a collection of his most scholarly papers; the late three volumes of the *Historical Atlas of World Mythology*, and another lecture collection, *The Inner Reaches of Outer Space*, as well as posthumous journals.[36] *Transformations of Myth Through Time* was the posthumous publication of his last lecture tours, also videotaped for a PBS series.[37] That final collection of lectures no doubt gratified Campbell's numerous fans, but did little to quiet critical concerns about the mythologist's oversimplification of historical matters and tendency to make myth mean whatever he wanted it to mean. Indeed, one has a familiar but disturbing sense of an old man becoming more and more set in his opinions as the years advance. That is apparent in his treatment of the Semitic element in European and American culture.

In *Transformations*, he recalls scolding a student of his at Sarah Lawrence for saying that if she didn't think of herself as Jewish, she wouldn't know her identity. Campbell told her that he knew who he was even apart from thinking of himself as an Irishman. On the same page (91) he presents a confrontation he had with the celebrated Jewish theologian Martin Buber, whom he took to task for expressing horror at the sacrifice of children to the pagan god Moloch despite Abraham's willingness to obey Yahweh's command to sacrifice his own son Isaac. Whatever the rights or wrongs of the argument, it is apparent that examples of what Campbell considers bad religion often seem to involve Judaism and its progeny. The return from East to West did not necessarily mean a return to *these* religions. In chapter 11 of the same book, "Where There Was No Path: Arthurian Legends and the Western Way," he makes those famous stories speak of a lingering pagan individualism standing over against an oppressive "Near Eastern tradition" imported by Christianity, buttressing the case through hopelessly selective use of the material, and despite the fact that we know King Arthur only as a Christian hero. Anyone who, despite great learning, could so forget both the ruthless and repressive sides of tribal paganism, and the stunning examples of Jewish and Christian individualistic heroes from David to Jesus, to embrace such a simplistic view of European culture, is beyond rational argument.

Regrettably, in Joseph Campbell one sees a man in whom, for all his celebratory status and accomplishment, some levels of promise remained unfulfilled. In place of ongoing growth in wisdom and understanding, there is a life too soon foreclosed around views that seem more firmly rooted in quirks of temperament than intellectual analysis. He seems one of those golden youths to whom too much came too soon and too easily, and who thereafter does little but repeat the homilies that first won him the laurels of popular acclaim.

Yet there is another Campbell, a counterpart to the charismatic public figure, a Campbell who was almost bafflingly inward. This mysterious persona surfaced in one of his most remarkable books, one that only he could have written, *The Mythic Image* (1974).

Perhaps that is the work with which to best end this narrative. *The Mythic Image* is a stunningly illustrated gift book and the quintessential Campbell, notable for its rich association, always important to Campbell, of myth and art, and of both to the reveries of dream. The first section is entitled "The World As Dream," and of course suggests that myths are the key to the interpretation of the oneiric fantasy we see all around us and take for real. The book received virtually awestruck notices in such media as the *New Yorker* and *Newsweek*, but the historian of religion Charles H. Long, in the *Religious Studies Review*, perhaps had the best take on it as he noticed that the organization of the work itself is dream-like. It wanders like a dream from one image to another: from rock paintings to "wild and erotic" Tantric art to gruesome sacrifices to the monumental buildings of lost civilizations, and on and on. By now Campbell is entirely uninhibited in his free association of symbols across space and time. The sleeping Kundalini serpent of Tantric yoga reminds him of something in Rembrandt's painting of Faust, and in one of the cave temples of Aurangabad the Buddha holds a "lotus ladder" reminiscent of both the Norse Yggdrasil and Jacob's ladder. There is no necessary cultural connection in these things, but there is a sort of dream melding of one image into another, an "oneiric logic," evocative of what here is Campbell's central concern, the relation of dream to myth. The book, Long concludes, reads as though it had been written in a dream, while asleep. It is passive, ambiguous, haunting.[38]

## BASIC IDEAS

What is mythology supposed to *do*? Here, from *Myths To Live By*, are four functions of myth. All four of these clearly have direct or indirect political ramifications, either in the way myths give spiritual power and identity to an individual—notice the primary emphasis on the individual in these lines—and so strengthens one's functioning within the political order, or by validating that order directly.

> The first [function] is what I have called the mystical function, to waken and maintain in the individual a sense of awe and gratitude in relation to the mystery dimension of the universe, not so that he lives in fear of it, but so that he recognizes that he participates in it, since the mystery of being is the mystery of his own being as well.
>
> The second function of the living mythology is to offer an image of the universe that will be in accord with the knowledge of the time, the sciences and the fields of action of the folk to whom the mythology is addressed.
>
> The third function of the living mythology is to validate, support, and imprint the norms of a given specific moral order—that, namely, of the society in which the individual is to live.
>
> And the fourth is to guide him, stage by stage, in health, strength, and harmony of spirit, through the whole foreseeable course of a useful life.[39]

Such fundamental notions as these remained constant throughout Campbell's career. They included also the idea of the unity of myth, that is, that myths throughout the world give an essentially identical message (with the exception, perhaps, of the "Near Eastern"). We have seen how the idea was expressed in quasi-Freudian terms in the preface to *Hero*. Also at the beginning of his career, he wrote in his preface to Maya Deren's *Divine Horsemen*:

> All mythology, whether of the folk or of the literati, preserves the iconography of a spiritual adventure that men have been accomplishing repeatedly for millennia, and which, whenever it occurs, reveals such constant features that the innumerable mythologies of the world resemble each other as dialects of a single language.[40]

No less important themes were the relation of myth to dreams and the unconscious; and, on the other hand, to the explication of comparable motifs in great literature. Insofar as there were differences in the apparent values of myths, that was attributable to the workings of the "cultural morphology" he had learned from Oswald Spengler and Leo Frobenius. For morphological changes in myth as culture changed was possible; the geographical universality of myth was not necessarily also a temporal sameness age after age. The exact level of mythic universality versus cultural specificity or of timeless versus temporally conditioned truth in myth, however, was not examined in depth by Campbell.

Both Spengler and Frobenius were among those who not only were immensely popular writers in the Weimar period, but also perpetuated a highly sophisticated version of the volkish mood: antidemocratic, pessimistic about the modern world. It is clear that, more than most Americans of his generation, Campbell was nurtured by the milk of that particular strand of Weimar intellectualism, and always maintained a soft place in his heart for the glories of German thought.

It may be recalled that Spengler also enjoyed a vogue in the early and mid fifties in America. Many intellectuals, including the Beats, took up with the pessimistic, antimodern mood of thinkers like Aldous Huxley, C. G. Jung, and the rediscovered Spengler, in opposition to the brave new world of television, fishtail cars, and Cold War capitalism appearing outside their study windows. In the days of *Hero* and the Eranos conferences, Campbell was far from alone in publicly bemoaning (and maybe covertly applauding) the decline of the West, but he clung to the ghosts of Weimar intellectual life longer than virtually anyone else.

What impressed Campbell about Spengler and Frobenius was not so much their explicit political views as their concept of the morphology of culture, the view that cultures have definite shapes in space and time, in which all features of a particular cultural era interlock to form a definite style that is as much a form of consciousness and character as of art and architecture.

For example, according to Spengler the Russians have a "flat plane" culture expressed in low buildings and an ethics of egalitarian fellowship; western Europe is "Faustian," with its soaring gothic spires, its distance perspective in art, its world exploration and world conquest, its long-distance weapons. Moreover, cultures pass through distinct stages of growth and decline, and it is here that Spengler's one celebrated book, *The Decline of the West*, expressed its prophetic judgment on a civilization that had already passed midlife. Campbell first read that book during the author's moment of post–World War I fame but he never forgot it, returning to its main themes again up to the end of his life.

Thus fundamental to Campbell's position all the way through were two ideas taken from Frobenius and Spengler about the myths of particular cultures. First was the concept of the spiritual unity of a culture. That unified essence is expressed through the myths of the culture but is also found in visual art and even in individual personality styles. The unity is further expressed in the culture's particular forms of the Jungian archetypes and in its great literature. Joyce and Thomas Mann were supreme examples, for Campbell, of modernity's particular cultural circle.

Second, Campbell affirmed, with Frobenius and Spengler, that cultural circles can evolve. The medieval Western style was not the same as the modern Western. Spengler, as is well known, and as is suggested in the very title of *The Decline of the West*, believed that cultural circles, like human beings and all organic life, pass through seasons of youth, maturity, and senescence, finally to die. But here Campbell preferred the more optimistic vision of his other German mentor, Frobenius.

He was struck by Frobenius's comparable concept that every race has its own *paideuma* or soul, its own way of feeling and its own spectrum of significant knowledge. This spirit is expressed in its art and its mythology, and may also evolve over time, so that the paideuma of a Neolithic agricultural people may be different from what it was when they were hunters and gatherers, or that of Renaissance Europe different from that of medieval Europe.[41]

Campbell clearly seized on this idea, to which his interest in myth, and his hardly less lively interest in art and literature, fitted so well. What was important was to look not so much at the dreary technical details of a story or sculpture as at the fascinating message encoded in its overall structures and leading archetypes. Who is on top? Who is the rebellious hero? What is the dominant representation of the divine, the mother goddess or the patriarchal male or what? Campbell was also much impressed by Frobenius's notion of three stages of human development, a concept outlined twice, for example, in his 1972 *Myths To Live By*.[42]

The first stage was that of primitive food gatherers, of nonliterate hunters, gatherers, planters. The second stage, commencing around 3500 B.C.E., was that of the "Monumental" cultures: Egypt, Mesopotamia, China, Greece, Rome, medieval Europe, modernity. All these civilizations were centered on a supposed divine cosmic order, often buttressed by a personal God, that gave the template for human achievement: cities were modeled on the those of heaven, empires were built in the name of God.

But today a new stage is emerging, a "global" culture based on realization that the sacred is within. Following Frobenius, Campbell also believed that we are now entering a new age, a third age of the spirit like that once prophesied by Joachim of Flora, a dawning "global age," an age of "boundless horizons" made up of the coming together of all the formerly separate cultural worlds of humanity. This idea seems to have especially crystallized for Campbell in interaction with the visionary sixties, despite his professed antagonism to some of its values. In this rising era, as in that esoteric decade, religion would move in a mystical direction. The laws and gods ruling Earth will be seen no longer as "out there," but within the hearts of humankind. In his most idealistic moods, Campbell no doubt viewed himself as a premier prophet of that new spiritual dispensation.

Campbell was clearly drawn to this modern version of the coming spiritual age. The first benighted stage had seen the sacred in the plant and the animal, the second projected it "aloft among the planets and beyond," but the third put it where it belonged, "in men, right here on earth." Its advent would be sung in modern myths, by men and women freed from the props of formal religion.

The last chapter of Creative Mythology, significantly called "The Death of 'God' and the Earthly Paradise," tells us that the "technological determinants" of the new age would be scientific method and power-driven machine, even as writing and "coercive government" had been for the Monumental age. Furthermore:

> The distinguishing feature of the new mankind—as heralded in the lives and works of those through whom it was announced—has already been suggested in Wolfram's Parzival: that is to say, a mankind of individuals, self-moved to ends proper to themselves, directed not by the constraint and noise of others, but each by his own inner voice.[43]

Campbell then cited José Ortega y Gasset to the same effect, and also Joachim, Ralph Waldo Emerson, Thomas Mann, and Paul Tillich— a modern gnostic catalogue of saints.

The Leo Frobenius to whom Campbell owed this vision, incidentally, had an unusual career. Never an academic in the strict sense, he was an explorer and collector who spent much of his life in the African bush on expeditions sponsored by museums and universities. Single-mindedly preoccupied with African culture, he took no interest in the social and political aspects of that changing continent, and though not racist himself did not argue with Eurocentric assumptions characteristic of his time. Indeed, during the Weimar years Frobenius was a member of the "Doorn circle," which met regularly with the exiled Kaiser Wilhelm II at his Dutch retreat for conversations on anthropology and archaeology, topics in which the former emperor had a lively interest. Although he may have had private reservations, Frobenius must also have listened courteously to the windy diatribes on religion, Jews, the superiority and inferiority of races, and the classical origins of German civilization, with which his imperial host, once described as a man of half-baked ideas and fully-formed prejudices, was well known to afflict his guests. Later, during the Nazi regime, Frobenius served as director of the Frankfort enthographical museum until his death in 1938.[44]

After reading Frobenius, Campbell wrote:

> I learned that the essential form of the myth is a cycle, and that this cycle is a symbolic representation of the form of the soul, and that in the dreams and fancies of modern individuals (who have been brought up along the lines of a rational, practical education) these myth-symbols actually reappear—giving testimony of a persistence, even into modern times, of the myth power.[45]

It was in the spirit of these words that Campbell was a student of modern mythology too. Always more of a literary scholar and critic at heart than a folklorist, much less an anthropologist, he always preferred to deal with myths as retailed by great writers and tellers from Homer and Hesiod through the medieval exponents of the Grail story to Joyce and Mann. In reviewing *The Hero with a Thousand Faces*, Stanley Edgar Hyman remarked that to Campbell folk literature is inferior, "undeveloped or degenerate" in relation to the "great mythologies" of the higher civilizations, which of course usually had worthy renditions.[46] The relative distance of literary myth from "the people" was no great price to pay. For if, as Campbell believed, myths tell truly universal truth, that truth is as true for a poet or novelist of the first magnitude as for anyone else, and that writer can probably tell it better, in more truly universal language.

In that light one may view Campbell's deep interest in two makers of contemporary mythologies, James Joyce and Thomas Mann, examples of consciousness shaped by the morphology of modernity. Campbell appreciated the Irish and the German novelists' ability to paint modern life as fractured and imperfect. Yet even the seemingly secular, unheroic, and comfortably middle-class lives of their characters come across as profoundly significant because the reader is also led to believe each contains an undying spark of the eternal flame. Campbell did not consider the shattering of heroic illusions in these modern literary myths as inconsistent with the archetypal thrust of mythology. To him the supreme modern meaning of myth was that all the imperfect persons we see around us, even the most vacant bourgeois, still have within them the same divine fire that animated the mythic hero. In *Myths To Live By*, Campbell points to Tonio Kröger in Mann's novel of the same name as such a hero, commenting:

> Perfection in life does not exist; and if it did, it would be—not lovable but admirable, possibly even a bore. Perfection lacks personality. (All the Buddhas, they say, are perfect, perfect and therefore alike. Having gained release from the imperfections of this world, they have left it, never to return. But the Bodhisattvas, remaining, regard the lives and deeds of this imperfect world with eyes and tears of compassion.) For let us note well (and here is the high point of Mann's thinking on this subject): what is lovable about any human being is precisely his imperfections. The writer is to find the right words for these and to send them like arrows to their mark—but with a balm, the balm of love, on every point. For the mark, the imperfection, is exactly what is personal, human, natural, in the object, and the umbilical point of its life.[47]

At the same time, Campbell followed Mann's political (or "unpolitical") thinking up to a point, for he believed it was precisely Mann's unpolitical nature that made possible the deep humanism, the universal understanding behind these remarkable words. It was that transcendent care for the lovable uniqueness in every imperfect human that Campbell persuaded himself Mann had abandoned as he took a "partisan" antinazi stand in the thirties. In the twenties Campbell, as we have seen, had been deeply influenced by Mann's *Reflections of an Unpolitical Man* (1918), a pessimistic end-of-the-war piece that defended the traditional state against democracy, and creative irrationalism against "flat" reason. Mann then called for moderns to develop personal internal culture despite the shallow values of civilization. In his journals Campbell wrote of that work:

> Mann spoke . . . however, against the one-sidedness of every political achievement, and celebrated the two-eyed, ironic powers of the artist. The strictly balanced deed of the artist's pen or brush represented a heroic clear-sightedness, and a salubrious affirmation of the balanced truth against every possible tendentious politicization.[48]

However, as Mann changed his ideas on politics and society in opposition to Nazism, Campbell withdrew into a moral equivocalism that tended to say only that faults obtain on both sides in the great ideological battles of the day. The true artist ought to observe the human scene from a transcendent perspective rather than choose sides. This view was expressed, of course, in the 1940 talk "Permanent Human Values." As time went on, Campbell became only more contrarian about the matter. He refused to let it die even in the different world of the decades after the war, except when he took sides against communism.

In *The Inner Reaches of Outer Space*, at the end of his life, he defiantly went out of his way to cite Mann's *Reflections* once again, long after the tract's author had himself left its stance far behind. This time the World War I essay was quoted to the effect that economic and military imperialism, conjoined with "hypocritical democracy," were more the legacy of Great Britain and the United States than of Germany. One can sense Campbell's Irish blood rising as he records Mann saying in 1918 that "To my soul's satisfaction, I find nothing in German history to compare with England's treatment of Ireland." It is with obvious disappointment that the American must also note that during World War II, as England stood almost alone against the Nazi menace, Mann had considerably changed his tune, now going so far as to say, "Can it be denied, that the world, in so far as it is English, finds itself in right good hands?"

Campbell then cites two other writers in support of Mann's 1918 views, men who remained faithful to the spirit of those views even amid the flames of World War II: the American expatriate poet and admirer of Mussolini Ezra Pound, who "was at that time in Italy, broadcasting condemnations of the Western Alliance that were very much like those of Mann's World War I *Betrachtungen*," and the also controversial T. S. Eliot. Campbell then returns to the question of eyes, quoting Strindberg to the effect that "politicians are one-eyed cats." But according to the mythologist, the artist sees with two eyes, "and alone to him is the center revealed: that still point, as Eliot saw, where the dance is. 'And there is only the dance.' "[49]

On the same theme, in *Creative Mythology* Campbell had cited a radio address Mann had addressed to the German people in December of 1941, on the eve of Pearl Harbor as it turned out. Campbell reproduced intact the lengthy catalogue of Nazi atrocities to date about which the novelist had informed any of his countrymen courageous enough to listen to him. Then, explaining his own role, Mann had remarked that the artist lives and works not for the glory of his country but out of individual "immanent need." Those last words Campbell italicized.

Campbell then went on to comment that Hitler's "monstrous empire" had now been replaced by "Stalin's no less monstrous slave state," to which was added "another Asian monster," the Chinese, and with it "a scientifically enforced Asiatization of world affairs." What does that mean? "This is the old Bronze age world image of an absolutely inexorable, mathematical cosmology of which the social order is but an aspect . . . both Indian and Chinese." To this is now added the "equally inexorable Marxian notion of the logic of history." The leading challenge to these monstrous but outdated social machines was, not unexpectedly, "the politics of the free individual."[50] One thinks of the small but heroic and individualist rebel alliance in *Star Wars* confronting the vast machines and faceless storm troopers of the evil empire.

Now we must confront directly the issue of anti-Semitism in Campbell's life and work. Robert A. Segal, in an article "Joseph Campbell on Jews and Judaism," has assembled a full collection of evidence to the effect that Campbell disliked both Jews and Judaism.[51] There are accounts of verbal diatribes on the subject from students and colleagues at Sarah Lawrence, and many illustrations from his books of the roundhouse condemnations of ancient Israel's violence and exclusivity of which Campbell was capable. "Campbell's would-be scholarly characterizations of Judaism evince all the stock anti-Semitic epithets." Judaism is said to be chauvinistic, fossilized, nationalistic, sexist, patriarchal, and antimystical. Even primal peoples, such as Campbell's beloved Native Americans, are said to "possess a broader vision than Jews." And these attitudes, Segal noted, became only more pronounced in the author's latest books.

As he became more interested in, and positive toward, feminine values in myth, Campbell spoke of the ancient Hebrew conquest of Canaan as a truly egregious example of pastoral fighting people subjugating the feminine and promoting warlike attitudes. In *The Power of Myth*, explaining the origins of the dolorous patriarchal monotheism that has long afflicted Western culture, Campbell declared that "The Yahweh cult was a specific movement in the Hebrew community, which finally won. This was a pushing through of a certain temple-bound god against the nature cult, which was celebrated all over the place. And this imperialistic thrust of a certain in-group culture is continued in the West."[52] In the "Secularization of the Sacred" essay, as we have seen, modern secularization is presented as an affirmation of values found in early Celtic-Germanic and Greco-Roman culture, which were later weakened by Christianity with its "Semitic" absolutizing of the particular sacred and its subsequent dualism.[53] In a significant article, Maurice Friedman touched on some of the same material as Segal, including Campbell's notorious encounter with Martin Buber, and also noted the mythologist's lack of attention to the Jewish holocaust—surely a deed whose blackness was of mythological dimensions, and which has shaped subsequent consciousness as certainly as has the bright mythologies of heroes and outer space.[54]

Yet there are other perspectives in Campbell's work. In the introduction to *The Masks of God: Primitive Mythology*, Campbell had referred to the destructive power of mythological racism and Aryanism in such writers of the nineteenth and twentieth century as Gobineau and Chamberlain, and he drew from them the moral that "mythology is no toy for children," but can have explosive power in our own as well as any other age.[55] On the same page he wrote: "And the world is now far too small, and men's stake in sanity too great, for any more of those old games of Chosen Folk (whether of Jehovah, Allah, Wotan, Manu, or the Devil) by which tribesmen were sustained against their enemies in the days when the serpent could still talk."

The major biography of Campbell to date, Stephen and Robin Larsen's *A Fire in the Mind*, states that Campbell was anti-Zionist but not anti-Semitic.[56] One relevant issue about which some misunderstanding seems to have arisen is that of Freud versus Jung in Campbell's work. Brendan Gill, in the *New York Review* article, claimed that Campbell liked Jung but disliked Freud, and thought this had to do with anti-Jewish prejudice; but it seems to me that even the original premise here can be questioned. One of Campbell's most powerful pieces of writing is a long section on "The Psychology of Myth" in *Primitive Mythology*, a real tour de force interpretation of myth in highly Freudian terms, from birth trauma to breast to discovery of genital sexuality. The most direct influence there was that very orthodox Freudian anthropologist Géza Róheim, to whose *festschrift* Campbell also made a significant contribution.[57] Róheim, and behind him Freud, is also prominent in *The Hero with a Thousand Faces*; we have noted the quote from Freud in the prologue to that work. But Campbell always seemed to accept the common wisdom that Freud is the best guide to the first half of life, Jung for the second. While Campbell appears to have become more Jungian and less Freudian as the years advanced, there is certainly no evidence of nonacademic bias. At the same time, his bias against the Hebrew God, and that deity's manifestations in three religions, is evident repeatedly. In the last year of his life, when he finally got a computer for writing, he named it Jahweh. "A lot of rules and no mercy," he explained.[58]

Yet it is not quite true that Judaism was always portrayed negatively. In *Hero* there are a few neutral or even positive citations. A "tender lyric from the miserable east-European ghettos" is compared favorably to Jonathan Edwards's portrayal of an angry God, at the end of the chapter on atonement.[59] We must also not forget Campbell's close and highly fruitful relations with Heinrich Zimmer and Kurt Wolff, both exiles from Hitler's Germany because of Jewish connections. Anti-Semitism was not his only prejudice: his Anglophobia was hardly less entrenched; England, English culture, and English persons also receive little if any favorable notice in Campbell's corpus. (Even his beloved Arthur and the Grail stories are cited mostly in German versions.) At the same time it cannot be denied that Campbell had some sort of recurrent emotional problem with both Jews and Judaism. Like the disturbing inability as late as the 1980s to forgive Thomas Mann for turning antinazi a half-century earlier, issues involving Jews were returned to and gnawed on over and over, more and more bitingly as time advanced. One is left with an unpleasant feeling of something very narrow lurking within the broad mind of the world-scanning mythologist.

A similar narrowness of focus is apparent as Campbell turned his capacity for creative mythology to the America he idealized. The mythic model American is clearly the free-enterprise "rugged individualist" of a romanticized past, one continuous with the earlier Grail quest, or with Tristan and Isolde's quest for authentic human love. What Campbell admired was somehow not the type of heroic individualism represented in his own day by, say, a Rosa Parks or a draft resister. How Campbell's political worldview was reconciled with his disdain for the Judeo-Christian tradition, out of which at least some of Western individualism derives, is not explained.

In the Moyers interviews, reproduced in *The Power of Myth*, Campbell talked at some length about the American "myth," or rather myths, for he held that the United States in its pluralism has never had a single, unified mythology. The classic American goals of life, liberty, and the pursuit of happiness, he said, are *for the individual*—but are buttressed by the cosmic orientation of the Great Seal, reproduced on the dollar bill. Its four-sided pyramid represents the earth, and the descending eagle, the bird of Zeus, indicates the "downcoming of the god into the field of time."[60] By now Campbell was clearly well beyond any serious scholarly study of the background of particular myths. He was concerned only to preach his sermon to the world.[61]

In the end, Joseph Campbell's political thought can only be considered a collection of unassimilated fragments, some brilliant, some not thoroughly thought through, some frankly based on prejudice. Toward the close of his life he seemed to realize that he was politically out of step with both left and right, and—like, eventually, Jung and Eliade as well—ready to give up on the whole political world. In a late interview he said:

> I don't know what politics can do. I think it's fair to say that I'm a little bit discouraged by the people who are involved in the political life of this country. I begin to feel it has been betrayed. Its potentialities have been sold for values that are inscrutable to me.[62]

This is not the place to psychoanalyze Joseph Campbell, but two features of his character may be noted. First, from childhood, he was possessed by a dream or fantasy of idealized, and individualized, Native American life. Together with this, he had, like some irrepressible young brave, an incorrigibly rebellious side, well articulated in his saying that he was Western in India and Eastern in New York.

Second, one notes his revulsion against the filth of the world, countered by a Germanic passion for order and personal cleanliness.

This trait was early registered on his college-age trip to Mexico and Central America, and presumably was expressed also in the long-lasting sexual inhibition his biographers mention. The syndrome was recovered on his later trip to India, where his interest in its ancient culture combined with deep distaste for the subcontinent's dirt, beggary, and inefficiency. It all ran together in his mind and left him feeling polluted. Whatever he took from India, or from other cultures, had to be on his own terms and leave him personally unstained. Individualism, standing apart from tribe and sect as an observer of the collective myths of others, and a preacher of those myths in forms that exalted the individual, was what was left.

## POLITICS TO LIVE BY

Campbell discussed politics overtly less than did Jung or Eliade in published writings. But he let broadly political views, together with his rebellious individualism and various social and quasi-political prejudices, permeate his general writing more than did the other two. It was clear he thought societies should have common myths, but they ought primarily to facilitate the self-realization of the individual, especially in the role of hero. Myth was therefore the wellspring of individual enterprise more than of collectivism. It was clear also that he increasingly thought even accessible collective myths ought not to be those of established religious institutions. Undoubtedly just for that reason, unlike a thousand institutional preachers, he apparently saw little individualist inspiration in the stories of David or Jesus. He looked instead, no doubt quite intentionally, to such half-underground alternatives as tales of Camelot and the Grail, stories powerful just because they were unblessed by scripture or pulpit, or the medieval ecclesiastical establishment.

Where did this leave Campbell politically? Maybe with Libertarianism, although participation in a small and disputatious political sect would not have been his style. He even had problems with Republicanism, although he considered himself a "classic" conservative.

But two kinds of conservatives are to be found in modern society. It is a matter of what past one wants to conserve. Tory conservatives yearn primarily for the traditionalist "organic" society, hierarchical, largely rural, religion based, and in many ways quite authoritarian, which they imagine to have obtained in the Middle Ages. This is the conservatism of Burke and in certain respects of Jung and Eliade. Then there is the Whig sort of conservative, far more common in the United States than the Tory. These conservatives are fundamentally more concerned with economic than social values; they idealize not the Middle Ages but the free enterprise, laissez-faire economics of the early industrial revolution. Whig conservatives like to think of themselves as rugged individualists, and insofar as they are social conservatives it is because they value the work ethic and productive stability they associate with traditional propriety.

Campbell was really mostly the latter, the Whiggish sort of conservative. Although he dealt with what, to the Tory or Germanic volkish mind, was the archaic and medieval raw material of the other conservatism, he managed—apparently hardly realizing he was doing so—to follow Jung by individualizing that material into models for personal inner realization and success.

What kind of society would Campbell's view of myth construct? Not Jung's Burkeanism of tradition and reasonable democracy, or Eliade's newfound American utopia of level pluralism. Rather, it would be a society of heroes like the principals of *Star Wars* who follow their own myths, and a ground crew of those who are not heroes but who sing about heroes, and the songs keep the social order together. For while Campbell might have liked a Jeffersonian utopia free of government coercion and egalitarian, he would probably have realized that, in a truly unconstrained social order, elites, by birth or talent or more likely both, will like himself rise naturally to positions of greater wealth and influence than the ordinary. But all of that will be according to myth. Whatever one does in this society, one identifies with the mythic archetype of that role: the soldier or policeman with the primal swordsman, the scientist with the white-coated heroes of his kind, the mother with the Great Mother one with the earth, lovers with Tristan and Isolde.

It would be a society like that of the tribes of Native America: the lone warrior and vision quester, the sacred dance complete with ritual clowns around the fire. A century or two in the future, it might be set in outer space, an epic of brave explorers of strange planets and staunch settlers conquering new worlds. In the process, they would be defying and defeating the armadas of collectivists who, like the Anglo whites, sought to reduce their lives to bureaucratic forms and their songs to paper music.

This is a fantasy, and an unlikely one at that. *Star Wars* notwithstanding, the brave new world of the conquest of outer space, or of any reasonable future for our overpopulated planet, will require cooperation and organization on a scale that would need to be managed by a powerful government, not by individual heroics. If a speculative book like Freeman Dyson's *Imagined Worlds* is on the mark, the technological creation of collective human minds through "radio telepathy," group minds and personalities that would prevail because they would be far more powerful than any individual could be, may be possible in as little as a thousand years—and their coming would mean the ultimate defeat of the individualist creed.[63] Indeed, Campbell himself was increasingly aware that he represented social values with more past than future, however much he argued otherwise.

There is, however, more to Campbell and politics than individualism. One must also look at the concept of myth as a political reality and political force. This is important, and is on a different level of discourse than the supposed message of the particular myths one favors. Three points may be made about political myth as Campbell presented it. First, societies need a cohesive story about who a people are, what they can accomplish, and what their deep-level values are. Second, the social myth can only be received and employed by individuals through individual choice. Third, dominant myths and symbols can change, and must as one order gives place to another, especially the coming third age of the Spirit.

Campbell would doubtless argue that the spiritual age will actually require the midwifery of apparently conservative politics, since the requisite emergence of the sacred within, rather than in the plant or animal or in the sky, calls for that near-total freedom for individual creativity and enterprise that Campbell considered the core value of conservatism. This, he considered, is the political position that fits better than any other the nonpartisan, antiideology, neutral-observer posture of the early Mann or the two-eyed artist. He may never have fully confronted the contradiction this stance presented in respect to the totalitarian regime Mann had fled, though he made up for that in his opposition to Stalin and Mao. At the end of his life he had only begun to face a similar contradiction in U.S. conservatism, in respect to such issues as its alliance with fundamentalist Christianity and the exploitation of nature.

But, however laden with contraries in the real world, Campbell's politics will have an impact in proportion to the extent his stories shape the fantasies and dreams of men and women, which they will then enact in their own ways in the twenty-first century. In a world of stories past, present, and to come, these will be dreams reminding us that our psychic origins are buried deep in a fabulous past, that in the present one can follow one's own bliss and become whatever one really is within, and that the unimaginable future of spaceships and heroes will be made for people who can follow inner joy wherever it leads.

# 5

# CONCLUSION: THE MYTH OF MYTH

What does the saga of the twentieth-century mythologists mean for the politics of myth and the myths of politics?

First, like many reconstructions of favored pasts, their enterprise said more about the time of their reconstruction of the past than of times past. Mythological scholarship in the nineteenth and twentieth centuries has been in deep tension between a meaning-laden assessment of myth—romantic in foundation and based on a view that myth is the voice of primordial organic society—and the kind of Enlightenment perspective more inclined to laugh at its absurdities and, at best, to make it a matter of philological and history-of-religion investigation. Victorians like Max Müller, or the pioneer anthropologists Edward Tylor and Sir James Frazer, come to mind as representatives of the latter camp. They saw in myth little more than a disease of language, prerational science, or the magic that preceded religion even as religion preceded science.

Other nineteenth-century figures, particular Germans like von Herder or Schelling, saw the significance of myth quite differently. They were the spiritual ancestors of Jung, Eliade, and Campbell. In their eyes, the distant world evoked by myth was numinous with significance for understanding the whole panorama of human life past and present, not merely of scholarly interest. Myths were like cryptic gnostic revelations, bound to be of unimaginable importance if one could only crack their code. Yet the fathers of modern mythology were also persons of the modern academy. This meant that, in their intellectual training, they were children far more of the Enlightenment than of the romantic reaction so far as scientific and scholarly values were concerned. They had to use modern language and methods in their mythological endeavors though their ultimate goals might have been better understood as a branch of gnosticism or mysticism. Such reactionary sympathies as they possessed stemmed from semiconscious and unresolved tension between the nature of their material, as it came out of a luminous but unretrievable archaic worldview lit by romanticism, and the modernist milieu within which they worked and whose concepts of knowledge they largely accepted.

The romantic school harbored within itself a further tension between the individual and the political potentials of myth as modern medicine, a cleavage closely related to what we have called apocalyptic and gnostic uses of myth. Should one really undertake a revolutionary rebuilding of the collective, or heal a smattering of individuals plucked out of the spiritual emptiness of the modern world? One can perceive in our mythologists the two eyes of which Campbell spoke. One eye turned to the social role of myth, perhaps envisioning the psychic security of a new organic society and/or the glory of a society based on a newly empowered individualism. The other eye, chastened, recoiling from the dragons that lurked in such dreams, looked back to individual therapy and private life for all practical purposes. While that turning toward inwardness might mean abandoning collective dreams for the sake of the sometimes despised modern individual, it also meant potentially making all the mythologist's clients or students heroes insofar as they enacted myth in their own lives.

While myth may have universal themes, concrete myths are always particular, of particular cultures and times, pointing to the specific form wisdom took in a certain people on a certain soil. Yet the second of François Lyotard's metanarratives of modernity, the unity of knowledge, evokes the universal languages—that is, those of science and social science—by which particular cultures and their particular knowledges can be interpreted universally. To these scholarly tongues the particulars are subordinated, for it is the universal that gives power. As we have noted, the modern university was above all the custodian and power dispenser of both of Lyotard's modern metanarratives—progress and the unity of knowledge. Our three mythologists were university people or closely related to university ways of thinking. Archaic myth was undeniably an outsider to the cognitive university world of nineteenth- and early and middle twentieth-century modernity. On the surface at least, myth is that which scientific progress has progressed beyond. From the scientific point of view, myth does not unify knowledge but fragments it into a thousand faces. Myth might be studied, but only as "mythology," that is, in a way that subordinated it to the metanarratives, treating it as prescientific and bringing to it the tools of the unified knowledge of modern science, social science, and philology.

The three mythologists were enough persons of modernity to profess to do this. As scholars, they took the panoptic privileged position of the modern observer, surveying the world past and present to bring all its myths into their purview, and subordinating them to various kinds of hermeneutics or styles of interpretation. But Jung, Eliade, and Campbell were not able to subject myth simply to the rationalist reductionism of the Victorians. They lived a little too late for that, in a world that seemed far more dangerous and nonrational than Queen Victoria's. Over against their modernity, the mythical world, the world of a cosmos that is alive and harmonizes soul and matter, in which processes of individual transformation obtain, and where heroes go on adventures of ultimate significance, seemed an appealing "otherness" to set beside the drab world of "mass man."

For by the midtwentieth century when the mythologists were in their prime, talk was rising to high decibels of how science and reason, far from unifying knowledge or humanity, had produced deep levels of alienation: humanity from nature, humanity from its own soul. The problems were becoming visible, but no antidote was at hand. Material progress was still happening, from jumbo jets to the computer revolution, but as the twentieth century advanced, hopes that it would, almost of itself, make human life unequivocally better and happier were clearly fading. It may be, first Jung and then Eliade and Campbell thought, that the archaic peoples whose language was myth had in some ways done it better.

But to make myth accessible to modernity as a remedy, it also had to become sufficiently modern to be heard: it had to be made compatible with what was left of the idea of progress, and speak some species of universal tongue. The mythologists sensed the vast saving potential of their archaic material, yet they were also people of their time. They could not simply become archaic, not even to the extent of the noisiest of volkists and nationalists, most of whom were nonacademic. Rather, the mythical empowerment would need to be advanced through the *means* of modernity, which meant in effect through the metanarratives of progress toward emancipation, and of the unity of knowledge. Whatever the case in archaic times, twentieth-century myth had to bespeak some kind of progress, individual or social, and become a universal language. It could talk the language of national redemption, or of personal psychotherapy, both familiar themes by midcentury. The mythologists explored both of those options, ending up more with the latter than the former.

The three mythologists lived for the most past before the frank deconstructive fragmentation of postmodernism; they lived in a time when it was still possible to think in terms of a grand theory or an overarching symbol system that could unify the world. But they did live at a late stage of modernism when scientific rationalism had sufficiently broken down that the proffered symbol system could, in fact, be mythical and nonrational, unifying history and experience in terms of the worlds of myth rather than of science or reason. It would be scientific in the sense that it was based on modern comparativist and psychological studies, but its appeal would be to levels of human nature deeper and more powerful than the rational. It would, in a word, say that all myths were one, that behind their thousand faces they had in effect one message, based on the psychic unity of humanity, and proclaimed one intrapsychic path to salvation. This was essentially the point of Jung's archetypes, Eliade's structuralism, and Campbell's one message behind all myths.

What about the myth of myth itself? Whether there was ever such a thing as living primordial myth in the sense the mythologists envisioned it may be questioned. Myth as we know it is always received from an already distant past, literary (even if only oral literature), hence a step away from primal simplicity. To be sure, such myths as the Iliad, the Odyssey, and the Aeneid in classical Greece and Rome, the Kojiki as it became a scripture of Japanese nationalism, or the Arthuriad in Tudor and Victorian England had, officially, broad cultural meaning, but they were hardly truly stories of "the folk." Even if widely disseminated in schools and at government-sponsored rallies, it was not the same. As any schoolboy knows, there are stories one learns in the classroom, and then there are the stories one tells in the playground to one's peers.

"Official" myths like these are inevitably reconstructions from snatches of folklore and legend, artistically put together with an eye for drama and meaning. But the real mythic images of a society, those that are so fresh they are not yet recognized as "myth" or "scripture," are fragmentary, imagistic rather than verbal, emergent, capable of forming many different stories at once—like the "myths" of UFOs in contemporary society, or the different ways in which the Civil War was told in different parts of the United States in the first generation after its end. Eventually perhaps UFOs will resolve into a new gnostic myth of cosmic salvation, as C. G. Jung anticipated, even as the Civil War has gradually, and still imperfectly, become a single myth of national crisis and healing.

It was at this last stage that myths took the form in which they were received by the three mythologists. For them, myth and therapeutic or saving purpose were inseparable because they saw myth only in its "finished" paradigmatic role, and so as something that inevitably came out of the past and calls us back to it, as to an Eliadean illud tempus of primordial power and singleness of heart. A myth, to them, was a story that came from elsewhere but had universal meaning. Its saving power came from the fact that it was *not* the "official" myth of its environing society, but like a gnostic savior, like Campbell's unofficial Western scripture of the Arthuriad to set against the West's official Judeo-Christian Bible, came from realms of gold elsewhere to succour us in our need. But a society's real myths are far less formally constructed even than the "loyal opposition" of recognized alternatives.

The mythologists' work was of great value, but we need also to be able to see that living myth, "creative mythology" in Campbell's term, is necessarily scattered, fragmentary, and ambivalent, even as are the stories of the personal dreams to which the mythologists often compared myth. Living myth tells us where we are culturally, but it does not tell us where to go, or what is right and wrong, until it has itself slipped into the past to become, officially or by consensus, received myth. To put it another way, myth is really a meaning category on the part of hearers, not intrinsic in any story in its own right. Myth in this sense is itself a myth.

However, the mythologists believed that a common myth was possible in the twentieth century, and desperately necessary. They viewed this task differently: Jung saw myth as an analytic tool for understanding and healing both history and the individual. Eliade at first yearned for a modern political and culture-creating myth of national resurrection for his country, but in the end he saw myth as better solace for an exile than ideology for a nation. Campbell wanted myths to have a role in the moral reconstruction of America, but he perceived that there is not just one American myth, though he had his favorites: individualism for the past, space for the future. In the end, all three came to prefer a deeply personal, intrapsychic role for myth over a political career. If myth helped society hold together, that would be because a sufficient number of people had interiorized and made their own myths thrusting in a similar direction: parallel individualism.

Even this upshot, however, is of some political significance. Whether or not myths from out of the past can really provide workable models for contemporary society, they can have certain definable functions.

First, myth is diagnostic. The idealized world of myth can suggest, as it did to the three mythologists, that actual modern society is too given over to one-dimensional "mass man." It is, depending on how one looks it at, too "atomistic" or too collectivized; but in any case the ills of modernity call for the depth and cohesion of an authentic "organic" society, and the heroism of the true individual.

Second, on another level the mythologists are able to remind us that though hopes for a remythologized world may be impractical, the hope itself must be protected, if need be politically. Their own lives and labors tell us that a society needs to be safe for individual myths and dreams. Much is lost if there is no place for the enhanced and enriched individualism of a person who has inwardly taken on a mythic identity, though she or he may be outwardly camouflaged as an ordinary modern person. What this entails politically, the mythologists seem to say, is a society based on a moderate and benign conservatism, wherein there is some access to tradition, where some honor is given symbols and values from the past, where there is freedom to read mythological books and to undertake private therapy, and the state has no heavy-handed mythological agenda of its own.

Third, the mythologists have found a way to make values and feelings very close to those of religion accessible to many at least partially secularized people. These persons are seekers who could accept the symbols and dramas of traditional religious lore as significant mythology, in Jung, Eliade, and Campbell's sense and from them as modern "wise men," but who would have more difficulty with the dogma of institutionalized religion. In them the spiritual quest is as alive as ever, but the literate, universalizing, and also individualizing language of the mythologists speaks to them better than churches or temples. That is because in the mythologists the question of *truth* can always be sidestepped; they emphasize instead *meaning*, and by meaning is denominated that which comes from a universal source but is congruous with one's own dreams and deepest significant fantasies. In a real sense, then, the mythical meanings articulated by the mythologists are subjectively self-validating, making irrelevant issues of objective or rational truth in religion. In a semisecularized and rampantly pluralized world in which the hold of objective religious truth is increasingly problematic, but in which religious questions and yearnings are certainly real, mythology is a viable and not ignoble alternative to a stark choice between dogmatic religion and sheer secularism.

What does this leave that is of enduring value?

Much is appealing and profoundly true in the sermons of the mythologists to the modern world. Undoubtedly that world is often alienating and dehumanizing, denying people easy access to the depths of their own souls. Myth, like all great literature, can become universal, transcending particular cultural settings to provide general models of the human predicament and ways out of it. This is true even though the mythologists, in their generalized reverence for their subject, did not always take into account that myth, like everything human, can be of quite varied moral worth: the Aztec myth by which the sun must be fed daily the blood of sacrificial victims, or the Babylonian myth, criticized by feminist scholars, in which Marduk created the world by carving up the body of the female entity Tiamat, are not necessarily to be received on the same level as love-suffused stories of Krishna or Jesus.

Moreover myth, unlike much later "civilized" literature, has one peculiar characteristic: it deals almost entirely in generic, "archetypal" categories, reducing individuals (and races or peoples) to types and roles, stereotyping them as Hero or Trickster, as Good or Evil. To be sure, mythology teaches us that abstractions are not the solutions to problems, but merely their distancing, and that the real truth is in story. This should mean that one must also avoid the pseudoabstraction of story that is merely stereotyping didacticism, as myth can be when it is no more than archetypal. We need also the complex humanism of Thomas Mann.

Here lies the great danger in applying mythic categories to contemporary affairs, above all political. The mythologists were aware of the danger, but not always sufficiently. The problem was not only their occasionally succumbing to dubious political myths, or in thinking of collectives of people from Jews to Storm Troopers in generic "bloc" terms, but also in a more general tendency to think of the modern world in a stereotyping, homogeneous, and pessimistic way—as mass man. They thereby came to peremptorily dismiss the world as hopeless for any kind of salvation but individual, or through some (equally hopeless) corporate reversion to the mythic world in a healthy sense. It was too late for that, and the pseudomythic worlds were far more dangerous than the ailment. But both alternatives left the mythologists political conservatives in effect: the individual-salvation option being politically reactionary by default, the reversionary endeavor reactionary in concrete political terms.

In summation, then, we need to listen to the mythologists in their wisdom, and make the world safe for myth and dream. But we need not expect to be saved by myth. We ought also to read the signs of the times and extrapolate from them our own myths of the future, enjoying the same freedom as the people of the beginning to decide for ourselves what the best human future would be like.

# NOTES

## CHAPTER 1. MYTH, GNOSIS, AND MODERNITY

1. Thomas Willard, "Archetypes of the Imagination," in Alvin A. Lee and Robert D. Denham, ed., *The Legacy of Northrop Frye*. Toronto: University of Toronto Press, 1994, pp. 15–27. See also, e.g., Northrop Frye, "Archetype" and "Jungian Criticism," in *The Harper Handbook to Literature*. With Sheridan Baker and George Perkins. New York: Harper, 1985; and relevant portions of Frye's major works, such as *Anatomy of Criticism*. Princeton, N.J.: Princeton University Press, 1957. On the general topic see Jos van Meurs and John Kidd, *Jungian Literary Criticism, 1920–1980: An Annotated Critical Bibliography of Works in English*. Metuchen, N.J.: Scarecrow Press, 1988, which contains twenty-eight entries on Frye.

2. "Personality," *Time*, July 7, 1952, p. 57.

3. Robert Hillyer, "Treason's Strange Fruit," *Saturday Review of Literature*, June 11, 1949, pp. 9–11+; letters July 9, p. 25; July 16, p. 23; and Sept. 10, p. 27.

4. "The New Radicals," *Time*, April 28, 1967, pp. 26–27.

5. Kurt Rudolph, *Gnosis*. San Francisco: Harper and Row, 1983, p. 56.

6. Hans Jonas, *The Gnostic Religion*. Boston: Beacon Press, 1958, especially the epilogue, "Gnosticism, Nihilism, and Existentialism."

7. Elaine Pagels, *The Gnostic Gospels*. New York: Random House, 1979, pp. xix–xx. Emphasis added by Pagels.

8. Harold Bloom, *The American Religion*. New York: Simon and Schuster, 1992, p. 49.

9. Eric Voegelin, *The New Science of Politics*. Chicago: University of Chicago Press, 1952.

10. Voegelin, *New Science of Politics*, pp. 166–67.

11. Ibid., p. 125 and passim.

12. Eric Voegelin, *Science, Politics and Gnosticism*. Chicago: Henry Regnery, 1968. Trans. of *Wissenschaft, Politik und Gnosis*, Munich: Koesel, 1959.

13. Erich Voegelin, *From Enlightenment to Revolution*. Durham, N.C.: Duke University Press,. 1995, pp. 28–29.

14. Robert A. Segal, "Introduction," Robert A. Segal, et al., ed. *The Allure of Gnosticism*. Chicago: Open Court, 1995, p. 6.

15. Stephen A. McKnight, "Voegelin and Gnostic Features of Modernity," in Robert A. Segal, *The Allure of Gnosticism*, pp. 137–38.

16. Kevin Michael Doak, *The Dream of Difference: The Japan Romantic School and the Crisis of Modernity*. Berkeley: University of California Press, 1994.

17. Jean-François Lyotard, *The Postmodern Condition: A Report on Knowledge*. Trans. Geoff Bennington and Brian Massumi. Minneapolis: University of Minnesota Press, 1984, p. ix.

18. Henry David Thoreau, *Journal*. New York: Dover Publications, 1962, v. 8, p. 134.

19. Jan de Vries, *The Study of Religion: A Historical Approach*. Trans. with intro. by Kees W. Bolle. New York: Harcourt, Brace and World, 1967, p. 46.

20. Joseph von Görres, *Mythengeschichte der asiatischen Welt*, I. Heidelberg: Mohr unt Zimmer, 1810, pp. 18–19. Trans. and cited in Jan de Vries, *The Study of Religion*, p. 48.

21. See Carl Otfried Müller, *Prolegomena zu einer wissenschafterlichen Mythologie*. Göttingen: Vandenhoek and Ruprecht, 1825, p. 293. Trans. and cited in Jan de Vries, *The Study of Religion*, p. 57.

22. Wilhelm Wundt, *Völkerpsychologie*; see Wundt, *Elements of Folk Psychology*. Trans. Edward Leroy Schaub. New York: Macmillan, 1916.

23. George L. Mosse, *The Crisis of German Ideology*. New York: Gosset and Dunlop, 1964, pp. 19–22.

24. Mosse, *Crisis of German Ideology*, pp. 42–43.

25. Karl Joel, *Nietzsche und die Romantik*. Jena: Diederichs, 1905.

26. On visionary German fiction and prophetic literature related to the rise of the Third Reich, see Jost Hermand, *Old Dreams of a New Reich: Volkish Utopias and National Socialism*. Trans. by Paul Levesque in collaboration with Stefan Soldovieri. Bloomington: Indiana University Press, 1992. This work presents valuable documentation and summaries of a vast array of rare volkish and nazi literature, such as nazi-oriented science fiction. However, the book is often hasty and must be used with some caution. For example, the one brief reference to C. G. Jung (pp. 237–38) portrays him one-sidedly as one who "extolled" the National Socialist movement, citing only a few out-of-context quotations in unspecified essays like "Wotan," to be discussed in our next chapter; Hermand's notes on this passage refer to no direct study of Jung's writings on his part but solely to an unnamed article in the popular magazine *Der Spiegel*.

27. Mark Girouard, *The Return to Camelot: Chivalry and the English Gentleman*. New Haven, Conn.: Yale University Press, 1981.

28. Heinrich von Treitschke, "A Word about Our Jews" (1879). Cited in Mosse, *Crisis of German Ideology*, p. 200.

29. Edward Said, *Orientalism*. New York: Pantheon, 1978.

30. For interesting essays studying this process in the case of Buddhism, see Donald S. Lopez, ed., *Curators of the Buddha: The Study of Buddhism under Colonialism*. Chicago: University of Chicago Press, 1995.

31. Luis O. Gomez, "Jung and the Indian East," in Lopez, ed., *Curators of the Buddha*, p. 211.

32. I am indebted to Zeev Sternhell, *The Birth of Fascist Ideology*. Princeton, N.J.: Princeton University Press, 1994, especially ch. 1, "George Sorel and the Antimaterialist Revision of Marxism," for background for this discussion of Sorel.

33. C. G. Jung, "The Undiscovered Self," *Collected Works*, vol. 16, *Civilization in Transition*. New York: Bollingen, 1964, p. 264. Orig. pub. 1957.

## CHAPTER 2. CARL GUSTAV JUNG AND WOTAN'S RETURN

1. See Sigmund Freud, *Civilizations and Its Discontents*. Trans. James Strachey. New York: Norton, 1961. Orig. German ed. 1930.

2. Paul A. Robinson, *The Freudian Left: Wilhelm Reich, Géza Róheim, Herbert Marcuse*. New York: Harper and Row, 1969, p. 122.

3. C. G. Jung, *Memories, Dreams, Reflections*. Recorded and edited by Aniela Jaffé. Trans. by Richard and Clara Winston. New York: Pantheon Books, 1961.

4. Peter Homans, *Jung in Context: Modernity and the Making of a Psychology*. Chicago: University of Chicago Press, 1979, p. 29.

5. Jung, *Memories, Dreams, Reflections*, pp. 86–88.

6. Ibid, p. 103.

7. C. G. Jung, "On the Psychology and Pathology of so-called Occult Phenomena," *Collected Works of C. G. Jung* (henceforth CW). Trans. R. C. F. Hull. New York: Pantheon Books, vol. 1, 1957, pp. 3–88. Orig. publ. 1902. See also F. X. Charet, *Spiritualism and the Foundations of C. G. Jung's Psychology*. Albany: State University of New York Press, 1993.

8. *Wandlungen und Symbole des Libido* (1912). Trans. as *The Psychology of the Unconscious* by Beatrice M. Hinkle. New York: Moffat, Yard, 1916, 1921. The causes of the break between Freud and Jung were more complex than the publication of this book alone. For some indicators see *The Freud/Jung Letters: The Correspondence between Sigmund Freud and C. G. Jung*. ed. William McGuire. Princeton, N.J.: Princeton University Press, 1974.

9. Jung, *Psychology of the Unconscious*, pp. 209, 295, 423.

10. Jung, *Psychology of the Unconscious*, pp. 128–29.

11. James Jackson Putnam, *Letters*. Cambridge, Mass.: Harvard University Press, 1971, p. 376. Cited in Richard Noll, *The Jung Cult*. Princeton, N.J.: Princeton University Press, 1994, p. 133.

12. Robert A. Segal, ed. *Jung on Mythology*. Princeton, N.J.: Princeton University Press, 1998. Introduction, p. 8.

13. C. G. Jung, "The Meaning of Psychology for Modern Man," CW 10, *Civilization in Transition*. New York: Pantheon, 1964, pp. 148–49. Orig. pub. 1933.

14. C. G. Jung, "The Role of the Unconscious," CW, vol. 10, *Civilization in Transition*, p. 26. Orig. pub. 1918.

15. Ibid.

16. C. G. Jung, "Psychological Types," CW 6, p. 10. Orig. pub. 1921.

17. All cited in C. G. Jung, *Psychology of the Unconscious*, pp. 23–24.

18. See Homans, *Jung in Context*, pp. 189–90.

19. C. G. Jung, "What India Can Teach Us," CW 10, p. 518. Orig. pub. 1939.

20. C. G. Jung, "The Dreamlike World of India." CW 10, p. 27. Orig. Pub. 1939.

21. C. G. Jung, "The Role of the Unconscious." CW 10, p. 27. Orig. pub. 1918.

22. For the uses to which folklore studies of this era were put in nazi Germany and Austria, see James R. Dow and Hannjost Lixfeld, ed. and trans., *The Nazification of an Academic Discipline: Folklore in the Third Reich*. Bloomington: Indiana University Press, 1994.

23. C. G. Jung, "Psychology and Literature." CW 15, p. 94. Orig. pub. 1930.

24. C. G. Jung, "Flying Saucers: A Modern Myth of Things Seen in the Skies," CW 10, pp. 307–436. Orig. pub. 1958.

25. C. G. Jung, *Answer to Job*. London: Routledge and Kegan Paul, 1954, p. 169.

26. C. G. Jung, "The Fight with the Shadow," CW 10, p. 219. Orig. pub. 1946.

27. C. G. Jung, "The Role of the Unconscious," CW 10, p. 13. Orig. pub. 1918.

28. José Ortega y Gasset, *The Revolt of the Masses.* New York: W. W. Norton, 1932, p. 11. Orig. Spanish ed. 1930.

29. Ibid., p. 133.

30. Ibid., p. 115.

31. Cited in Homans, *Jung in Context*, p. 180.

32. C. G. Jung, "After the Catastrophe," CW 10, pp. 200–201. Orig. pub. 1945.

33. Cf. C. G. Jung, "Epilogue to 'Essays on Contemporary Events,' " CW 10, p. 235. Orig. pub. 1946.

34. C. G. Jung, "The Undiscovered Self," CW 10, pp. 258–59. Orig. pub. 1957.

35. See C. G. Jung, "The Mana Personality," CW 7, orig. pub. 1912, rec. 1945.

36. At this point it may be appropriate to present Richard Noll's controversial books *The Jung Cult: Origins of a Charismatic Movement* (Princeton, N.J.: Princeton University Press, 1994) and *The Aryan Christ: The Secret Life of Carl Jung* (New York: Random House, 1997). Noll, clearly no sympathizer with Jung or his "cult," endeavored to show that the sage of Zurich created a "pagan" "Nietzschean religion" with himself as its divine "Christ" or Messiah. The roots of the "cult," as over against merely a school of analytic psychology, lay in the years around 1913–1916, when, in conjunction with the split from Freud, Jung underwent his spiritual crisis, and emerged from it fully armed with the archetypes and the individuating self adumbrated in the *Wandlungen* of 1912. In constructing this "religion" Jung is said to have drawn heavily not only from Nietzsche, but also from volkish mysticism, spiritualism, theosophy, and "sun worshiping" movements; from Ernst Haeckel's "monism" and vogues with names like *lebensphilosophie* and *naturphilosophie*, which embraced mythic and Bergsonian vitalist concepts.

There is no doubt that Jung was influenced by all of this, and was capable of bouts of megalomania. At the least, as *Myths, Dreams, and Reflections* shows, he viewed the outer world in very large part through the powerful lens of his own inner psychic life. But as a defining interpretation of Jung, it seems to this writer that Noll's case, like other simplistic charges about the man, collapses under the weight of the sheer complexity of the Jungian corpus. Only a selective reading of the material, informed by a prior hypothesis, could come to such unambiguous conclusions. The fact is that there is no consistent religious, political, or social doctrine in Jungiansim; only a consistent *approach* based on conviction that such outer expressions of the human psyche are but reflections of inner processes, in turn controlled by the archetypes of the unconsicous. But this mentality on the part of Jung as analytic therapist made his role more descriptive than prescriptive. Jung was not necessarily advocating everything he saw Abraxas or Wotan doing, nor was he always abjuring it. His mind, unlike those of activist bent, was far too inward and contemplàtive for that. Rather he was, like his No. 2, a world observer, and more and more prepared to direct the energies behind the world out of the turbulent stream of history and into personal transformations.

Attention should also be directed to serious and documented criticisms that have been made of Noll's scholarship about Jung, especially in Sonu Shamdasani, *Cult Fictions: C. G. Jung and the Founding of Analytic Psychology*. New York: Routledge, 1998.

37. Jeffrey Herf, *Reactionary Modernism*. Cambridge, England, and New York: Cambridge University Press, 1984, pp. 1, 2.

38. Andrew Hewitt, *Fascist Modernism*. Stanford, Calif.: Stanford University Press, 1993.

39. Heidegger, "Deutsche Männer und Frauen," cited in Herf, *Reactionary Modernism*, p. 113.

40. Rüdiger Safranski, *Martin Heidegger: Between Good and Evil*. Cambridge, Mass.: Harvard University Press, 1998, p. 254.

41. According to Safranski, by around 1939 Heidegger had "discovered that National Socialism was itself the problem whose solution he had once thought it was. He saw the furor of the new age rampant in National Socialism: technological frenzy, government, and organization—in other words, inauthenticity as total mobilization." Safranski, *Martin Heidegger*, p. 293.

42. C. G. Jung, "The Role of the Unconscious," CW 10, pp. 12–13. Orig. pub. 1918.

43. Letter of Jung to Oskar A. H. Schmitz, dated May 26, 1923; *C. G. Jung Letters*, selected and edited by Gerhard Adler in collaboration with Aniela Jaffé, Princeton, N.J.: Princeton University Press, 1973, I: 1906–1950, pp. 39–40. Cited also in Steven F. Walker, *Jung and the Jungians on Myth*. New York: Garland Publishing, 1995, pp. 106–107.

44. C. G. Jung, "After the Catastrophe," CW 10, p. 204. Orig. pub. 1945.

45. C. G. Jung, *Jung Speaking*, ed. William McGuire. London: Thames and Hudson, 1978, pp. 773–79. Cited in also Andrew Samuels, *The Political Psyche*. London and New York: Routledge, 1993, p. 282.

46. C. G. Jung, "Wotan," CW 10, pp. 179–93. Orig. pub. 1936.

47. Ibid., p. 185.

48. Samuels, *Political Psyche*, p. 301. Jung had given seminars with Hauer, an Indologist, on Kundalini Yoga. On the movement, see Jacob Hauer et al., *Germany's New Religion: The German Faith Movement*. London: Allen and Unwin, 1937.

49. James A. Zabel, *Nazism and the Pastors*. Missoula, Mont.,: Scholars Press Dissertations Series 14, 1976, p. 1.

50. See Geoffrey Cocks, *Psychotherapy in the Third Reich: The Göring Institute*. London and New York: Oxford University Press, 1991.

51. C. G. Jung, "Epilogue to 'Essays on Contemporary Events,'" CW 10, p. 236.

52. Aniela Jaffé, "C. G. Jung and National Socialism," in her *Jung's Last Years and Other Essays*. Dallas, Tex.: Spring Publications, 1984.

53. Laurens van der Post, *Jung and the Story of Our Time*. New York: Random House, 1975, pp. 195–96.

54. C. G. Jung, "The State of Psychotherapy Today," CW 10, p. 165. Orig. pub. 1934.

55. Ibid.

56. Adolf Hitler, *Mein Kampf*. Trans. by Ralph Manheim. Boston: Houghton Mifflin, 1943, 1971, p. 301.

57. See Samuels, *Political Psyche*, especially chapters 12 and 13, for further discussion and documentation, especially regarding articles that appeared under Jung's general editorship of the *Zentralblatt für Psychotherapie* in the 1930s, and the extent to which his editorship was more than nominal. We cannot here undertake a full analysis of the situation, and Samuels's treatment is highly recommended. In the end, and I think Samuels would agree, the situation remains profoundly and puzzlingly ambiguous. However much evidence is piled up to support one side of the debate over Jung's conscious complicity with Nazism, there always appears to be about as much that can be adduced on behalf the other, and the mystery remains. Samuels believes that one reason for Jung's sometimes twisting path was simply a desire to maintain his own presidency and leadership in the psychotherapeutic movement, for both personal and well-meaning reasons; he was often willing to make what political moves were necessary to that end.

58. Gerhard Adler, ed., *C. G. Jung Letters, I: 1906–1950*, pp. 164–65.

59. In a 1933 editorial in the *Zentralblatt* of the society, published in Leipzig, Jung went on to say at this incendiary moment, "the differences which actually do exist between Germanic and Jewish psychologies and which have long been known to every intelligent person are no longer to be glossed over, and this can be only be beneficial to science . . . at the same time I should like to state expressly that this implies no depreciation of Semitic psychology, any more than it is a depreciation of the Chinese to speak of the peculiar psychology of the Oriental." *Zentralblatt für Psychotherapie und ihre Grenzgebiete* VI:3, Dec. 1933. CW 10, pp. 533–34.

60. Adler, ed., *C. G. Jung Letters I*, p. 224.

61. Richard Stein, "Jung's 'Mana Personality' and the Nazi Era," in Aryeh Maidenbaum and Stephen A. Martin, *Lingering Shadows: Jungians, Freudians, and Anti-Semitism*. Boston: Shambhala, 1991, pp. 89–116.

62. See, for example, "After the Catastrophe," CW 10, pp. 194–217. Orig. pub. 1945.

63. See the chapter, "National Socialism: 'Yes, I Slipped Up,'" in Gerhard Wehr, *Jung: A Biography*. Trans. David M. Weeks. Boston: Shambhala, 1987, pp. 304–30. The phrase, "Yes, I slipped up," concerning Jung's initial failure to recognize the Nazis for the evil force they were, was allegedly said by Jung to the former concentration camp inmate Rabbi Leo Baeck, during a long conversation after the war, following which the two men were reconciled.

Wehr, 325–26, based on an account given by Gershom Scholem to Aniela Jaffé.

64. Frank McLynn, *Carl Gustav Jung: A Biography*. New York: St. Martin's Press, 1996, p. 367.

65. Laurens van der Post, *Jung and the Story of Our Time*, p. 194.

66. Adler, ed., *C. G. Jung Letters I*, p. 276.

67. Ibid., p. 282.

68. C. G. Jung, "The Undiscovered Self," CW 10, p. 278. Orig. pub. 1957.

69. Hans Schaer, *Religion and the Cure of Souls*. New York: Pantheon, 1950, p. 121.

70. Homas, *Jung in Context*, pp. 185–86.

71. "Answers to Questions from the Rev. David Cox," CW 18. Orig. text 1957.

72. McLynn, *Jung*, p. 528.

73. Voegelin, *Science, Politics and Gnosticism*, p. 12.

74. "Conscious, Unconscious, and Individuation," in *The Archetypes and the Collective Unconscious*, CW 9, p. 288. Orig. pub. 1939.

75. C. G. Jung, "Symbols and the Interpretation of Dreams," CW 18. Orig. pub. 1961.

76. Volodymyr Walter Odajnyk, *Jung and Politics: The Political and Social Ideas of C. G. Jung*. New York: Harper and Row, 1976, p. 182.

77. "The Swiss Line in the European Spectrum," CW 10, pp. 579–88. Orig. pub. 1928. Jung wrote: "Does neutral Switzerland, with its backward, earthy nature, fulfill any meaningful function in the European system? I think we must answer this question affirmatively. The answer to political and cultural questions need not be only: Progress and Change, but also: Stand still! Hold fast! These days one can doubt in good faith whether the condition of Europe shows any change for the good since the war" (p. 587).

78. C. G. Jung, "After the Catastrophe," CW 10, p. 196. Orig. pub. 1945.

79. Alan Morris Schom, *Survey of Nazi and Pro-Nazi Groups in Switzerland 1930–1945*. Los Angeles: Simon Wiesenthal Center, 1998.

80. Alan Morris Schom, *The Unwanted Guests: Swiss Forced Labor Camps 1940–1944*. Los Angeles: Simon Wiesenthal Center, 1998. It should be pointed out that Swiss officials have disputed some of these contentions of both these reports, and that Rabbi Marvin Hier, Dean and Founder of the Simon Wiesenthal Center, states in his Preface to The Unwanted Guests that "It is not the purpose of this report to condemn the entire Swiss people during World War II," and goes on to indicate that there were "many Swiss people from all segments of society—nurses, businessmen, members of the clergy and ordinary people— who showed great courage and humanity toward their fellow men during those difficult years."

81. Ann Brenoff, "Alan Morris Schom: Ferreting Out Switzerland's True Relationship With Nazi Germany." *Los Angeles Times*, August 23, 1998, p. M3.

82. McLynn, *Jung*, p. 1.

83. Samuels, *Political Psyche*, p. 287.

84. Ibid., p. 313.

85. Ibid., p. 325.

86. See Homans, *Jung in Context*, p. 199.

CHAPTER 3. MIRCEA ELIADE AND NOSTALGIA FOR THE SACRED

1. Apart from some articles directed against the communist regime in his homeland, which appeared up to 1954 in Romanian émigré periodicals.

2. Vol. 1: *1907–1937, Journey East, Journey West*, San Francisco: Harper and Row, 1981; vol. 2: *1937–1960, Exile's Odyssey*, Chicago: University of Chicago Press, 1988.

3. Mircea Eliade, *Journals*. All University of Chicago Press, vol. 1: *1945– 1955*, 1990; 2: *1957–1969*, 1989; 3: *1970–1978*, 1989; *1979–1985*, 1989.

4. Mac Linscott Ricketts, *Mircea Eliade: The Romanian Roots, 1907–1945*. 2 vols. Boulder, Colo. East European Monographs, 1988. Distributed by Columbia University Press, New York.

5. See the discussion in Bryan S. Rennie, *Reconstructing Eliade*. Albany: State University of New York Press, 1996, chapter 13, "Eliade's Political Involvement." This chapter contains summaries and critiques of Ivan Strenski, *Four Theories of Myth in Twentiety-Century History*, London: Macmillan, 1989; Adriana Berger, several articles, especially "Fascism and Religion in Romania," *The Annals of Scholarship* 6, no. 4 (1989), pp. 45–65 and "Mircea Eliade: Romanian Fascism and the History of Religions in the United States," in *Tainted Greatness: Antisemitism and Cultural Heroes*, ed. Nancy A. Harrowitz, Philadelphia: Temple University Press, 1994; Leon Volovici, *Nationalist Ideology and Antisemitism: The Case of Romanian Intellectuals in the Thirties*. New York: Pergamon Press, 1991; and Daniel Dubuisson, *Mythologies du XXe Siécle: Dumézil, Lévi-Strauss, Eliade*. Lille: Presses Universitaires de Lille, 1993. See also criticisms of Eliade in Russell McCutcheon, *Manufacturing Religion: The Discourse on Sui Generis Religion and the Politics of Nostalgia*. New York: Oxford University Press, 1997.

6. Published serially in the journal *Cuvantul*, 1926; French translation, *L'adolescent miop*. Paris: Acte Sud, 1992.

7. Ricketts, *Mircea Eliade*, 1, p. 31.

8. That dissertation in turn was the basis of his French book, *Yoga: Essai sur les origenes de la mystique Indienne* (Paris: Guenther, 1936), his first important work in history of religions, which after further major alterations became *Yoga: Immortality and Freedom* (London: Routledge and Kegan Paul, 1958).

9. English translation, University of Chicago Press, 1994. There is an interesting sequel: Maitreyi herself, by now a prominent writer and public figure in her own right, eventually learned of Eliade's story and wrote her own autobiographical novel, Maitreya Devi, *It Does Not Die* (Bengali, 1974; English translation by the author, Calcutta: Writers Workshop, 1976), giving her version of the affair, climaxing with a scene in which she confronts the now-distinguished historian of religion in his Chicago office about the slanderous insinuations and defamation of her character she contends were presented in the youthful novel; Eliade has no answer but to look at her with eyes "turned to stone." She acknowledged in a letter to Mac Ricketts that the high drama of this unforgettable novelistic scene was actually a conflation of several meetings in 1973 (Ricketts, *Mircea Eliade*, 1, p. 483).

10. Ted Anton, *Eros, Magic, and the Murder of Professor Culianu*, Evanston, Ill.: Northwestern University Press, 1996, p. 43.

11. A useful summary of the Legion's history and ideology can be found in the relevant parts of Stanley G. Payne, *A History of Fascism 1914–1945*, Madison: University of Wisconsin Press, 1995, especially pp. 136–38, 279–81, 391–97. The fullest account in English is Radu Ioanid, *The Sword of the Archangel*, Boulder, Colo.: East European Monographs, 1990. This is a translation of a Romanian work, which shows some signs of its provenance under the Communist regime, but contains essential documentation unavailable elsewhere in English. There is reference to Eliade as a spokesperson for Legion ideology. For a proLegion apologetic see Alexander E. Ronnett, *Romanian Nationalism: The Legionaray Movement*. Chicago: Loyola University Press, 1974. Ronnett, whose real surname was Rachmistriuc, was a Guardist and medical doctor who settled in Chicago after the war. In a 1995 interview, Ronnett told Ted Anton that he had been Eliade's personal physician in his Chicago years, and also claimed that Eliade had been a prominent Guardist. Anton, *Eros, Magic, and the Murder of Professor Culianu*, p. 117.

12. Leon Volovici, *Nationalist Ideology and Anti-Semitism*, pp. 64–65.

13. See, in addition to the works cited above, F. L. Carsten, *The Rise of Fascism*. Berkeley: University of California Press, 1967, 1982 ed., pp. 181–93.

14. See, for example, Ricketts, *Mircea Eliade*, 2, pp. 909–12, 915–17. It should be pointed out that in some places Eliade urged merely that the minorities be assimilated, and unlike other rightists even at his harshest did not urge the use of force against such groups collectively.

15. Strenski, *Four Theories of Myth*, p. 125.

16. Mircea Eliade, *Autobiography*, 1, Volovici, *Nationalist Ideology and Antisemitism*, pp. 101–105; Ricketts, *Mircea Eliade*, 2, pp. 727–41.

17. "Contra dreptei si contra stangi," *Credinta*, 14 February 1934, p. 3. Cited in Ricketts, *Mircea Eliade*, 2, p. 893.

18. "Noul Barbar," *Vremea*, 27 January 1935, p. 3. Cited in Ricketts, *Mircea Eliade*, 2, pp. 893–94.

19. "Catevacuvinte mare," *Vremea*, 10 June 1934, p. 3. Cited in Ricketts, *Mircea Eliade*, 2, p. 915.

20. Ricketts, *Mircea Eliade*, 2, p. 918.

21. "Renastere romaneasca," *Vremea*, Easter, 1935, p. 7. Cited in Ricketts, *Mircea Eliade*, 2, p. 903.

22. "Democratia si problema Romaniei," *Vremea*, 18 December 1936, p. 3. Cited in Ricketts, *Mircea Eliade*, 2, pp. 900–901. Ricketts comments that at the time *Vremea*, for which Eliade wrote regularly, had recently switched from a moderate to a far right political position.

23. Mircea Eliade, *Autobiography*, 2, p. 65.

24. Payne, *A History of Fascism*, p. 280.

25. "Noua aristocratie legionara," *Vremea*, 23 Jan. 1939. Cited in Volovici, *Nationalist Ideology and Antisemitism*, p. 91.

26. Ricketts, *Mircea Eliade*, 2, pp. 928–29. The statement, "De ce cred in biruinta miscarii legionare," appeared in *Buna vestire*, 17 December 1937.

27. Mircea Eliade, *Ordeal by Labyrinth: Conversations with Claude-Henri Rocquet*. Trans. by Derek Coltman. Chicago: University of Chicago Press, 1982, p. 53. Orig. pub. in French 1978.

28. Mircea Eliade, *No Souvenirs: Journal, 1957–1960*. New York: Harper and Row, 1977, p. 220.

29. Cited in Ricketts, *Mircea Eliade*, 2, p. 926. Cf. Volovici, *Nationalist Ideology and Antisemitism*, p. 142, n.134. The diaries of Sebastian, who was killed in an accident in 1945, were the source of the article that opened current debate on Eliade's Romanian political stance, "Dosarul Mircea Eliade" [Mircea Eliade File], probably by Theodor Lavi, published in the Israeli journal *Toladot*, January–March 1972.

30. Volovici, *Nationalist Ideology and Antisemitism*, p. 73, n.90.

31. Eliade, *Autobiography*, 2, p. 65.

32. Cited Rickets, *Mircea Eliade*, 2, pp. 1108–1109. The book by Eliade is *Salazar si revolutia in Portugalia*. Bucharest: Editura Gorjan, 1942.

33. Eliade, *Autobiography*, 2, p. 69.

34. Ibid, p. 85.

35. The horrors climaxing on January 21, 1941, happened as Antonescu, disillusioned with the Legion's excesses and incompetence, was preparing to turn against them with Hitler's approval; the January pogrom was part of a sort of preemptive revolt by the Legion. But it failed, and Antonescu soon outlawed the Legion while remaining firmly in the Axis camp. The worst single event in Romania, the murder of several thousand Jews in Iasi, was in late June 1941, just after German and Romanian troops had invaded Russia; Jews were regarded as Soviet sympathizers. Apparently German forces, Romanian soldiers, and Legionary elements all had a hand in the terror with the connivance of the Antonescu government. General Antonescu did order an investigation and later, to his credit, tried seriously to protect Romanian Jews. But Jews were routinely massacred by Romanians as they advanced into the formerly Romanian, now Soviet, territories of Bukovina and Bessarabia.

36. Letter of January 24, 1978. Cited in Anton, *Eros, Magic, and the Murder of Professor Culianu*, p. 98.

37. Eliade, *No Souvenirs*, p. 116.

38. Mircea Eliade, *Myths, Dreams and Mysteries*. New York: Harper and Brothers, 1960, pp. 25–26.

39. Rennie, *Reconstructing Eliade*, p. 177. See all of ch. 13, "Eliade's Political Involvement."

40. Eliade, *No Souvenirs*, p. 120.

41. In his journal entry for June 30, 1965, Eliade stated that he was doing a review of Scholem's book on the Kabbala, adding that "in the Kabbala we have to do with a new, real creation of the Judaic religious genius." *No Souvenirs*, p. 266.

42. Eliade, *Autobiography*, 2, p. 138.

43. Ion Culianu, Review of Eliade, *Journals*, etc., *The Journal of Religion* 72/1 (January 1992), p. 60.

44. Ted Peters, *Eros, Magic, and the Murder of Professor Culianu*, p. 235.

45. Seymour Cain, "Mircea Eliade, the Iron Guard, and Romanian Anti-Semitism," *Midstream* 25 (Nov. 1989), p. 29. cited in Culianu, Review . . . , pp. 60–61.

46. Culianu, Review . . . , p. 61.

47. Eliade, *Autobiography*, 2, pp. 106–107.

48. Rennie, *Reconstructing Eliade*, p. 165.

49. Eliade, *Autobiography*, 1, pp. 6–7.

50. Eliade, *Myths, Dreams, and Mysteries*, p. 43.

51. Mircea Eliade, *Cosmos and History: The Myth of the Eternal Return*. New York: Harper and Row, 1959, pp. 74–75.

52. Ibid., p. 156.

53. Ibid., p. 157.

54. Payne, *History of Fascism*, p. 8; see also L. Birken, *Hitler as Philosophe: Remnants of the Enlightenment in National Socialism*. Westport, Conn.: Greenwood, 1995.

55. Mircea Eliade, *The Forbidden Forest*. Trans. Mac Linscott Ricketts and Mary Park Stevenson. Notre Dame, Ind.: University of Notre Dame Press, 1978, p. 250.

56. Eliade, *Autobiography*, 1, p. 254.

57. Eliade, *Autobiography*, 2, p. 13.

58. Mircea Eliade, *Shamanism: Archaic Techniques of Ecstasy*. London: Routledge and Kegan Paul, 1951; New York: Pantheon, 1964.

59. Mircea Eliade, *The Sacred and the Profane*. New York: Harcourt, Brace and World, 1959, p. 205.

60. Thomas J. J. Altizer, *Mircea Eliade and the Dialectic of the Sacred*. Philadelphia: Westminster, 1963.

61. Eliade, *No Souvenirs*, p. 179.

62. Mircea Eliade, *The Quest*. Chicago: University of Chicago Press, 1969, p. 3.

63. Eliade, *Ordeal by Labyrinth*, p. 127.

64. Eliade, *No Souvenirs*, pp. 88, 113.

65. Eliade, *Ordeal by Labyrinth*, p. 127.

66. Strenski, *Four Theories of Myth*, p. 102.

67. Ibid, p. 108.

68. Eliade, *Cosmos and History*, p. 9.

69. Mircea Eliade, *The Sacred and the Profane*, p. 33. The story comes originally from B. Spencer and F. J. Gillen, *The Arunta*, London, 1926, I, p. 388; for the claim that the account is unreliable see Jonathan Z. Smith, *To Take Place*. Chicago: University of Chicago Press, 1987, pp. 1–15. Among other critiques, Smith points out that the tense of Eliade's account is wrong; instead of a current, observed event the broken pole was itself a mythical story of the Achilpa (or Tjilpa), set in the mythical time of the beginning. Eliade acknowledges this in the later treatment of the narrative in his *Australian Religions*. Ithaca, N.Y.: Cornell University Press, 1973, p. 53.

70. Eliade, "A New Humanism," in Eliade, *The Quest*. Chicago: University of Chicago Press, 1969, p. 3.

71. Ibid., preface.

72. Eliade, *No Souvenirs*, p. 313.

73. Eliade, "A New Humanism," p. 6.

74. Eliade, *No Souvenirs*, p. 182.

75. Wendy Doniger, "The Implied Spider: Politics and Theology in Myth." *Religious Studies News*, February 1997, p. 9.

76. Eliade, *No Souvenirs*, p. 121.

77. Mircea Eliade, *Ordeal by Labyrinth*, pp. 80–81.

78. Ibid., p. 117.

79. Mircea Eliade, "The Quest for the 'Origins' of Religion," pub. in Eliade, *The Quest*, pp. 37–53.

80. Cited in Virgil Ierunca, "The Literary Work of Mircea Eliade," in Joseph M. Kitagawa and Charles H. Long, eds., *Myths and Symbols: Studies in Honor of Mircea Eliade*. Chicago: University of Chicago Press, 1969, p. 351. Originally from *Journals* for June, 1954.

81. Eliade, *The Sacred and the Profane*, pp. 166–67.

82. Mircea Eliade, *Patterns in Comparative Religion*. New York; Sheed and Ward, 1958, p. 405.

83. Ibid, p. 424.

84. Eliade, *Myth and Reality*, p. 95.

85. Eliade, *Ordeal by Labyrinth*, p. 138.

86. Ibid., p. 136.

87. Eliade, *The Sacred and the Profane*, p. 206. See also his *Occultism, Witchcraft, and Cultural Fashions*. Chicago: University of Chicago Press, 1976.

88. Eliade, *Autobiography*, 2, p. 187.

89. Ibid, p. 203.

90. Mircea Eliade, "Paradise and Utopia: Mythical Geography and Eschatology," in Eliade, *The Quest*, pp. 88–111.

91. Mircea Eliade, *No Souvenirs: Journal, 1957–1969*. New York: Harper and Row, 1977, p. 130.

92. Thomas J. J. Altizer, "America and the Future of Theology," in Altizer and William Hamilton, *Radical Theology and the Death of God*. Indianapolis: Bobbs-Merrill, 1966; Hamilton, "Thursday's Child," in ibid. p. 87.

93. Eliade, *No Souvenirs*, pp. 227–29.

94. Ibid, pp. 73–74.

95. Ibid, pp. 303–304.

96. Ibid., pp. 310–311.

97. Joseph J. Ellis, *American Sphinx: The Character of Thomas Jefferson*. New York: Knopf, 1996, p. 302.

98. Eliade, *No Souvenirs*, p. 232.

99. Eliade, *The Forbidden Forest*, p. 314.

## CHAPTER 4. JOSEPH CAMPBELL AND THE NEW QUEST FOR THE HOLY GRAIL

1. Mary R. Lefkowitz, "The Myth of Joseph Campbell," *The American Scholar*, 59–3 (summer 1990), p. 429.

2. Stephen and Robin Larsen, *A Fire in the Mind: The Life of Joseph Campbell*. New York: Doubleday, 1991, pp. 540–43.

3. Joseph Campbell, with Bill Moyers, *The Power of Myth*. New York: Doubleday, 1985, p. 5.

4. Karen L. King, "Social Factors in Mythic Knowledge: Joseph Campbell and Christian Gnosis," in Daniel C. Noel, ed., *Paths to the Power of Myth: Joseph Campbell and the Study of Religion*. New York: Crossroad, 1990, p. 69.

5. Robert A. Segal, "The Romantic Appeal of Joseph Campbell," *Christian Century*, April 4, 1990, pp. 332–35.

6. Robert A. Segal, *Joseph Campbell: An Introduction*. New York: Garland Publishing, 1987, p. 137.

7. Brendan Gill, "The Faces of Joseph Campbell," *New York Review of Books*, Sept. 28, 1989, pp. 16–19.

8. Larsen and Larsen, *A Fire in the Mind*, pp. 32–35.

9. The talk is published in its entirety in ibid., pp. 287–90.

10. Ibid., p. 298.

11. Ibid., p. 297.

12. Ibid., p. 363.

13. Joseph Campbell, *The Hero with a Thousand Faces*. Bollingen series 17. New York: Pantheon, 1949. 2d ed., Princeton University Press, 1968.

14. See the summary of this scenario in ibid., pp. 245–46.

15. Stanley Edgar Hyman, "Myth, Ritual, and Nonsense," *Kenyon Review* 11 (summer 1949), pp. 455–75.

16. Richard M. Dorson, "Mythology and Folklore," *Annual Review of Anthropology* 2 (1973), pp. 107–26, citation pp. 107–108.

17. J. Zemljanova, "The Struggle between the Reactionary and the Progressive Forces in Contemporary American Folkloristics," *Journal of the Folklore Institute* 1 (1964), pp. 130–44; citation p. 132.

18. Cited in Larsen and Larsen, *A Fire in the Mind*, p. 357.

19. Alan Watts, *In My Own Way: An Autobiography 1915–1965*. New York: Pantheon, 1972, p. 229.

20. Joseph Campbell, *Baksheesh and Brahman: Indian Journal 1954–1955*. Ed. Robin Larsen, Stephen Larsen, and Antony Van Couvering. San Francisco: HarperCollins, 1995.

21. Larsen and Larsen, *A Fire in the Mind*, p. 373.

22. Campbell, *Baksheesh and Brahman*, p. 76.

23. Ibid., p. 65.

24. Ibid., p. 203.

25. Ibid., p. 157.

26. Joseph Campbell, *The Masks of God*. Vol. 1, *Primitive Mythology*. New York: Viking, 1959; vol. 2, *Oriental Mythology*, New York: Viking, 1962; vol. 3, *Occidental Mythology*. New York: Viking, 1964; vol. 4, *Creative Mythology*. New York: Viking, 1968.

27. Stephen P. Dunn, review of *The Masks of God: Occidental Mythology*, in *American Anthropologist* 67 (February 1965), p. 140.

28. Joseph Campbell, "The Secularization of the Sacred," in Donald L. Cutler, *The Religious Situation*, 1. Boston: Beacon, 1968, ch. 17.

29. Ibid., p. 629.

30. Larsen and Larsen, *A Fire in the Mind*, pp. 465–66.

31. Toby Johnson, *The Myth of the Great Secret*. Berkeley, Calif.: Celestial Arts, 1992, pp. 48–49.

32. Joseph Campbell, *Myths To Live By*. New York: Viking, 1972.

33. Emmett Wilson, Jr., *Saturday Review* 55 (June 24, 1972), p. 68.

34. Campbell, *Masks of God: Creative Mythology*, p. 5.

35. J. A. Appleyard, *Commonweal* 96 (September 29, 1972), p. 530; Peden Creighton, *Journal of Religious Thought* 30 (1973), pp. 64–68.

36. Joseph Campbell, *The Flight of the Wilder Gander: Explorations in the Mythological Dimension*. New York: Viking, 1969; *Historical Atlas of World My-thology*: vol. 1: *The Way of the Animal Powers*. San Francisco: Harper and Row, 1983; vol. 2: *The Way of the Seeded Earth*. San Francisco: Harper and Row, 1983. *The Inner Reaches of Outer Space*. New York: A. van der Marck Editions, 1986. Published journals have commenced with *Baksheesh and Brahman*, op. cit.

37. Joseph Campbell, *Transformations of Myth through Time*. New York: Harper and Row, 1990.

38. Joseph Campbell, *The Mythic Image*. Bollingen Series; Princeton, N.J.: Princeton University Press, 1974. Reviews: Peter S. Prescott, *Newsweek* 85 (March 31, 1975), pp. 75–76; Winthrop Sargeant, *New Yorker* 51 (July 21, 1975), pp. 86–88; Charles H. Long, "The Dreams of Professor Campbell: Joseph

Campbell's *The Mythic Image,*" *Religious Studies Review* 6 (October 1980), pp. 261–71.

39. Campbell, *Myths To Live By,* pp. 214–15.

40. Joseph Campbell, foreword to Maya Deren, *Divine Horsemen: The Living Gods of Haiti.* London and New York: Thames and Hudson, 1953, p. 1.

41. See Léopold Sédar Senghor, foreword to Eike Haberland, ed., *Leo Frobenius 1873–1973: An Anthology.* Wiesbaden: Franz Steiner Verlag, 1973, p. vii.

42. Campbell, *Myths to Live By,* pp. 85–867, 244–45.

43. Campbell, *Creative Mythology,* p. 575.

44. Lamar Cecil, *Wilhelm II,* vol. 2. Chapel Hill: University of North Carolina Press, 1996, pp. 317–21.

45. From the "War Journal," a journal Campbell kept during World War II. Cited in Larsen and Larsen, *Fire in the Mind,* p. 226.

46. Stanley Edgar Hyman, "Myth, Ritual, and Nonsense," *Kenyon Review* 11 (summer 1949), p. 474.

47. Campbell, *Myths To Live By,* p. 167.

48. Cited in Larsen and Larsen, *A Fire in the Mind,* p. 325. From Campbell's Journals.

49. Campbell, *Inner Reaches of Outer Space,* pp. 147–48.

50 . Campbell, *Creative Mythology,* p. 321.

51. Robert A. Segal, "Joseph Campbell on Jews and Judaism," *Religion* 22 (1992), pp. 151–70.

52. Joseph Campbell, *The Power of Myth.* New York: Doubleday, 1988, p. 21. From the Public Broadcasting System series.

53. Campbell, "The Secularization of the Sacred," in Donald R. Cutler, ed., *The Religious Situation 1968.* Boston: Beacon, 1968, pp. 601–37, and in Jo-

seph Campbell, *The Flight of the Wild Gander*. New York: Viking, 1969. Quote from Cutler, ed., p. 629.

54. Maurice Friendman, "Why Joseph Campbell's Psychologizing of Myth Precludes the Holocaust as Touchstone of Reality," *Journal of the American Acadmey of Religion* 66/2 (summer 1998), pp. 385–401.

55. Campbell, *The Masks of God*, p. 12.

56. Larsen and Larsen, *A Fire in the Mind*, pp. 510–11.

57. "Bios and Mythos: Prolegomena to a Science of Mythology," in *Psychoanalysis and Culture: Essays in Honor of Géza Róheim*, ed. George B. Wilbur and Warner Muensterberger. New York: International Universities Press, 1951.

58. Larsen and Larsen, *A Fire in the Mind*, p. 539.

59. Campbell, *Hero*, p. 149.

60. Campbell, *The Power of Myth*, p. 27. See also Dabney Gray, "Campbell, America, and the Individual as New Hero," in Kenneth L. Golden, ed., *Uses of Comparative Mythology: Essays on the Work of Joseph Campbell*. New York: Garland, 1992, pp. 235–48.

61. Joseph Campbell, *Transformations of Myth through Time*. New York: Harper and Row, 1990.

62. John M. Maher and Dennis Briggs, eds., *An Open Life: Joseph Campbell in Conversation with Michael Toms*. New York: Harper and Row, 1989, p. 101. The interviews in this book are undated but took place over a ten-year period beginning in 1975.

63. Freeman Dyson, *Imagined Worlds*. Cambridge: Harvard University Press, 1997.

# INDEX

MEER SHA    ALEE ODD

Breinigsville, PA USA
10 May 2010
237709BV00002B/7/A